AF292500

Asahi Pentax and Pentax SLR 35mm Cameras 1952-1989

Danilo Cecchi

HOVE FOTO BOOKS

Asahi Pentax and Pentax SLR 35mm Cameras 1952-1989

Danilo Cecchi

First published in Great Britain February 1991 by
Hove Foto Books
34 Church Road
Hove, Sussex BN3 2GJ

British Library Cataloguing in Publication Data
Cecchi, Danilo
Asahi Pentax and Pentax SLR 35mm cameras 1952-1989.
1. Cameras
I. Title
771.32

ISBN 0-906447-62-3

Translated from Italian by Susan Chalkley

Design: Wendy Bann, Twyford, Berks.

Typesetting and layout: Annida's Written Page, Sussex BN15 0NR
Printed in Germany by Kösel GmbH, Kempten.

Contents

USA Model Names

At different periods in their history Asahi Pentax and Pentax cameras have been given different model names in the USA, or the wider north American market. The Asahiflex cameras sold through Sears Roebuck were called "Tower". When the Honeywell corporation took over the distribution in the USA, through its Heiland division, the cameras were called "Heiland Pentax", soon changed to "Honeywell Pentax". In more recent times Pentax, who now distribute themselves in the USA, have given different designations to some models for marketing reasons.

Japanese and European Name	American Name
ASAHIFLEX ERA	
Asahiflex	Tower (Sears Roebuck only)
Asahiflex IIb	Tower 23 (Sears Roebuck only)
Asahiflex IIa	Tower 22 (Sears Roebuck only)
SCREW MOUNT CAMERAS (1958-1975)	
Asahi Pentax	Tower 26 (Sears Roebuck only)
Asahi Pentax H2 or Asahi Pentax S2	Heiland Pentax H2
Asahi Pentax S1	Heiland Pentax H1 or Honeywell Pentax H1
Asahi Pentax S3	Heiland Pentax H3 or Honeywell Pentax H3
Asahi Pentax S1a	Honeywell Pentax H1a

Asahi Pentax SV | Honeywell Pentax H3v
Asahi Pentax S2 (Super) | not imported into USA

Asahi Pentax Spotmatic | Honeywell Pentax Spotmatic
 | (a few H4)

Asahi Pentax SP II | Honeywell Pentax SP II
Asahi Pentax SP 500 | Honeywell Pentax SP 500

 | Honeywell Pentax SP IIa
 | only for American market

Asahi Pentax SPF | Honeywell Pentax SPF
Asahi Pentax SP 1000 | Honeywell Pentax SP 1000
Asahi Pentax Electro Spotmatic | not imported into USA
Asahi Pentax ES | Honeywell Pentax ES
Asahi Pentax ES II | Honeywell Pentax ES II

PROGRAM CAMERAS (1983-1990)

Pentax Super A   (black) | Pentax Super Program (chrome)
Pentax Program A (black) | Pentax Program Plus (chrome)
Pentax A3 | Pentax A 3000
Pentax P50 | Pentax P5
Pentax P30, P30n | Pentax P3, P3n

AUTOFOCUS CAMERAS (1987-1990)

Pentax SFX, SFXn | Pentax SF1, SF1n
Pentax SF7 | Pentax SF10

Introduction

The story of the Pentax camera is the story of the reflex - according to an eloquent piece of publicity on the occasion of the 10,000,000th Asahi Optical camera being produced. Apart from publicity, Asahi Pentax cameras have inspired the writing of many pages in this enthralling history. They have contributed to the development of the SLR concept, with many revolutionary innovations which have resulted in as many commercial successes.

At the beginning of the 1950's, Asahi Kogaku (Asahi Optical Company) boldly stepped onto the reflex stage with its first Asahiflex model. The subsequent fame of the Asahiflex derived from its being the very first Japanese-manufactured 35mm reflex. As the pioneer, it was symbolic. It was an act of faith in the reflex system and a bold choice. The Asahiflex was designed at a time when the big names in the burgeoning Japanese camera industry were a long way from thinking about reflex models: Nikon and Canon were producing excellent rangefinder cameras, inspired by the prewar German Contax and Leica models.

In the mid-1950's, Asahiflex cameras suddenly came to world attention on account of a number of new facilities they offered. They were the first reflex cameras to incorporate a mechanism for the automatic return of the mirror to the working position. Following the success of the Asahiflex, almost all other reflex cameras were fitted with a rapid-return mirror and by the beginning of the 1960's, the automatic mirror had become one of the distinguishing features of high-class single lens reflex cameras.

In 1957, Asahi Optical put on sale the first Japanese reflex cameras equipped with a fixed pentaprism viewfinder. "Pentax" was the auspicious name given to these cameras and it was used for twenty years in association with the word "Asahi". The dual-name, "Asahi Pentax", characterized all screw mount cameras made between 1957 and 1975. With the change to a bayonet mount, the name Asahi became almost illegible on the pentaprism, until it finally disappeared all together. Thus the trademark "Pentax" prevailed and eclipsed the name of the company, which was taken off the cameras and deleted from the catalogues. From the beginning of the 1980's, the name Pentax alone characterized all Asahi Optical output.

During the 1960's, Asahi Pentax secured another important first with the Spotmatic model. The Spotmatics were the first reflex cameras to feature light metering through the lens. A system to be used by all reflex camera manufacturers from the second half of the 1960's.

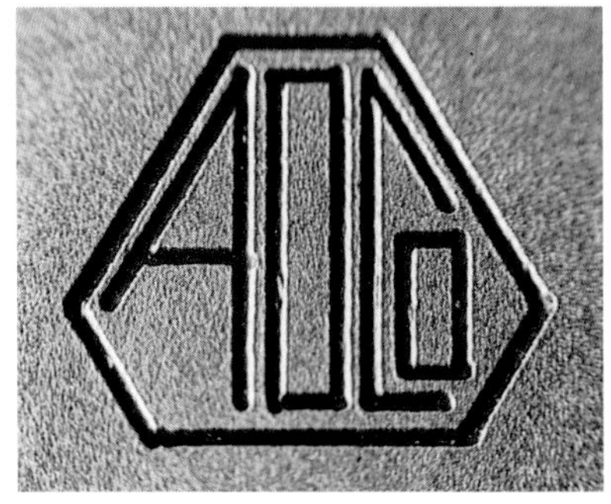

The Asahi Optical company's logo was engraved on finders and pentaprisms from 1952 to 1980. The last cameras to bear this symbol were the Asahi Pentax MX and Asahi Pentax K1000.

At the beginning of the 1970's, the Asahi Pentax Electro Spotmatic was presented, the first electronic reflex to have automatic aperture priority. Once again, it was revolutionary and transformed the design of SLR cameras, opening the way for a technological explosion which has still not subsided.

In thirty-five years, Asahi Optical has fully justified its entry into the field of 35mm reflex cameras. Few other companies can boast as many patents and as much tenacity. Almost all modern SLR cameras owe something to the various Asahi Pentax models.

For almost twenty years, SLR camera manufacturers took Asahi Pentax as a model. In the 1960's and 1970's, a great many Japanese and German companies built 35mm reflexes fitted with the Pentax screw lens mount, and similar in appearance to the Asahi Pentax. Imitation is indeed the sincerest form of flattery.

Having pioneered many technical advances in 35mm SLR cameras, and strengthened by its experience, Asahi Pentax diversified into other types of camera. It introduced reflex models in bigger formats, leading the way with the Asahi Pentax 6x7 in the early 1970's. Fifteen years later the Pentax 645, an advanced reflex for 120 rollfilm, repeated the success. It then notched up another first by building the smallest reflex in the world with interchangeable lenses for the 110 format. At the beginning of the 1980's, Asahi Optical became interested in a sector of the photographic market which had hitherto been neglected. After a half-hearted attempt with the Viva cameras, it introduced a full range of 35mm compact cameras, from the economical Pino 35 to the sophisticated Zoom 70.

After almost seventy years, Asahi Optical is one of the oldest Japanese photographic enterprises. With over ten million reflex cameras sold, it has also become one of the largest. Cameras and lenses are not its sole products, however. As with the majority of Japanese companies, Asahi aims for diversification in production and has produced binoculars and geodesic equipment for years. Recently it entered the computer field. For some years it has been increasingly engaged in the camcorder sector, reconfirming its dedication to the recording of images.

The most fascinating era in Asahi Optical's history was the period of the famous screw mount Asahi Pentax cameras. Made up to 1975, they epitomised a way of photography. Out of production for many years, supplanted by cameras equipped with much more advanced technology, the old screw mount Pentaxes have became objects of affection and collectable items. Many continue to be used daily and others, in perfect working order, are sold around the world. To evoke their history is to relive a period in the history of photography.

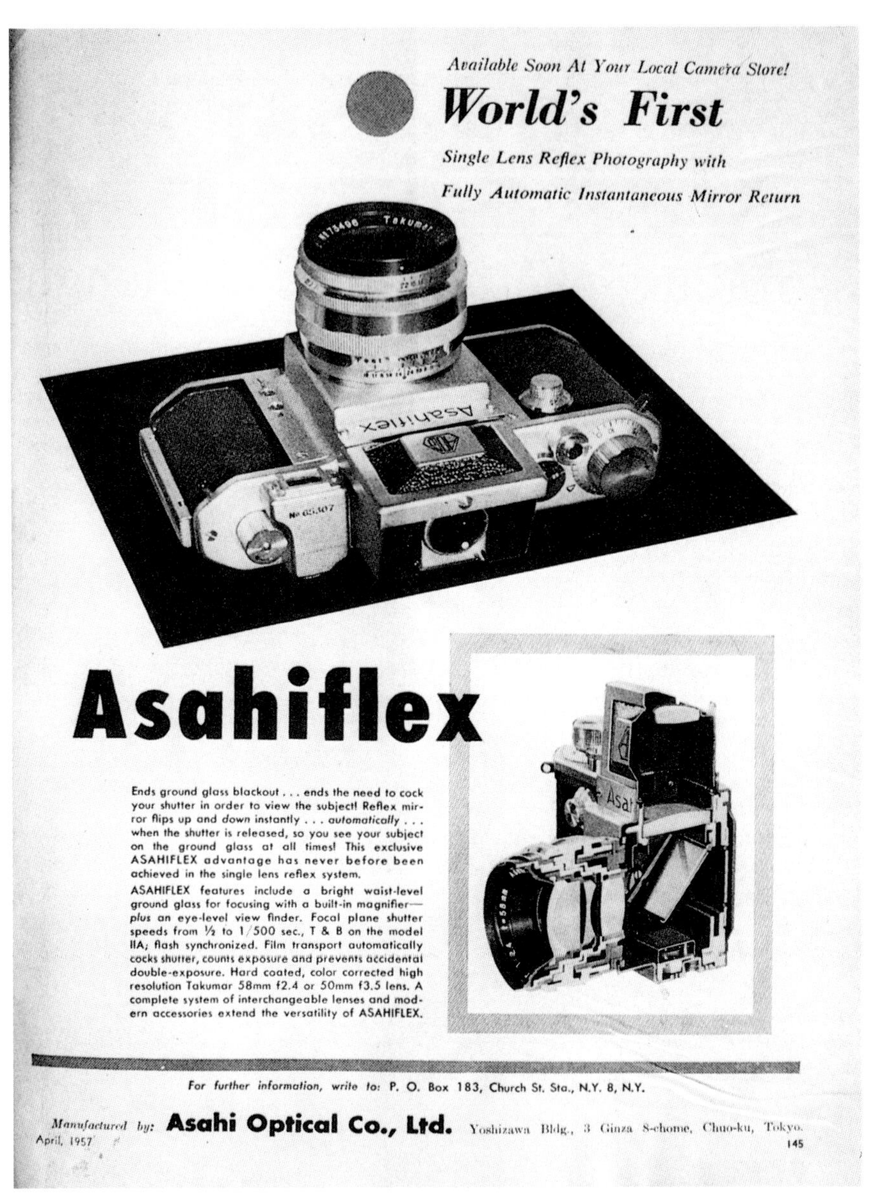

Advertisement for Asahiflex IIa in *Popular Photography* in April, 1957. The breakthrough in single lens reflex cameras was the instant return mirror - Asahi Optical company's first major contribution to camera design.

C H A P T E R 1

Rise and Fall of the Screw Mount

The Asahi Pentax originated in the 1950's from an established optical company that had been active in the period between the two Wars. The company was founded in 1919 to produce lenses for spectacles, telescopes and other civil and military instruments. The original name of the company was Asahi Kogaku Goshi Kaisha. It had its headquarters in the Toshima district of Tokyo, and the working of the ophthalmic lenses, carried out by Kumao Kajiwara, was its most important activity. In the period between the two Wars, Asahi Optical was never directly involved with photography or photographic equipment.

The first contact Asahi Kogaku had with photography came indirectly in 1931 when it was invited to produce photographic lenses for the Molta Company, owner of the Minolta brand, which was soon to change its own name to Chiyoda Kogaku Seiko and later become famous as the Minolta Camera Company. In 1931, Asahi Kogaku built for the Molta Company a 105mm,f/4.5 Corona Anastigmat triplet which was mounted on the Molta Happy Hand Camera for 6.5x9 plates. The Happy was the first fully Japanese-manufactured camera from the Molta Company and marked the start of technological independence from Germany. In 1933, the 105mm,f/4.5 Actiplan Asastigmat triplet was made for the Minolta and Auto Minolta rangefinder 6.5x9 cameras, the first cameras to be given the Minolta name. In 1935, a 75mm,f/4.5 Corona Anastigmat triplet was made for the Semi Minolta cameras, which used 4.5x6 format on 120 film. Collaboration with the Molta Company continued until the end of the prewar period, with the production of two Tessar-type f/3.5 four-element lenses, called Promar Anastigmat, in 75mm and 105mm focal lengths, for the Auto Semi Minolta and Auto Press Minolta.

Between 1932 and 1933, Asahi Kogaku worked with another large camera manufacturer, Konishi, which has today become the industrial giant Konishiroku. In 1932, they made a two-element 75mm,f/6.3 Optor anastigmatic lens and a 75mm,f/8 fixed-focus meniscus lens for Konishi's 127 Pearlette folding cameras. The following year, the 105mm,f/4.5 Optor Anastigmat triplet was produced to replace the German 105mm,f/6.3 Tinar Anastigmat lenses mounted on previous models of the Idea Showa 8 and Pearl Showa 8, 6.5x9 cameras. Japanese photographic production in the 1930's was aimed exclusively at the internal market. The different companies collaborated to reduce the foreign influence on the national industry and to satisfy an expanding domestic market in a situation where government policy blocked imports.

The early years of the Asahi Kogaku company were marred by an unusual event. In 1937, the Riken group, which today produce Ricoh cameras, founded an optical company with the name "Asahi Optical Works", in spite of the fact that "Asahi Optical" was already in existence. Asahi Optical Works in the 1930's produced Olympic cameras for 35mm, 120 and 127 films and the Leitex 127 cameras. After 1940, the name of the company was changed to Riken Optical Industry. At the beginning of the 1950's, a company called Asahi Precision Industry produced a 6x6 folding camera, called the Ricoh Six. This bizarre episode reflected the haphazard growth of the Japanese photographic industry at the time. The word "asahi" - the rising sun - is very common in Japan, the country of the rising sun. It is a goodwill name chosen to describe various activities. The most widely-read Japanese daily, which has nothing to do with Asahi Optical, is called *Asahi Shimbun*.

The damage suffered during the War forced the break-up of Asahi Kogaku Goshi, but the company reappeared in 1948 under the name Asahi Kogaku Kogyo and devoted itself to the manufacture of binoculars for export. Adapting itself to the new era and to the demands of Japan's industrial reconstruction, Asahi Kogaku, or Asahi Optical to the Americans, followed the example of other Japanese optical companies and added cameras and binoculars to their product line. But they went against prevailing fashion and produced a 35mm reflex camera which, although not very original in itself, was to herald a revolution.

In the early 1950's the Japanese photographic industry began to make its mark abroad, especially in the United States. The Japanese had for some years been producing good precision cameras and high level lenses but had only marketed them internally. The export of Japanese cameras was encouraged in the immediate postwar period during the American occupation. The foreign markets looked very promising, but Japanese cameras were accused of blatantly imitating prewar German models. The German cameras were taken as a model and copied with almost obsessive care, screw for screw. It was not a question of plagiarism, but of homage to the very advanced German technology. As in academia, copying of the classics represented an attempt at assimilation. But the Japanese did not limit themselves to copying; they often managed to modify the cameras taken as models in some small detail, thereby improving them in some way. However, lack of experience and being unable to obtain the best raw materials prevented them from equalling the quality, sturdiness and durability of the German cameras.

The Japanese photographic industry was protected and boosted by the American occupying administration, who were there to encourage the conversion of Japan's war industry to peaceful uses. In the immediate postwar period Nippon Kogaku and the Canon Camera Company, produced rangefinder cameras inspired by the Contax and Leica, and sold them in the United States. Other Japanese firms produced 6x6 twin-lens cameras, similar to the Rolleiflex, for the same market. When Asahi Optical came to design its first single lens reflex, there was no such famous name from which to take their inspiration. At the beginning of the 1950's, 35mm reflex cameras produced in Europe were few and far between.

The largest producer of precision cameras, Germany, was divided by the Iron Curtain. Dresden, which had been the main centre of camera production before the war, was in the Eastern zone. Still existing from the old companies was Ihagee Kamerafabrik, which in 1936 had introduced the world's first 35mm reflex; the Kine Exakta. In 1950, Ihagee brought out the Exakta Varex, developed from the prewar model but the first fitted with interchangeable viewfinders for the first time in the history of 35mm reflexes. The other Dresden factories were regrouped into Kombinat VEB Pentacon to produce, from 1948, the Contax S, which was illicitly sold with the Zeiss trade mark. The Contax S was the first reflex with a fixed pentaprism viewfinder and interchangeable lenses with the 42x1 screw mount. Meanwhile Zeiss Ikon itself, forcibly transferred from Dresden to Oberkoechen, did not produce a reflex model until 1951 when it introduced the fixed lens 35mm Contaflex.

Outside Germany there was the Swiss Alpa, the English Wrayflex and the Italian Rectaflex. These were prestigious and quite costly models, with diverse and original design solutions, which were complex and did not lend themselves to imitation.

As their starting point, Asahi Optical chose the most modest from amongst the 35mm reflex models available, the very cheap Praktiflex, brought out in 1938 by Kamera Werkstatten of Dresden. After the war its manufacture was resumed for a time under the aegis of Pentacon. It was followed by the Praktica, derived from the Praktiflex and made from 1948 by Kombinat VEB Pentacon.

Asahi Optical's first reflex appeared on the market in 1952, after a long period of research and experimentation, and was given the fairly unimaginative name of Asahiflex. It resembled the Praktiflex in name as well as appearance and specification. Like the Praktiflex, the Asahiflex had a very simple waist-level finder, focal plane shutter, and was equipped with a standard 50mm,f/3.5 interchangeable screw-mount lens.

In 1954, the mechanism for the rapid return of the mirror to the working position was tried out in the Asahiflex IIb. The experiment was an encouraging success. The rapid-return mirror was improved and incorporated in the Asahiflex IIa, with a shutter which offered a range of speeds extending down to half a second. The slow speeds were controlled by a separate dial situated on the

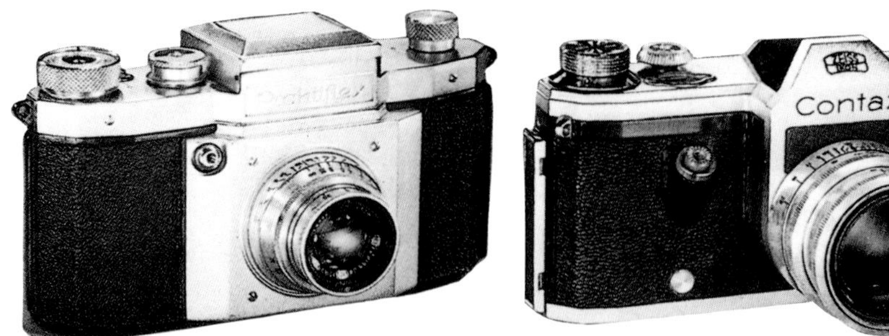

The Praktiflex KW (1938) and the Contax S (1949) were the German cameras taken as models for the development of the Asahiflex and Asahi Pentax.

front of the camera, as in the contemporary Leica. Thanks to the rapid-return mirror, the Asahiflex won fame as a revolutionary camera and gained a place in the history of photography. The make came to the attention of the public at large and the United States market in particular. The Asahiflex IIb and IIa remained in production until 1957. After its first commercial success, the little Tokyo factory was ready for its big leap into the photographic world.

At the end of 1957, a new reflex from Asahi was introduced in the United States. It broke with the Asahiflex in having a 42x1 screw lens mount, first seen ten years before with the Praktica and Contax S. It was also the first Japanese reflex to have a fixed pentaprism viewfinder for eye-level vision. They gave it the name Asahi Pentax. The choice of name was a tacit tribute to Pentacon's Contax, whose screw mount Asahi used, but in appearance the Pentax was far removed from its contemporaries, either Japanese or European.

The Asahi Pentax was the first reflex with a stylish design. Its appearance was extremely attendant to detail, its line very well drawn and most appealing. With the Pentax model, Asahi Optical inaugurated a series of cameras which were to be constantly revised and improved in their technical facilities and construction features, but which remained aesthetically unchanged for over ten years.

There was much more than simple evolution between the Asahiflex and the Asahi Pentax. Asahi Optical had made a generation leap. Despite the innovation of the automatic mirror, the Asahiflex did not bear comparison with the classic cameras of the 1950's. Set against the sacred models of German photography, Leica and Contax, the rising stars Exakta and Pentacon, and the burgeoning names of Japanese photography, Nikon and Canon, the Asahiflex looked like Cinderella. With the Asahi Pentax, Cinderella was completely transformed. Not yet a beautiful princess, but with all the qualities for becoming so. The extremely stylish bodywork of the Asahi Pentax concealed a shutter very similar to that of the Asahiflex. The slow-speed dial was on the front and maximum shutter speed was limited to $^1/500$ sec. The sophisticated image of the Asahi Pentax merited something more and Asahi Optical's designers dedicated themselves to improving the technical facilities of the camera.

16

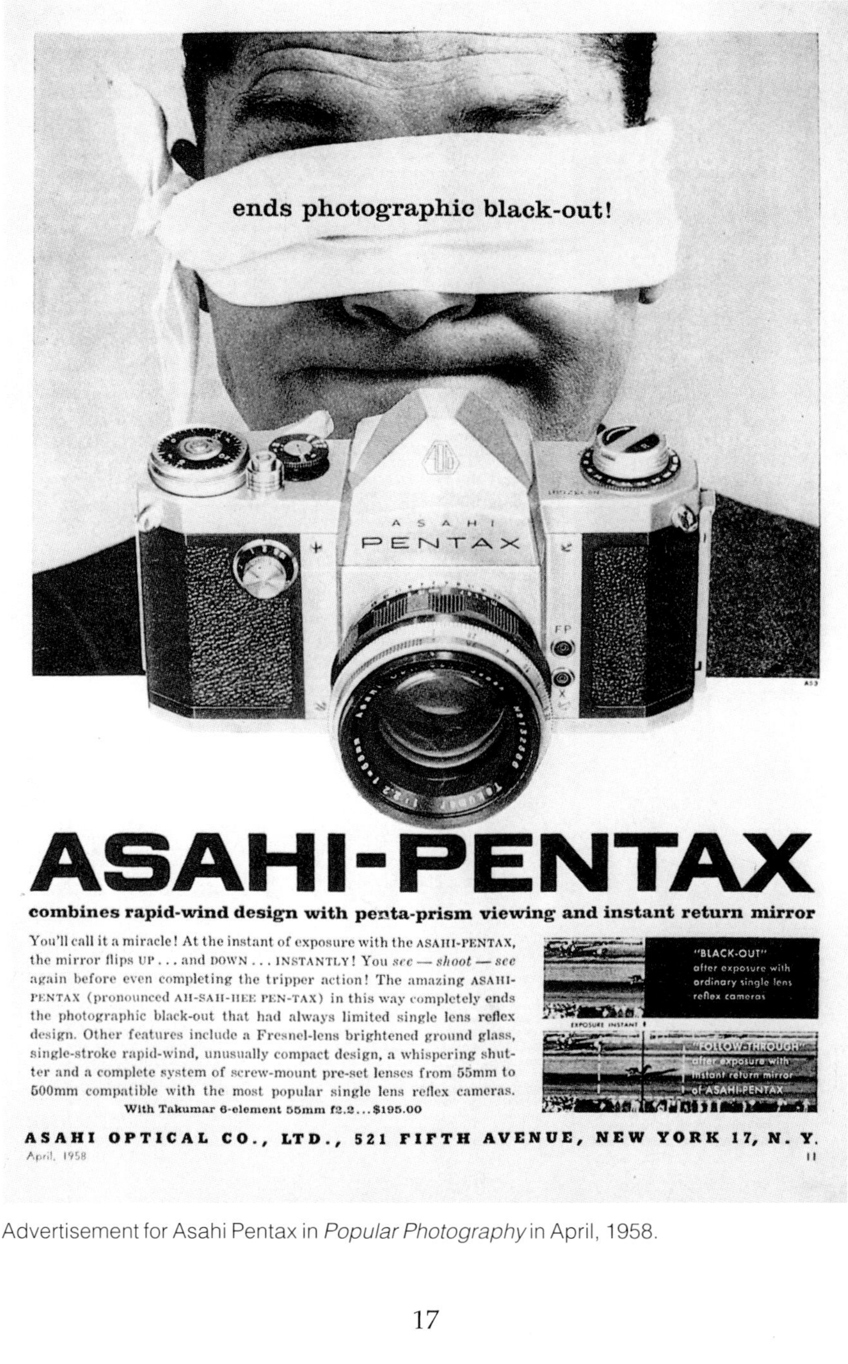

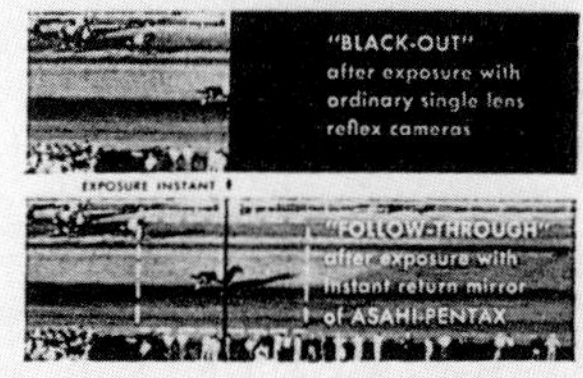

Advertisement for Asahi Pentax in *Popular Photography* in April, 1958.

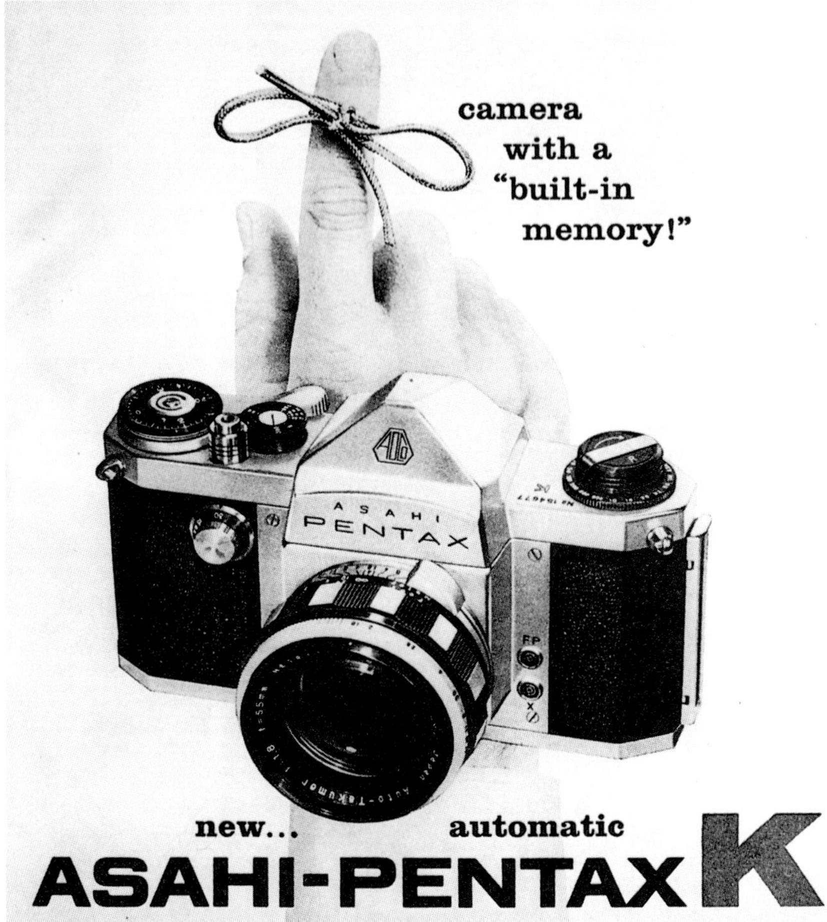

Advertisement for Asahi Pentax K, November 1958.

The spearhead model of the first generation Asahi Pentax was brought out in 1958 and designated with the letter K. The shutter was still controlled by two dials, one on the top and one on the front of the camera, but the highest speed was increased to $^1/1000$ sec. The standard lens with the Asahi Pentax K was a 55mm,f/1.8 Auto Takumar. The "Auto" referred to the semi-automatic working of the diaphragm. At the instant of release, a spring automatically closed the diaphragm to the preset value. To reopen it to the maximum value, one pressed a small button on the lens barrel. Semi-automatic working of the diaphragm was not a complete novelty. In Europe many cameras used semi-automatic lenses with external transmission linkages. The Exakta and the Pentacon had the shutter release on the front of the camera, so the semi-automatic lenses had a big button on the outside which was pressed in conjunction with the camera's shutter release. Where connection was not possible, recourse was made to very complex mechanical transmissions. A simple internal transmission for the screw mount was invented by Asahi Optical technicians and promoted on a wide scale. The idea was applied by many Japanese and German manufacturers and contributed to the mass acceptance of screw mount interchangeable lenses.

With the rapid return of the mirror, Asahi Optical had done away with the viewfinder black-out which followed shutter release. Now the almost instantaneous manual reopening of the diaphragm eliminated the darkening of the viewfinder typical of manual lenses. The 35mm reflex camera had begun to overcome its inferiority with respect to rangefinder cameras and to gain acceptance with professional photographers.

By this stage the Asahi Pentax was not the only Japanese reflex on the market. Alongside them was the Miranda, with interchangeable lenses, and a wave of new reflexes was appearing on the horizon. At the end of the 1950's, and in rapid succession, came Canon, Topcon and Minolta SLR's. In 1959, Nippon Kogaku brought out their reflex, intended to replace the rangefinder Nikons. The eternal and mythical Nikon F went on to gain an overwhelming and lasting success. Germany replied with its most prestigious reflex, the Zeiss Contarex.

Thanks to its greater flexibility, the reflex camera became dominant in the market, gradually superseding rangefinder cameras with interchangeable lenses. In the 1940's and 1950's the numerous cameras inspired by Leica and Contax had proved to be the most reliable and versatile professional instruments for the 35mm format. Thanks to them, 35mm had become a valid alternative to larger formats. With the arrival of the 35mm SLR, with its improved facilities, rangefinder cameras had a worthy rival and were to be virtually ousted from the equipment carried by professionals. During the early 1960's, *LIFE* photographers replaced the Leica M with the Nikon F. Impassioned debate on the merits of the rangefinder camera versus those of the reflex raged in the photographic world during the second half of the 1950's. By the 1960's the mass market had decreed the inevitable end of the rangefinder system. The original courageous and lone choice of Asahi Optical was imitated by the other companies. The 35mm reflex

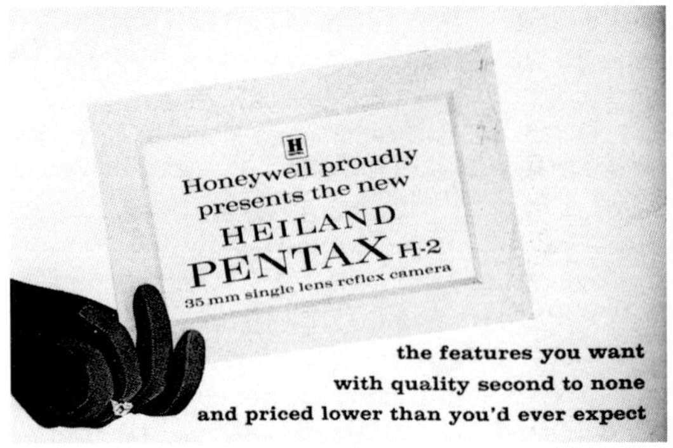

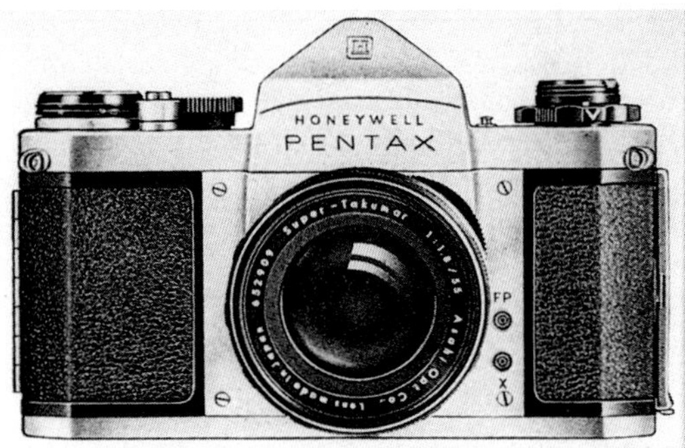

Why the Honeywell Pentax has become America's favorite 35mm single-lens reflex camera--

In 1959 the Honeywell corporation took over the marketing of the Asahi Pentax in the USA through its Heiland division. Initially the cameras were called "Heiland Pentax", later changed to "Honeywell Pentax". Above: Heiland H2 Advertisement. Below. Honeywell Pentax I I3v advertisement.

market became crowded with different models. Agressive commercial strategies and further leaps in quality were necessary.

In 1959, Asahi Optical's agency in the United States and Mexico was taken on by the giant Honeywell through the Heiland Corporation. The agreement with Honeywell led to the division of the world market into two distinct areas, with the US.A. and Mexico on one side and Europe and Japan on the other. The cameras produced for the Honeywell-controlled market bore the "Heiland Pentax" mark engraved on the pentaprism, subsequently changed to "Honeywell Pentax". In order to remove any doubts as to the intended market for Asahi Pentax cameras, the model names were designated by an initial. This was "H" for models sold by Honeywell and "S" for those for the European and internal Japanese markets.

In 1959, the first model of the second generation Asahi Pentax came out. Under the usual body was a new shutter controlled by a single dial. This had a maximum speed of $1/500$ sec. In the U.S.A. the second generation Asahi Pentax carried the model designation H2, whilst in Japan S2 was used. The European market was strewn with cameras labelled either H2 or S2.

A number of variations of the Asahi Pentax S2 were produced. Some models had a maximum speed of $1/1000$ sec. At the beginning of the 1960's the Asahi Pentax was marketed under various model designations. The cheapest model was called S1 and the most prestigious S3. The different numbers often applied to camera bodies which were basically identical but equipped with standard lenses with different maximum apertures.

In the early 1960's work on the prototype Spot-Matic was in full swing at Asahi. This did not prevent the Asahi Pentax SV model being brought out in 1963, bearing the designations H3v in America.

The Asahi Pentax SV was the first Pentax to be fitted with a delayed-action shutter release. The Super Takumar lenses were put onto the market in conjunction with the Asahi Pentax SV, equipped with a fully automatic diaphragm. Stop-down took place at the moment of release and the spring-loaded reopening was virtually instantaneous. This represented another step forward in the spread of the 42x1 screw mount which became dominant in the 1960's.

Alongside the Asahi Pentax SV came a simplified version, known on the various markets as S1a or H1a. It lacked the self-timer mechanism and met the need for a modestly priced reflex with similar facilities.

The series S Asahi Pentax could be fitted with a cadmium sulphide (CdS) exposure meter, the Asahi Pentax Meter, which clipped over the prism housing. It coupled directly to the shutter speed dial on the camera. Although bulky and awkward, the Asahi Pentax Meter proved to be very useful and was produced in two successive versions.

The success of the Asahi Pentax Meter persuaded Asahi Optical to improve and put into production an extremely refined professional exposure meter, brought out in prototype in 1960. Because of its narrow metering angle it was called the Spotmeter. The instrument had a cadmium sulphide (CdS) photocell and used a new reflex viewfinder to locate the subject. This precision exposure meter was improved in subsequent years and remained in production until the 1980's. The final version of the Spotmeter used a silicon photocell and gave a digital read-out.

By the end of the 1950's exposure meters had reached an advanced stage of development and had become essential. Photographers had become much more demanding, the market was rapidly expanding, and colour films, requiring extremely accurate exposure, were overtaking black-and-white in popularity.

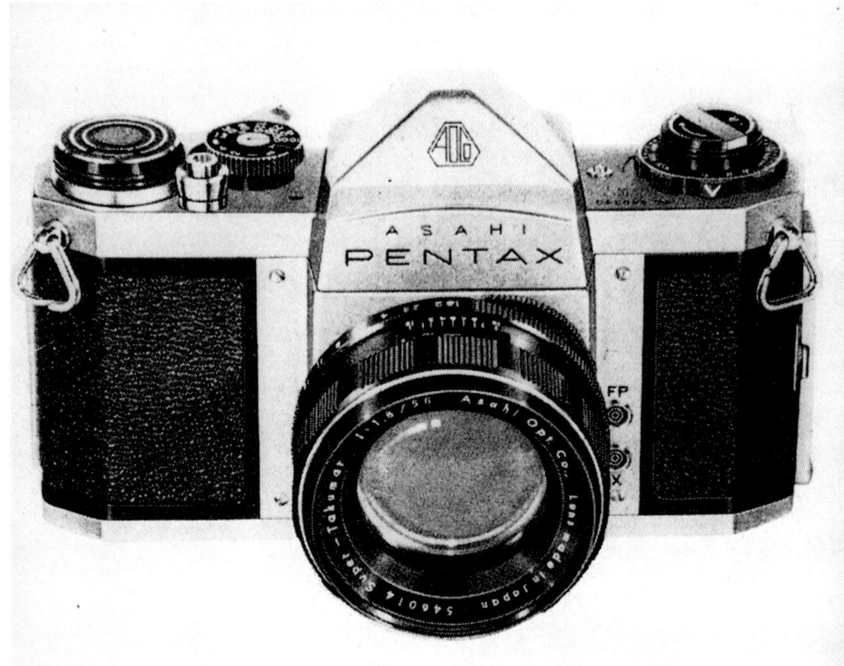

apertura automatica del diaframma

Nella nuova Asahi Pentax " SV " il diaframma è completamente automatico; si chiude sull' apertura prefissata al momento dello scatto e ritorna a piena apertura dopo lo scatto. Una levetta consente il controllo visivo della profondità di campo.

Italian advertisement for Asahi Pentax SV.

An exposure meter built into the camera became a necessity.

The first professional camera to be equipped with a built-in, but not coupled, exposure meter had been the Contax III in 1936. Many more followed in the postwar period. Selenium exposure meters were fitted to the most common rangefinder cameras of the 1950's. At the end of the decade, built-in exposure meters appeared on reflex cameras. In order to be sufficiently sensitive and accurate, selenium exposure meters need a large light cell. The market became flooded with reflexes whose pentaprisms were surmounted by incredible, bulky superstructures containing the photocell. In the early 1960's, selenium photocells were supplanted by tiny, very sensitive and accurate CdS photocells. In contrast to the selenium photocells, which were self-energizing, the CdS cells depended on external batteries which had to be replaced from time to time.

The market blossomed with a great many SLR's with external CdS meters. Minolta produced the SR7 and Nikon its first Photomic. Asahi Optical experimented with a number of cameras with external exposure meters which never reached the market. These prototypes were abandoned in order to pursue a new idea which proved to be a winner and fruitful beyond expectation. They designed a prototype with the photocell set on the inside of the pentaprism. Light metering was carried out directly on the ground glass where the image was formed. Only the enormous sensitivity of the CdS photocell made this possible, it would have been impossible with selenium.

This first Asahi Pentax with its internal photocell was officially introduced under the name Spot-Matic, at the 1960 Photokina. Its success was destined to radically change the world of photography. The big names in the photographic industry competed to develop the idea. Asahi Optical itself went back to reappraise its prototype, adopting new technical solutions. The new camera was completely changed in comparison with the original prototype, but almost unchanged in name, being called "Spotmatic" instead of "Spot-Matic". It was first shown in 1964. The body had been completely redesigned and the light meter circuit had undergone considerable development. The Asahi Pentax Spotmatic was ready for the mass market, but it was not the only reflex of this type.

Its direct competitors had prestigious names: Topcon, Nikkormat, Alpa, Praktica. All manufacturers had adopted the internal exposure meter system and had introduced interesting solutions to the problem. The Japanese and German manufacturers quickly adapted to the prevailing trend. Their design departments worked frantically to produce updated models and modify existing ones.

This metering system was instantly dubbed TTL by the Americans and has been universally known as such ever since.

In spite of imitations and competition, the Spotmatic retained its individuality, rapidly gaining a large slice of the market. Besides the TTL exposure meter, the Spotmatic offered the utmost operating simplicity, scrupulous attention to detail, and a very stylish design which was worthy of an international prize. Light metering took place through a pair of photocells and with the aperture closed to

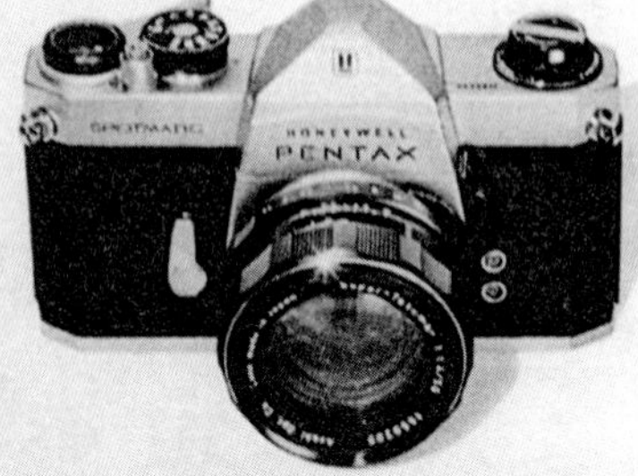
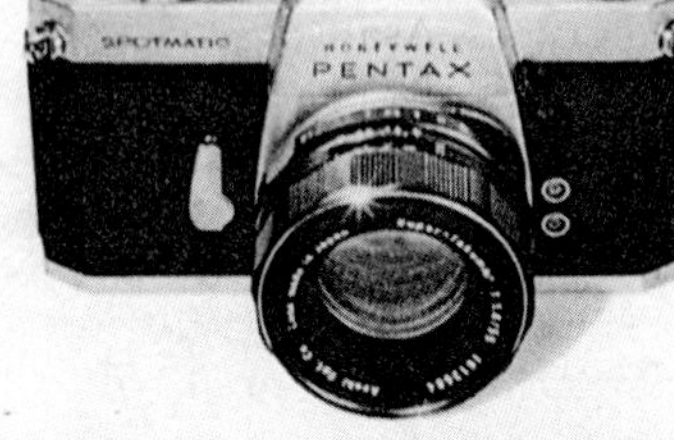

Advertisement for Honeywell Pentax Spotmatic.

the working value. The temporary black-out of the viewfinder was the price to be paid for ensuring accurate metering.

The Spotmatic quickly proved a real gem from the technical and aesthetic point of view. Fully automatic Super Takumar lenses were designed for it. The Super Takumars were made available in a number of focal lengths and apertures and came to form one of the most complete photographic systems of the 1960's. The universal screw mount made it possible for screw mount lenses produced by other manufacturers to be used with confidence, expanding the working potential of the camera to the full. In spite of this, the fact of having available a full system of original lenses played a fundamental role in establishing the Spotmatic. Matching innovation with tradition, Asahi Optical continued to retain the earlier models in its catalogue. The Asahi Pentax SV and S1a were improved and updated and presented as cheaper alternatives to the more expensive Spotmatic.

In 1968, Asahi Optical rationalized its production lines to make way for the large Asahi Pentax 6x7. The Asahi Pentax SV was pensioned off and in its place came the Asahi Pentax SL, without TTL exposure metering. It had the same body as the Spotmatic, and was to be the last model without a photocell. It was introduced as the poor relation of the Asahi Pentax system, but it did not gain wide acceptance and remained in production slightly less than three years.

The success of the Spotmatic was overwhelming and lasting. The very personal features of the camera imposed themselves beyond fashion and technological evolution itself. Far from thinking of the Spotmatic as the peak of achievement, the Asahi technicians devised new strategies and confronted the problem of the next Spotmatic. The screw mount presented many constraints and design problems. It limited the use of modern automatic diaphragms and subsequent development of the system. Whilst the Spotmatic was going through its most eventful period, serious thought was being given to abandoning the screw mount in favour of a bayonet mount. The 1960 experimental bayonet mount prototypes; Asahi Pentax Metalica and Spot-Matic, were dusted off. At the 1966 Photokina, a prototype Asahi Pentax Metalica II was put on display. Apart from the bayonet mount, it also introduced automatic exposure.

However, the prototypes were not developed immediately. They were temporarily set aside and remained at the level of a theoretical proposal. Despite changes round them, Asahi Optical remained faithful to the screw mount and the classic Spotmatic line. The market for the 35mm reflex was in growth phase and Asahi Optical shared this success without changing its image. But the traditionalist choice proved difficult to defend and maintain.

At the end of the 1970's TTL was no longer a novelty. Japanese and German companies competed in producing more or less successful imitations of the Spotmatic. There was a great increase in the number of reflexes equipped with screw mounts and TTL exposure meters. Some of these were cheaper than the Spotmatic but not so light, compact or elegant. The best-known amongst the Japanese were the Mamiya/Sekor, the Yashica and the Ricoh. Amongst the European there were the East German Praktica Mat and Praktica TL and the West German Edixa. In Russia the Zenit screw mount reflexes had been manufactured for years, equipped with an external exposure meter. Even Zeiss Ikon Voigtlander put a version of its Icarex, with screw mount and TTL exposure meter, into production.

A European branch, Asahi Optical Europe, was established with its head office in Belgium, followed by another branch in Hamburg and one in Brazil for South America. The North American success of the Spotmatic remained entrusted to Honeywell Pentax. Some Spotmatic models destined for the USA market were most inappropriately renamed H4, but in Japan the designation S4 was immediately put aside in favour of the name Spotmatic. At this time Asahi Optical also took an original initiative in opening the Pentax Gallery in Tokyo in December 1967. It was a sort of Museum of the Camera, combined with a photographic gallery. Alongside the Asahi Pentax models, some six hundred cameras belonging to various periods were on exhibition, making it possible to relive the history of photography. Some years later the company launched a magazine *Pentax Photography*.

With the success of the Spotmatic the number of imitators increased. The names Chinon and Cosina were added to the array of Japanese screw mount TTLs. At the end of the 1960's the SLR market divided into two sectors: the screw mount cameras, mass-produced and fitted with a universal mount for the lenses, filled the popular sector. The higher class reflexes had an exclusive bayonet mount which meant it was only possible to mount lenses of one particular make. The bayonet mount reflexes were expensive, stylish and complex.

The 1960's were dominated by the debate which raged between supporters of the screw mount reflex and those of the bayonet mount reflex. The screw mount reflex was widely available and mirrored the success of the screw mount Leicas of the 1930's and the 1950's. They could take lenses of almost any make and were therefore described as universal.

In practice, not all screw mount lenses suited all screw mount cameras. The inevitable errors due to over-wide tolerances sometimes created problems of in-compatability between different makes, causing disappointment to users, so the tendency to remain faithful to a particular make was reinforced. The most prestigious screw mount reflex of the time, the Spotmatic, rarely came with cheaper lenses than the Super Takumars. The so-called "universal lenses" found most favour amongst the owners of bayonet mount cameras. The high cost of original Nikon, Topcon or Minolta lenses led to the choice of less expensive ones from the independent makers. The screw mount, which had seemed to be the Spotmatic's weak point, proved throughout the 1960's to be its strong point. It became the symbol of the universal reflex by remaining unsurpassed in its originality.

Asahi Optical thrived in this favourable climate and the Spotmatic, unchanging, thrived with it. The special Motor Drive model was brought out, almost a challenge to the most famous motor drive reflex of the time, the Nikon F. Many special accessories appeared and the lens range became greater, year after year, with fast, lightweight lenses as well as very specialized and expensive ones.

Having gained experience with the 35mm format, Asahi Pentax moved into the so-called professional formats. Once again inspired by Pentacon, which for many years supplemented the Praktica 35mm with the Praktisix 6x6, Asahi Optical studied a prototype for a medium format. In 1966, at Photokina, the first Asahi Pentax of a larger format was introduced. This was a huge reflex built like a 35mm and provisionally named the Asahi Pentax 220. It used 120 and 220 rolls for images of a 6x7, the ideal format corresponding to the proportions of printing paper. The prototype was exhibited again two years later at the next Photokina. This giant Asahi Pentax only made its market entry at the beginning of the 1970's, with the name Asahi Pentax 6x7, and it had an electronically-controlled focal plane shutter.

At the beginning of the 1970's there was great excitement in the 35mm SLR world. Competitors put very sophisticated TTL models on the market. The automatic diaphragms made accurate and continuous metering possible with the aperture remaining fully open. Some of the new generation reflexes adopted selective metering of the spot or semi-spot type. Others made it possible to go from spot metering to integral metering by means of a simple switch. The first re-flexes appeared with automatic exposure based on servo-diaphragms controlled by the exposure meter. Rivals to the Spotmatic were the Nikon Photomic Tn, Nikkormat FTn, Topcon RE Super, Minolta SRT 101, Konica Autoreflex T and others of the same quality.

Competition took on the most bizarre forms. Canon suffered a set-back with the semi-transparent fixed mirror Pellix model. In order to redeem itself, it brought out the traditional FT QL, with bayonet mount and stop-down TTL metering. Canon placed itself within a decidedly low price bracket, offering good facilities and high standard optical equipment. Reflexes of this kind directly undermined the predominance of the Spotmatics.

Zeiss Ikon responded to the invasion of the Japanese TTLs with their Contarex and Contaflex models, fitted with an internal exposure meter. The most prestigious of the German firms, Leitz, introduced the TTL Leicaflex SL in 1968.

The Spotmatics continued unperturbed. With three million sold they held their own slice of the market. They were placed in an medium price bracket and continued to offer excellent quality for the price. But times were changing and the little Spotmatics found themselves surrounded on most fronts.

In 1970, the Fujica ST 701 was created by the Japanese giant, Fuji Film. Aesthetically, it closely matched the style of the Spotmatic, but its designers managed to make it even smaller and lighter. The TTL exposure meter used a silicon photocell which was far more sensitive than the CdS. This camera ushered in the fashion of the compact reflex and new approaches were indicated in the field of light metering. Olympus brought out a traditional screw mount 35mm reflex full of original features. For the first time a screw mount TTL reflex had a diaphragm simulator making metering possible at any aperture. The other screw mount reflexes for a long time remained confined by the stop-down system.

Rollei, gainsaying a long tradition bound to the 6x6 format, put into production a compact 35mm reflex with stop-down metering, calling it the Rolleiflex SL 35. In line and body Rollei was clearly inspired by the Spotmatic. To distinguish it from the crowd it was fitted with a new bayonet coupling for the exclusive Zeiss lenses.

Asahi Optical's countermove came at the end of 1971 with the Spotmatic II. Expectations of an innovative model were dashed by this camera. The SP II differed from the previous model only in minor details. The pentaprism was changed in appearance and, for the first time on an Asahi Pentax, included a shoe for the flash. The sensitivity scale was extended and there were a few cosmetic changes. A series of very interesting lenses were brought out at the same time as the SP II. The elements of these lenses were treated with an exclusive multi-layer, anti-reflective coating. They were designed for metering at any exposure aperture and the name was changed from Super Takumar to Super Multi Coated Takumar.

In spite of the apparently stagnant climate Asahi Pentax was preparing a few surprises. A few months after the SP II was introduced, a revolutionary camera, the Electro Spotmatic, was brought out. An electronically-controlled shutter was

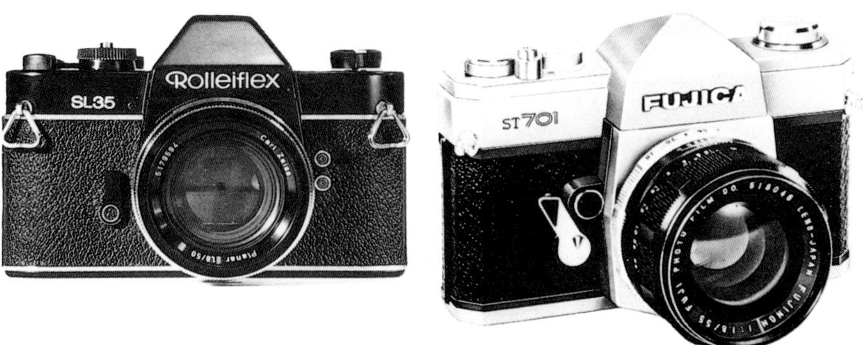

The Spotmatic design inspired the Rolleiflex SL 35 and the Fujica ST701, introduced at the 1970 Photokina.

hidden under a body derived from that of the Spotmatic II. For the first time in an SLR the shutter was programmed to set the right speed according to the exposure meter. The Electro Spotmatic was the first reflex with automatic aperture priority. There was no need for special lenses for it to function with fully automatic working. The Electro Spotmatic automatically selected the shutter speed with any lens or accessory not designed for the transmission of the traditional mechanical automatic workings. With the SMC Takumar lenses, the Electro Spotmatic was able to give light metering at all apertures. This feature was not greatly stressed and ran second to the automatic exposure.

The automatic electronic shutter revolutionised the SLR. Competitors were caught off balance and could find no better reply than to copy the line already taken. Electronic automatic reflexes sprang up like mushrooms. Nikon brought out the Nikkormat EL and Minolta put its spearhead XM model on the market followed by the cheaper XE models. Asahi Pentax was not content with having been the first and continued to design new models. The Electro Spotmatic was improved inside and out and became the ES II.

The continued production of screw mount cameras seemed anachronistic to many, but the cheaper SP 500 and SP 1000 models were made alongside the flagships ES and SP II. They were derived directly from the camera body of the Spotmatics and had no self-timer mechanism. They were intended to cover a sector of the mass market. Beside the latest generation cameras they seemed like survivors prolonging the Spotmatic line nostalgically and with little conviction.

A less happy exploit of the Pentax company was the Spotmatic F, heralded for some years and presented to the public in 1973. The technical specification was similar to that of the Spotmatic II with light metering at any aperture. The SPF arrived on the market considerably behind the competition and turned out to be a partial failure. It used the SMC Takumar lenses intended for connection with the diaphragm coupler but left many structural problems unresolved. The light

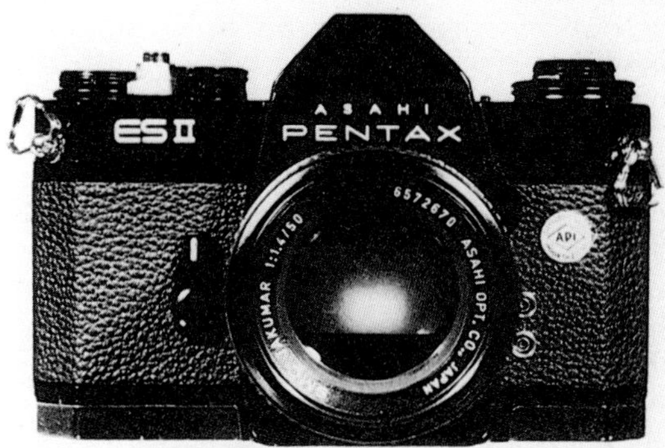

1954

Asahi Pentax crea la prima reflex con specchio a ritorno rapido. Da questo momento la reflex è rapi-

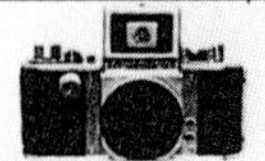

da nell'uso quanto gli apparecchi a telemetro.

1971

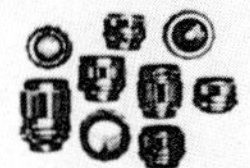

Asahi Pentax crea i primi obiettivi Super Multi Coated. Da questo momento è praticamente abolita ogni perdita di luce e di contrasto per riflessioni interne fra le lenti.

1960

Asahi Pentax crea la prima reflex con esposimetro TTL, per misurare la luce che attraversa effettivamente l'obiettivo. Da questo momento è

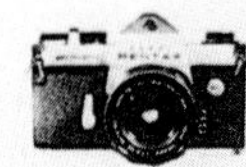

possibile conoscere la esposizione esatta, qualsiasi sia l'obiettivo montato sulla fotocamera.

OGGI

Asahi Pentax produce la Asahi Pentax ES II, la prima reflex automatica a controllo elettronico. La prima reflex dotata di circuito di memoria, con l'otturatore in grado di sce-

gliere una gamma infinita di tempi fra 1/1000 ed 8 secondi, per un'esposizione sempre perfetta. La reflex elettronica più venduta nel mondo - perché Asahi Pentax è ancora una volta all'avanguardia del progresso.

API SpA - Via Leonardo da Vinci, 16 - 50132 Firenze

Italian advertisement for Asahi Pentax ESII, stressing the continuous development of Asahi Pentax cameras.

meter reading circuit was activated automatically on securely screwing home the lens, without a special switch, but disconnecting the exposure meter meant unscrewing the lens from its mount. The Spotmatic F did not meet the requirements of photographers and it was technologically obsolete at birth. Asahi Optical did not worry too much about attending to the Spotmatic F because it had a winning ace up its sleeve. The introduction of the Spotmatic F had been a move made in expectation of subsequent events.

Within the span of a few years the photographic scene underwent radical changes. In 1972, Zeiss closed down camera manufacture, almost sanctioning with this gesture the foreseen end of the German camera industry. The technological and commercial competition was now solely between the Japanese manufacturers. Canon gained ground with its F1 and with the more modest FTb and EF. Some reflexes, like the Mamiya/Sekor, Yashica and Olympus abandoned the screw mount and adopted unique bayonet mounts. On the horizon a new star was born from collaboration between Zeiss and Yashica. It was called Contax RTS and had German lenses and very sophisticated Japanese electronics.

Competition between German and Japanese manufacturers had ceased. With the coming of the 1970's the duel was replaced by a kind of enforced collaboration. Leitz and Minolta formed an alliance better to confront the problems of a market which was becoming difficult to dominate. The crisis hit the Japanese manufacturers heavily. Big companies like Topcon and Miranda, who had gained significant commercial successes in the 1960's, closed their factories because they had not been able to produce new models quickly enough.

Times were ripe for a radical turn-around at Asahi. In 1975 the screw mount, which had characterized production for twenty-five years, was finally laid to rest. In the face of integrated circuits, motorization and new production technologies, the screw mount had exhausted its capabilities and had become an obstacle. The company caused a stir by bringing out three bayonet mount reflexes at once. The Asahi Pentax K2, KX, and KM replaced the Spotmatic line overnight. A full series of lenses was introduced for these cameras, covering a range of focal lengths from 15 to 1000mm. They were called SMC Pentax K and used the same optical construction as the SMC Takumar lenses. They were in elegant, chequer-patterned, rubber-covered barrels and had the exclusive K-bayonet mounting. With the end of the Spotmatics the Takumar lenses were taken out of production. The names Spotmatic and Takumar were brutally struck from the catalogues and buried in the memory.

This move by Asahi Optical brough to an end the development of screw mount SLR's. Many manufacturers had already abandoned the screw mount, others quickly followed their example. The screw mount Fujicas were supplanted by the X-bayonet mount Fujicas. Under licence from Asahi Optical, Ricoh, Cosina and Chinon adopted the K-bayonet mount. Pentacon and the Russian makers continued to produce screw mount reflexes very cheap and technically obsolete until the first half of the 1980's.

The disappearance of the Spotmatics meant extinction for a generation of cameras which had become a legend. The Spotmatic had been considered the most compact, lightweight, simple and universal reflex in the world. The cessation of their production closed a chapter in the history of the SLR and of the company. The introduction of the Asahi Pentax bayonet mount signalled the start of a prolific period which saw the Asahi Pentax system rise at a heady pace and assert itself in the race for better, automatic, compact and reliable cameras. The Asahi Pentax screw mounts retired from the scene with much ado, but also with dignity, to leave room for the new technologies. It was a bitter-sweet departure for things had been done well, with affection, good taste and honesty.

C H A P T E R   2

The Asahiflex

During the years of the American occupation, numerous Japanese optical companies, including Asahi Optical, were coerced into photography. Asahi Optical saw this as an opportunity to differentiate themselves from the other Japanese manufacturers. In line with this policy, they began to work on a reflex for the 35mm format. The first cameras to be produced were marketed from 1952 under the name Asahiflex. The Asahiflex was very modest and hardly original, either in name or design. In general structure it was heavily inspired by the prewar Praktiflex.

Other Japanese companies, in the immediate postwar period, produced numerous rangefinder cameras with fixed or interchangeable lenses. The Asahiflex represented the first attempt on the part of the Japanese to market a 35mm reflex which could in some way compete with the Europeans. At that time the 35mm single lens reflex was still very new and fraught with problems. The ability to frame the subject through the lens held an irresistible fascination for many professional photographers. In spite of its manufacturing complexity and slowness in operation, the single lens reflex was an unbeatable instrument in some fields of photography, like telephotography and close-up photography. So, in an audacious and unpredictable move Asahi Optical launched itself into 35mm reflex production.

Asahiflex

The first camera built by Asahi Optical showed many analogies with the 1938 Praktiflex. The Asahiflex had a waist-level focusing screen with a folding magnifier eyepiece and collapsible hood. The focal plane shutter had five speeds: $^1/20$, $^1/50$, $^1/100$, $^1/200$ and $^1/500$ sec. and B setting. It also reflected many of the aesthetic features of the Praktiflex as well as the technical ones. The octagonal form of the body, with its rounded corners, was similar to that of the German model but more accentuated. The layout of the main controls and the design of the front were also strongly influenced by the Praktiflex. The mirror box was square, projecting only slightly, and emphasized by broad metal side bands, like

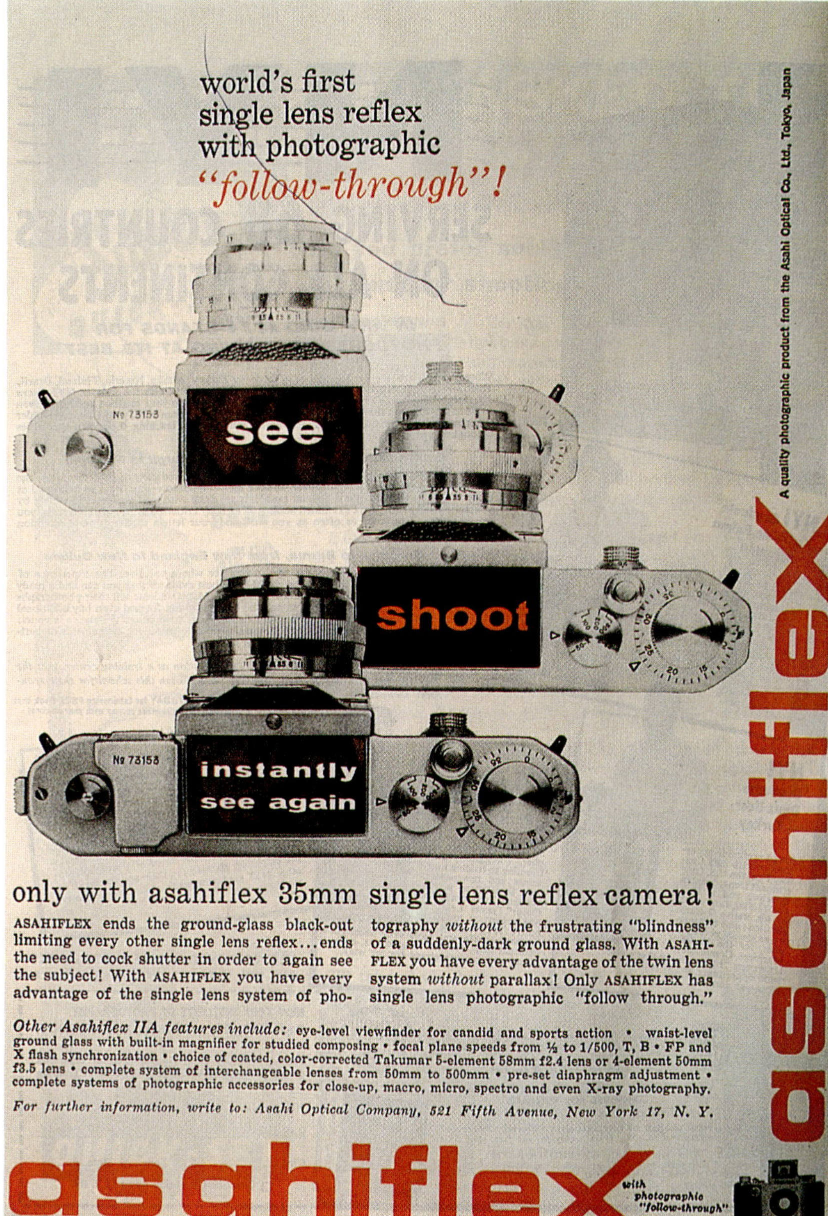

Asahiflex advertisement, 1957

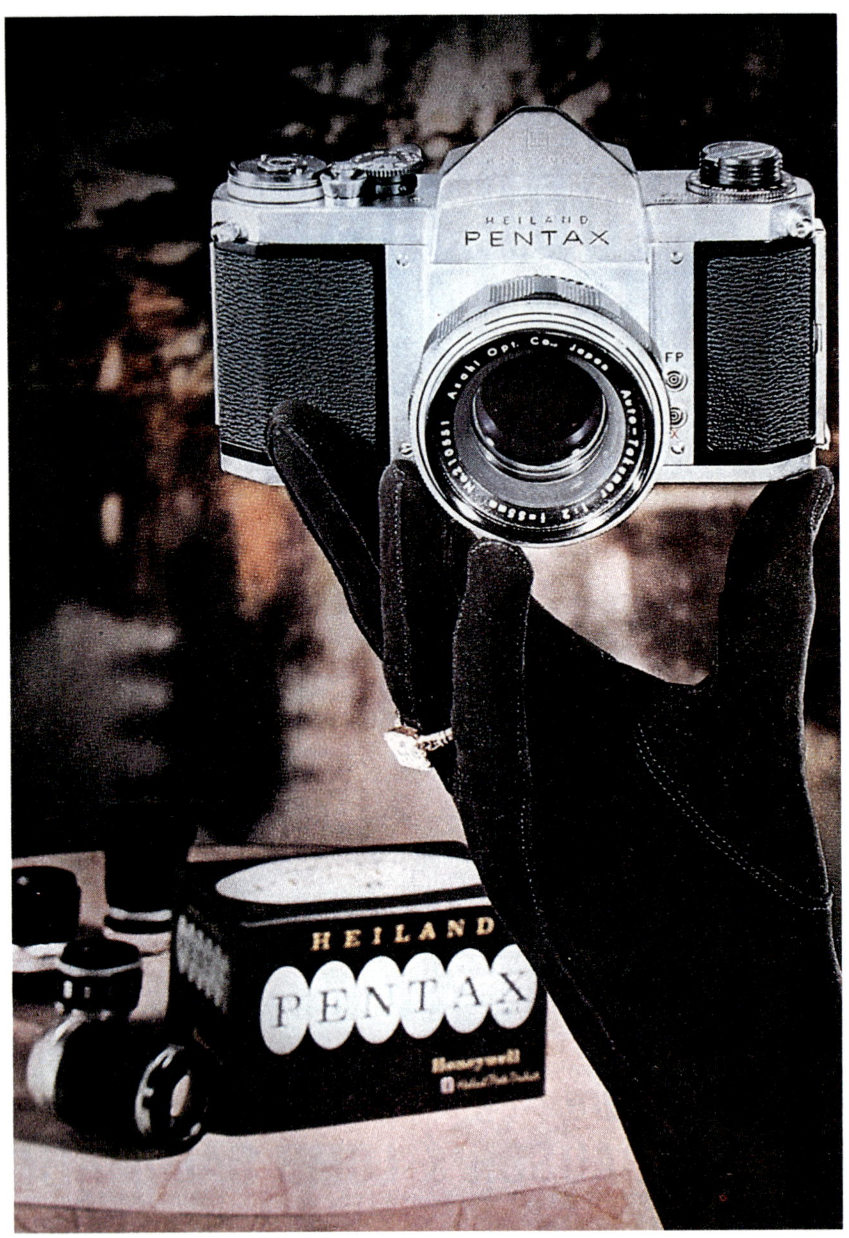

U.S.A. Heiland Pentax H2 advertisement, 1959.

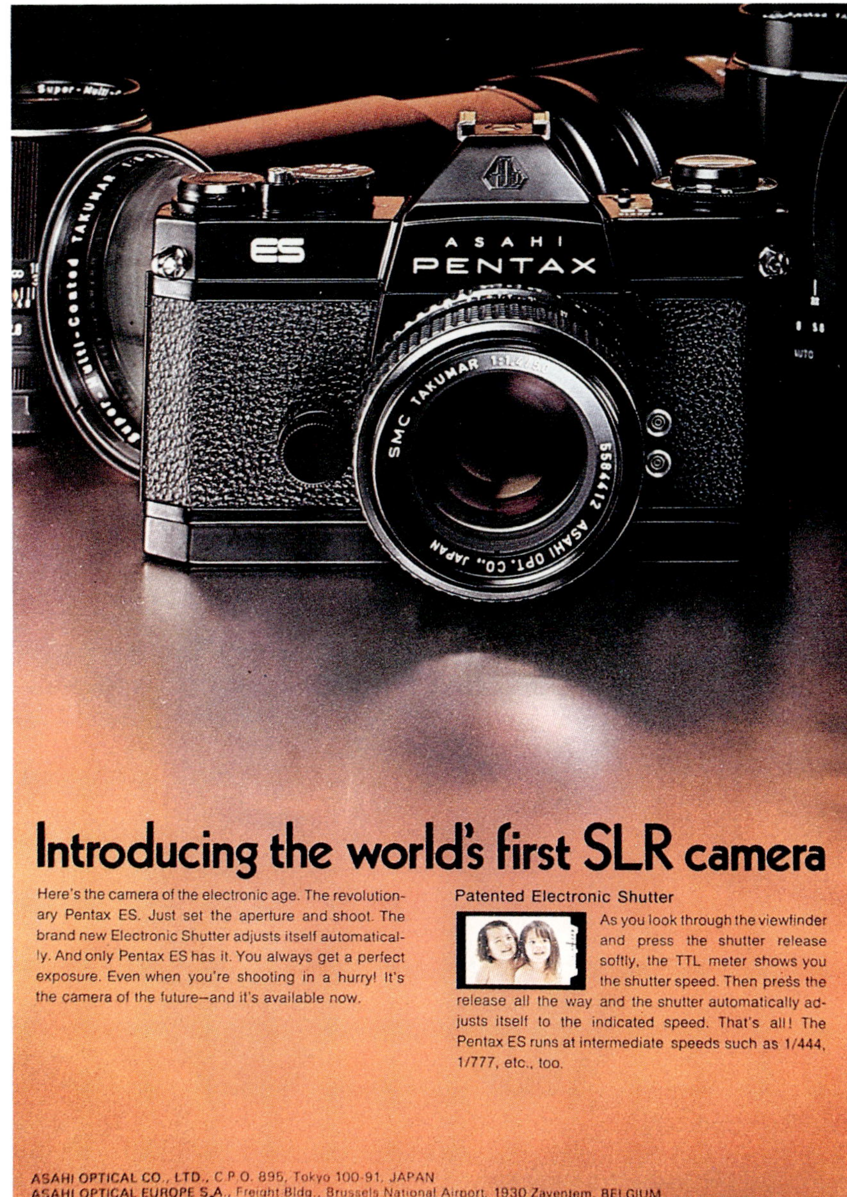

Asahi Pentax ES advertisement, circa 1972.

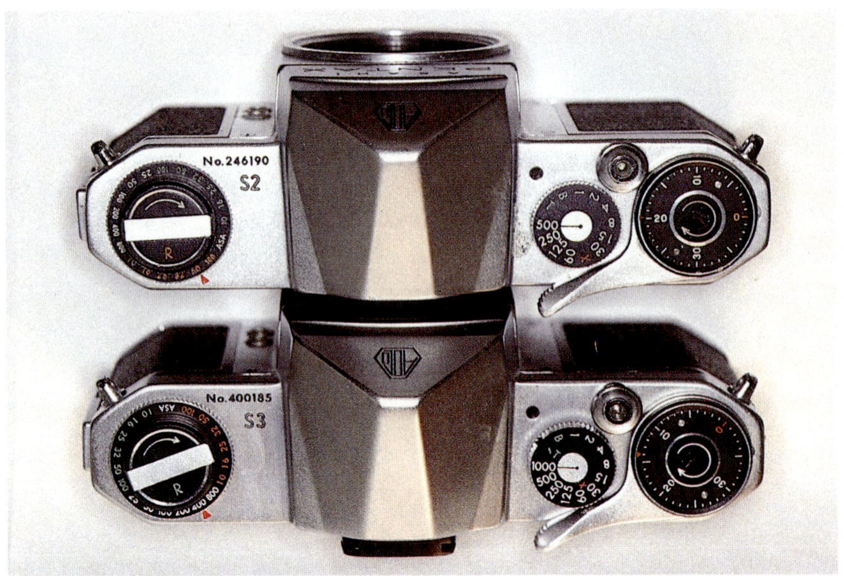

Asahi Pentax S2 and S3 compared.

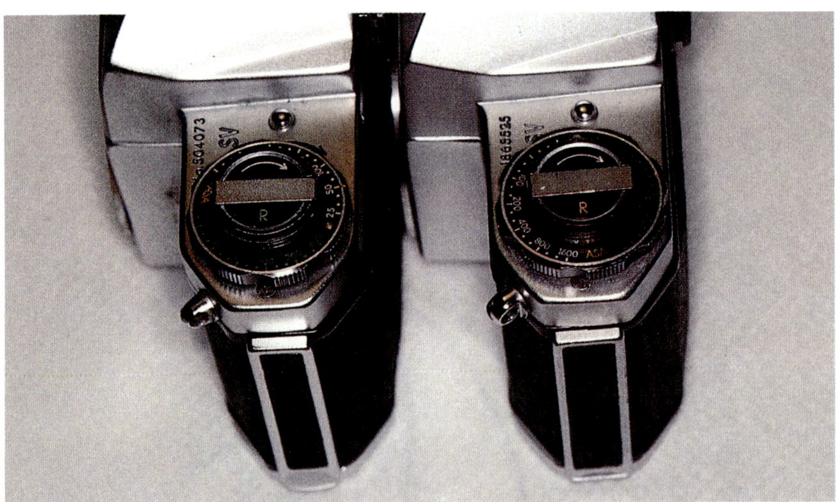

Asahi Pentax SV details. The scalloped wheel under the wind knob for winding the self-timer mechanism can be clearly seen. In the early models (left) the letter "R" on the rewind knob was green but it was orange on the late models (right). This camera was the Honeywell Pentax H3v in the U.S.A.

the German model. The main controls were small serrated knobs, similar to those on the Praktiflex and almost all contemporary cameras. The bigger knob, to the right of the viewfinder, was used for winding on the film, rewinding the shutter and resetting the mirror. The smaller one, to the left of the viewfinder, was used for rewinding the exposed film. The shutter release was located on the top plate.

The only original feature on the Asahiflex was the addition of a Galilean viewfinder. This second viewfinder was useful for following moving subjects. It was probably inspired by the Alpa Reflex, but was not connected to a rangefinder as on the Swiss camera. The serial number, of five digits, was engraved on the roof of the Galilean viewfinder.

The Asahi Optical trade mark, to be engraved on the pentaprism of all future Asahi Pentax cameras, made a fine showing on the folding cover of the waist-level viewfinder.

The Asahiflex took a standard 50mm, f/3.5 Takumar lens in a screw mount. The screw mount adopted for the Asahiflex did not correspond to any European one, having a slightly larger diameter than that of the 40mm of the Praktiflex, but smaller than the standard 42mm used on the Contax and Pentacon SLR's. The Asahiflex had a single FP flash terminal at the bottom left of the lens mounting.

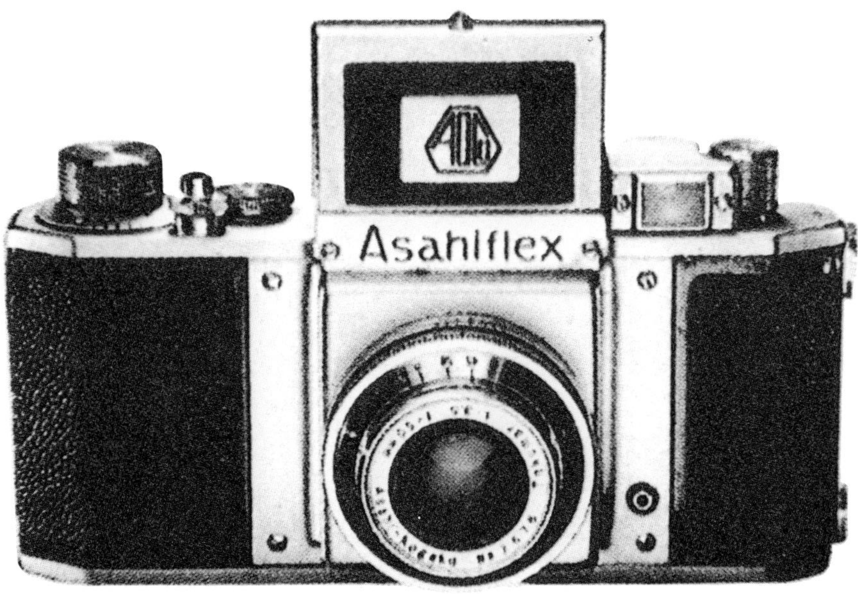

The original Asahiflex of 1952.

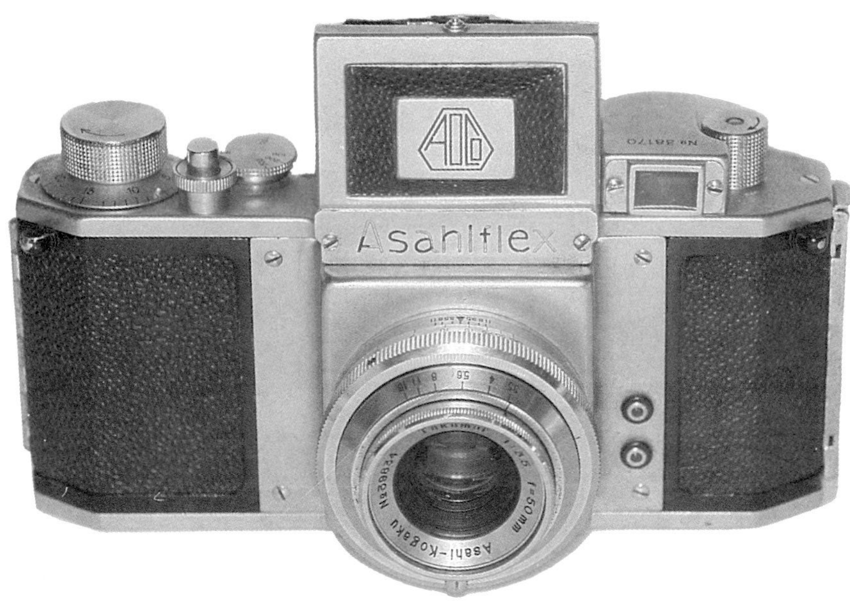

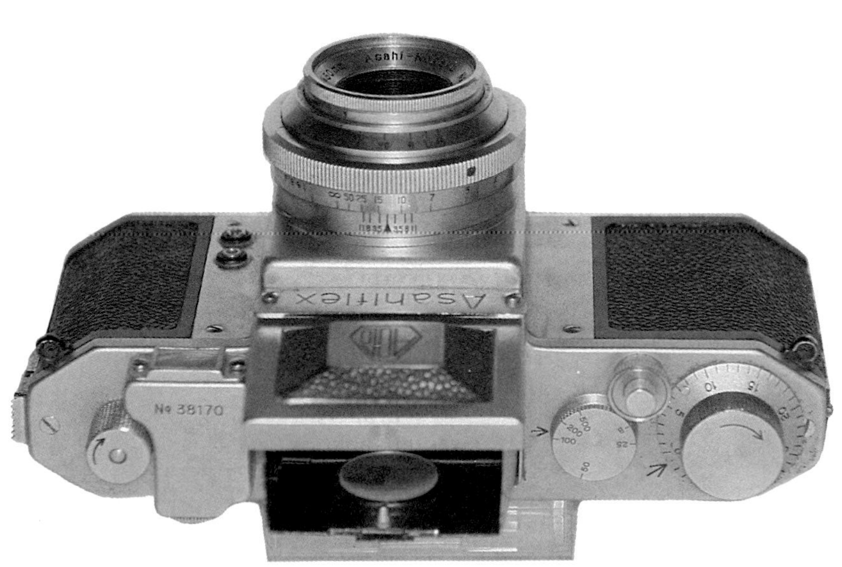

Asahiflex Ia

In 1953, several minor improvements were introduced to the original model. The slowest shutter speed was made $^1/25$ sec. and a second X terminal for the flash was added. There were no identifying letters on the camera body but the modified model was called the Asahiflex Ia by collectors to distinguish it from the previous model, Asahiflex I.

Asahiflex IIb

In 1954 Asahi technicians managed to solve the old problem of automatically raising the mirror after release. Priority for the invention can be contested by the Hungarian Gamma Duflex reflex brought out in 1947, but the Gamma patent was based on a different inventive step and was not followed up on a commercial basis.

The snag with all SLR's up to that time was the total black-out of the viewfinder when the mirror was raised prior to shutter release. The mirror had to be returned to the working position to restore vision, usually by the same action used for rewinding the shutter. With the introduction of the rapid-return mirror the SLR made a major step forward and became quick and practical in use like the rangefinder cameras.

The model on which the rapid-return mirror was installed was known as the Asahiflex IIb but it was not labelled as such. The camera was identical to the Asahiflex Ia in all general features including the shutter. The Galilean viewfinder, the usefulness of which was greatly diminished by the rapid-return mirror, remained obstinately in place.

Asahiflex IIa

In 1955 the automatic return mirror, proven by this time, was incorporated in the Asahiflex IIa. This was identical to the Asahiflex IIb, except for the shutter which had slow speeds $^1/2$, $^1/5$ and $^1/10$ sec. The additional shutter speeds required a separate selector knob which was placed on the front of the camera.

In spite of the revolutionary change brought to reflex photography by the automatic return mirror, the little Japanese company found it hard at first to gain recognition of its merits. Success finally came in 1957 when the innovation became known and appreciated beyond Japan. The American magazine, *Popular Photography*, reviewed the Asahiflex IIa enthusiastically in June 1957. A few months earlier the magazine had carried an advertisement for the camera taken out by Asahi Optical. Asahi Optical was thus able to gain a foothold in the United

---

Left: The 1953 Asahiflex, known by collectors as the Ia, had a second flash terminal for X synchronisation and a slowest shutter speed of 1/25 sec. instead of 1/20 sec. This example with Takumar 50mm,f/3.5 lens.

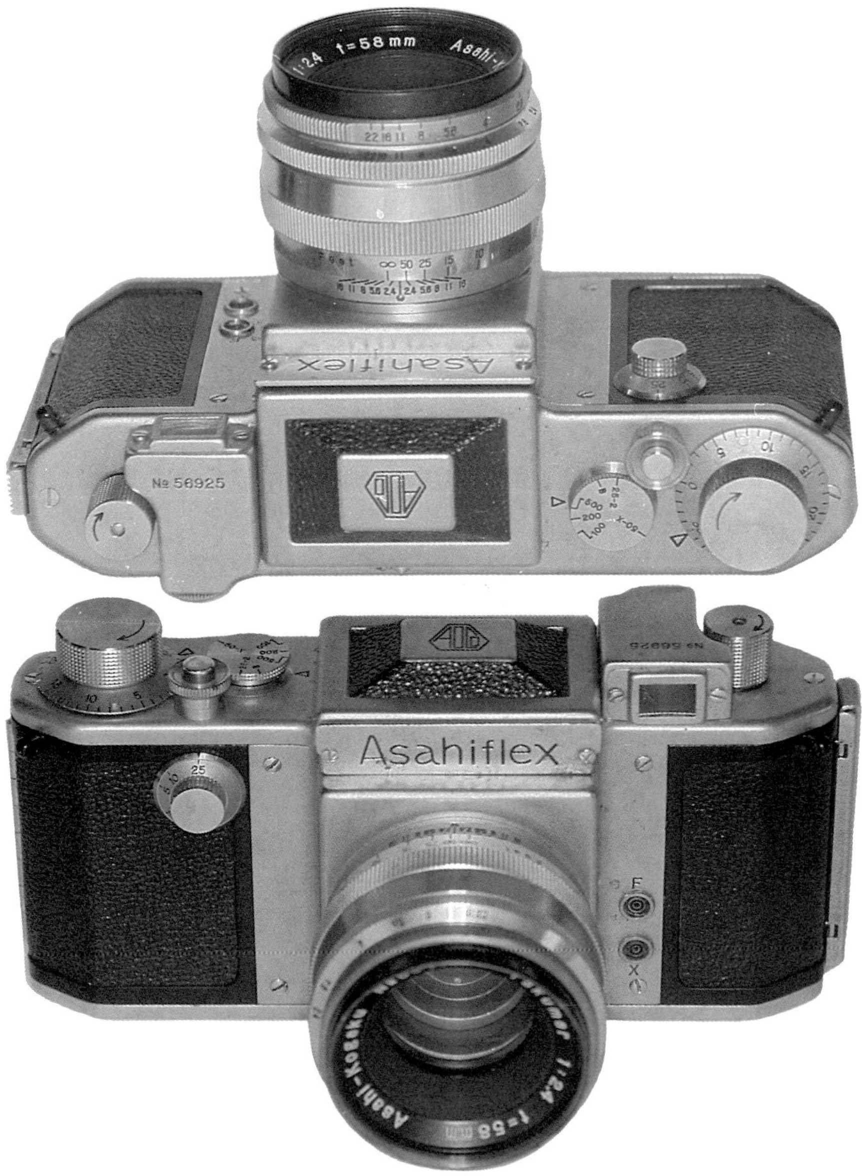

Asahiflex IIa of 1955 with Takumar 58mm,f/2.4 lens in 40mm screw mount.
This model had the rapid-return mirror and additional slow shutter speeds, set by the second dial on the front. The Asahiflex IIb, which preceeded it in 1954, was identical but had no slow speeds. Later IIb models used IIa body shells and had a round plate covering the hole where the slow speed dial would have been on a IIa.

States market, the richest and most coveted of the time. However, products coming out of Japan were still viewed with suspicion and the Asahiflex had to be content with second place beside the nobler European reflex cameras. With the initiative and dynamism which characterized the Japanese postwar industry, Asahi Optical cleverly exploited the opportunities offered to it and managed to establish a close-knit network of business relationships. In 1957 they opened a sales office in New York's Fifth Avenue.

Besides the new technical features, the Asahiflex was attractively priced. On the USA market the Asahiflex IIa, with the 50mm,f/3.5 lens, went for $99.50, and for $119.50 with the 58mm,f/2.4 Takumar lens with preset aperture. The Asahiflex IIb was sold at an even lower price; $89.50 with the 50mm,f/3.5 Takumar lens. The Asahiflex IIb was the cheapest 35mm single lens reflex available on the United States market. A few interchangeable screw mount lenses were sold for the Asahiflex. The 1957 price list showed two medium telephoto lenses; 83mm,f/1.9 and 100mm,f/3.5, together with a 135mm,f/3.5 and a spectacular 500mm,f/5.

Later Modifications to Asahiflex IIa and IIb

The Asahiflex underwent a few subsequent minor modifications during the second half of the 1950's. Some of the Asahiflex IIa cameras were made with the

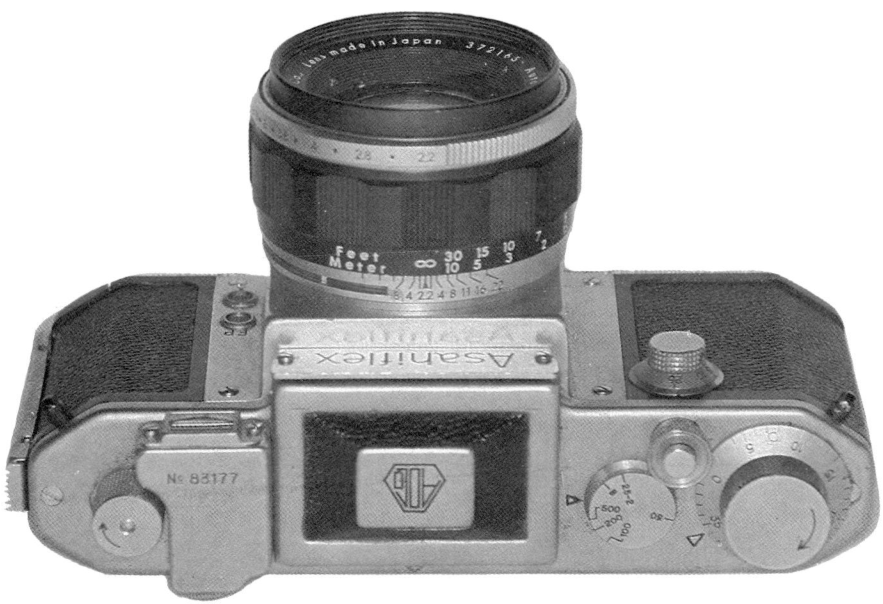

Later Asahiflex IIa, with 42mm screw lens mount and fitted with Auto Takumar 55mm,f/2.2.

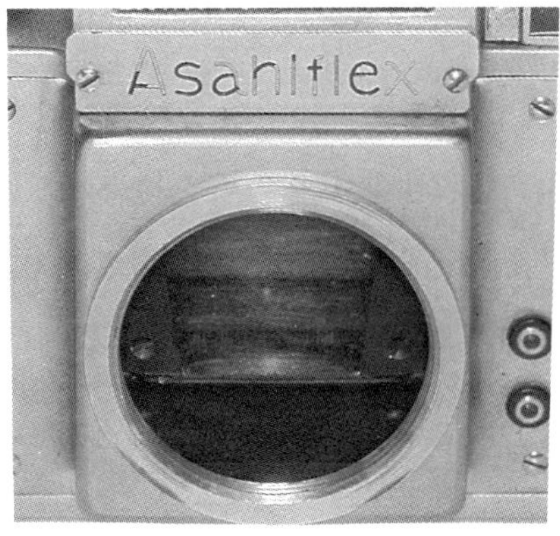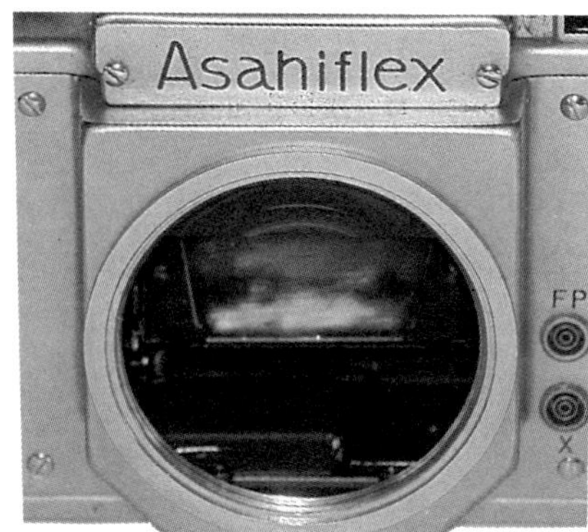

Asahiflex IIa
Left: 40mm screw mount.
Right: 42mm screw mount.

standard 42x1 screw mount. The last Asahiflex IIb was a modification of the IIa model. A little round cover hid the hole left by the absence of the slow speed dial. Some Asahiflex cameras were marketed in the USA under a different name. These were called Tower 22, 23 and 24 and were Asahiflex models being marketed by Sears Roebuck. The Tower cameras were supplied with Takumar lenses.

The success of the Asahiflex, spartan and efficient, encouraged Asahi Optical to offer the photographic public something better. The Asahiflex had opened a road which led far away into the distance and which Asahi Optical managed to travel right to the end.

CHAPTER 3

The First Asahi Pentax Family

In their December 1957 issue the American magazine, *Popular Photography*, published an advertisement for Asashi Optical. It was devoted to a new type of reflex. The camera was shown from the rear and not named in so many words. In the next issue of the magazine the camera was shown from the front with the name "Asahi Pentax" displayed on the base of the pentaprism. The camera went on sale at the beginning of 1958. The name "Pentax" was similar to the German mark "Pentacon" whose design influenced Asahi Optical in regard to a number of technical points. Compared with the Contax S and the Pentacon F the only resemblance was the fixed pentaprism and the standard 42x1mm screw mount for the lenses. In appearance, the Asahi Pentax differed radically from the German models.

The choice of the name Pentax was the ultimate tribute to Pentacon who in 1948, for the first time in Europe, brought out a screw mount reflex with a fixed pentaprism. The origin of the name most likely derived from a blending of the words PENTaprism and ContAX. (Interestingly, in 1946 Nippon Kogaku had used the names Bentax and Pentax to identify a number of 35mm prototype cameras.) The choice of name "Pentax" emphasized the importance attached to the viewfinder system.

The Asahi Pentax bore little resemblance technically or aesthetically to the Asahiflex, which was related to the German reflexes of the 1930's and 1940's. The Asahi Pentax heralded a new era and was to meet the demands of the 1960's. It was part of a careful business strategy aimed at potential new markets. The Asahiflex had succeeded in penetrating the rich, fruitful United States market, it was now set to assail the somnolent European market.

With the advent of the Asahi Pentax, the era of the waist-level viewfinder ended for 35mm cameras in general use. The pentaprism provided a direct image of the subject for horizontal and vertical shots without it being laterally reversed. The prism viewfinder proved to be very fast in use and very practical in searching for the right framing. The waist-level viewfinder was still the only practical

39

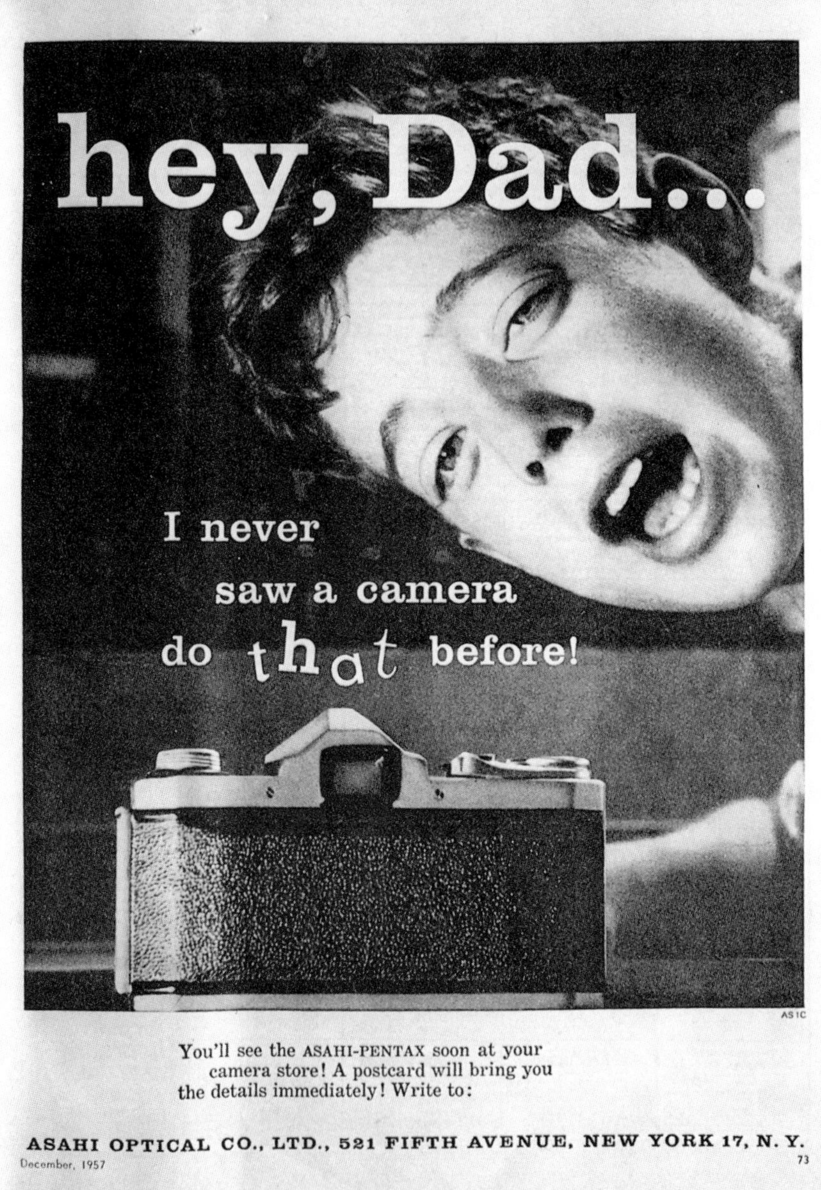

Advertisement for new Asahi Pentax in *Popular Photography* in December 1957.

solution for shooting from a very low position, or when one wished to point the camera discreetly. For this reason a number of professional reflexes preserved the possibility of using both types of viewfinder. The Nikon F, Topcon RE Super and a few others offered interchangeable viewfinders, with a waist-level finder being one choice.

Visually appealing and technically sound, the Asahi Pentax offered a comprehensive specification at a reasonable price and so stood out in the 35mm SLR market, which was at the beginning of a period of great expansion.

The camera had an octagonal body with very pronounced corners and a logical layout of controls, different from the reflexes which had preceded it. They were arranged on the top-plate, with the exception of the slow-speed dial, which remained on the front as on the Asahiflex II. The slow speeds were 1, $^1/2$, $^1/5$ and $^1/10$ sec. and the fast speeds $^1/25$, $^1/50$, $^1/100$, $^1/200$ and $^1/500$ sec. There was also B setting and X synchronization. The shutter was reset by means of a rapid-wind lever with built-in frame counter, which could be manually reset to zero. The frame counter dial was divided into forty notches, corresponding to the thirty-six frames on a standard roll plus four extra.

The wind lever, shutter release and fast-speed dial were grouped together on the top-plate, to the right of the pentaprism, according to a layout which became standard and remained unchanged for decades. The folding rewind crank was placed on the left. Coaxial with it was a dial on which it was possible to set the type of film used. The dial was divided into three sections, one for colour films, one for slides and one for black and white films. Each section was ASA calibrated, from 10 to 64 for colour and slides, and 25 to 800 for black-and-white. It was intended to serve simply as a reminder for the photographer, but generally people forgot to use it.

The front of the Asahi Pentax was square and emphasized by two vertical chrome bands on the sides of the lens mounting. The mirror box was rounded off at the bottom and at the top, culminating in the elegant fixed pentaprism. The shape of the pentaprism was attractively angled and very distinctive. The base of the prism projected a few millimetres above the top plate. The back of the camera could be opened by means of a vertical sliding latch on the left.

Elegant, small and light, the Asahi Pentax attracted attention with its unmistakable outline and technical features, which were improved on later models. It gained considerable success thanks to its extremely well-planned and inspired design. For a number of years to come, refinement in design was to be an unfamiliar factor of European cameras and other Japanese models.

Continual improvements were made to the internal mechanical elements of the camera and introduced on later models. The very successful body remained unchanged for several years until the mid-1960's.

The Asahi Pentax serial number was brought up to six digits and engraved on the top plate, next to the rewind crank. The first model did not have any identification letter and was formally characterized with the initials AP. It was

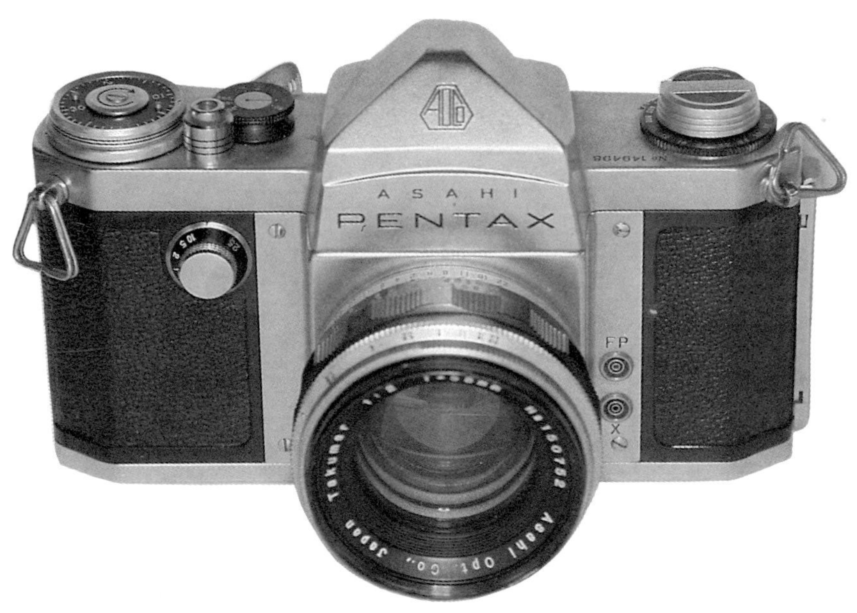

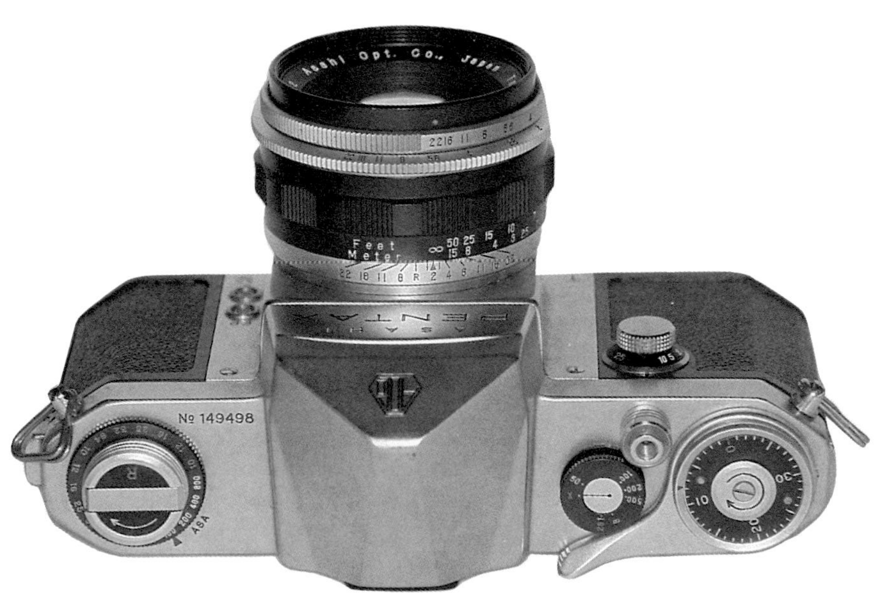

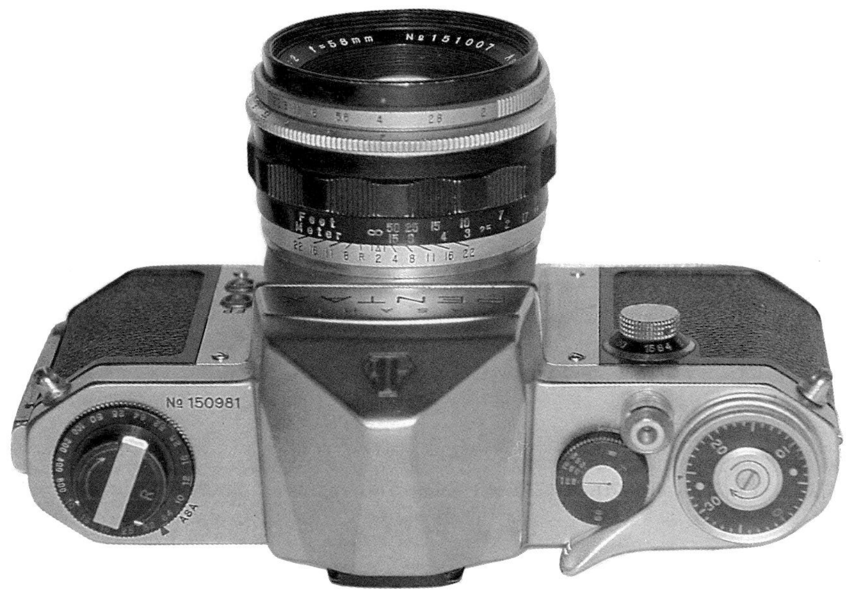

The Asahi Pentax S was the improved model of the original Asahi Pentax. The shutter speed range was in geometric progression.

sold with a f/2 or f/2.2 standard 58mm lens. With the aid of a small intermediate ring it was possible to mount Asahiflex screw mount lenses onto the Asahi Pentax.

In the United States the Asahi Pentax with the 55mm,f/2.2 lens was put on sale at $195. It was also sold there as the Tower 26 with a 58mm, f2.5 Takumar lens.

Asahi Pentax S

During 1958 the original Asahi Pentax underwent its first modification and became the Asahi Pentax S. The two models were identical except in minor details such as the finish on the rewind lever, which became black instead of chrome. The only substantial difference was in the shutter speed calibration which was rationalized. The slow speed dial on the front showed 1, $^1/2$, $^1/4$, $^1/8$, $^1/15$ and $^1/30$ sec. and the fast speed dial on the top plate $^1/60$, $^1/125$, $^1/250$ and $^1/500$ sec. A faster standard lens, the 55mm,f/1.8 Takumar with manual pre-setting was fitted. These early Asahi Pentax models did not bear any identifying

---

Left: The original Asahi Pentax is named "AP" by collectors. It has the standard Praktica 42x1 screw mount, pentaprism and two shutter speed dials. This example has a Takumar 58mm, f/2 lens.

mark or initial, and were made in a limited number. At the end of 1958 they were replaced by an improved version called Asahi Pentax K.

Asahi Pentax K

The Asahi Pentax K camera was presented at the 1958 Photokina. It introduced a few small technical and functional improvements over the original Asahi Pentax. The maximum shutter speed was raised to $^1/1000$ sec. The slow speeds continued to be controlled by the dial on the front. The standard lens for the Asahi Pentax K was the 55mm,f/1.8 Auto Takumar, fitted with a mechanical device for automatic closure of the diaphragm.

In the screw mount cameras there had been ample mounting tolerance between the lens and camera body. For this reason it was not easy to effect a sufficiently accurate coupling for the mechanical transmission of automatic working of the diaphragm. The Asahi Pentax K solved the problem by incorporating a movable plate within the mounting which was activated by the shutter release. On pressing the shutter release the plate was pushed forward and depressed a small pin on the rear of the lens. This pin released the spring which caused the preselected aperture to close automatically. The dimensions of the plate were sufficiently wide to ensure contact with the pin even when the lens was not perfectly aligned.

Reopening of the aperture was done manually by pressing a small button on the Auto Takumar lens mount. The semi-automatic diaphragm with internal transmission was a minor invention which was imitated and used by other manufacturers of screw mount reflex cameras.

The Asahi Pentax K cameras were outwardly identified by the letter "K" engraved on the top-plate above the serial number. The film memo dial was modified to indicate the increased sensitivity of colour or slide films to ASA 100.

The focusing screen was also improved by the inclusion of a microprism circular area in the centre for more accurate focusing than was possible on traditional ground glass.

The optical equipment for the Asahi Pentax K included three Auto Takumar lenses with preselector diaphragm: 35mm,f/4 wide-angle, 105mm,f/2.9, and 135mm,f/3.5, together with three non-automatic Tele Takumar telephoto lenses: 300mm,f/4; 500mm,f/5; and 1000mm,f/8. It was not a particularly big range of lenses, even for the 1960's, but it was the sign of a burgeoning system. The reflex system was not yet able to accommodate ultra-wide-angle lenses, which remained the prerogative of the rangefinder cameras, but the best reflex system included numerous telephoto lenses, appreciated by photographers of the time for their optical quality and the photographic possibilities they offered.

In the USA the Asahi Pentax K was sold with the 55mm,f/1.8 Auto Takumar lens at $249.50. A few Asahi Pentax K cameras were imported into Europe where they sold at an equivalent price.

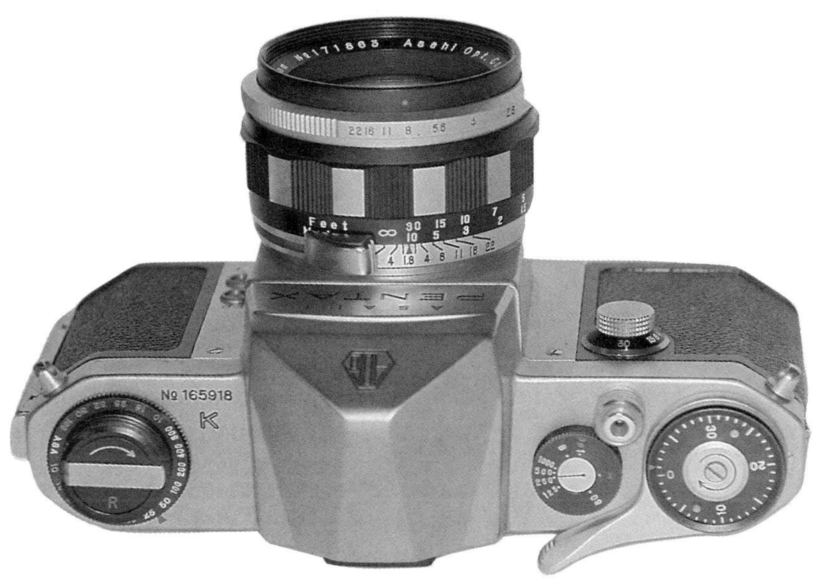

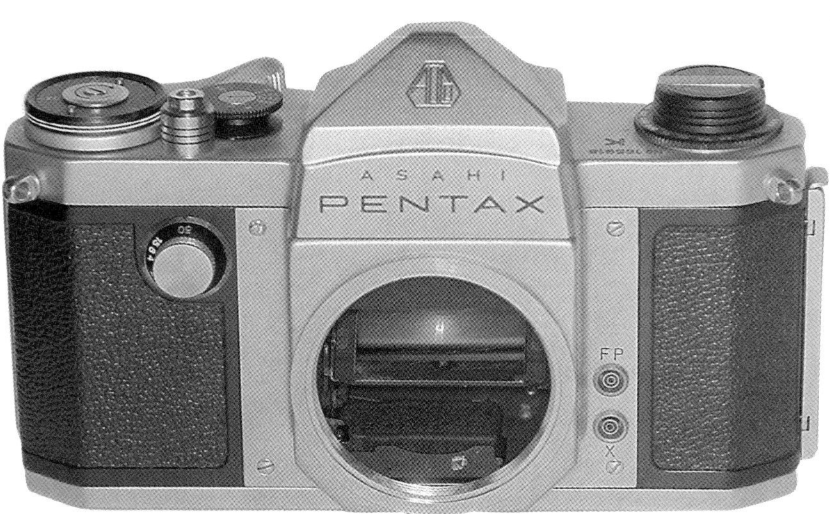

The Asahi Pentax K was the improved model of the Asahi Pentax S, with a top speed of 1/1000 and a mechanism for automatic diaphragm stop-down. Here with Auto Takumar 55mm, f/1.8.

C H A P T E R   4

The Asahi Pentax Before TTL

In the autumn of 1959 the S2 model was introduced. Its main feature was the single dial situated on the top plate for control of the shutter speeds. It was the rationalization and simplification of the Asahi Pentax K.

In 1960, the prototype Asahi Pentax Spot-Matic, the first reflex in the world to have an internal photocell with TTL metering, was unofficially displayed at the Photokina exhibition. The prototype left a few problems unresolved and was comprehensively redesigned during the years that followed. Four years went by before the Spotmatic could be put on the market. During this period Asahi Optical abandoned plans for a reflex with an external photocell.

The Asahi Pentax cameras produced from 1960 to 1962 adopted different initials and numberings depending on the markets for which they were destined. They were called S2, S3, S1, H2, H3, H1, SB or SB2. The many initials characterized versions more or less developed from the same basic model. The differences consisted of a few details. Some models had a maximum shutter speed of $1/1000$ sec. and the mechanism for diaphragm coupling.

The "S" designated cameras were destined for Japan and Europe. Those with "H" marking were destined for the North American market. Those marked "SB" were destined for exclusive sale in Japanese military shops. None of these cameras differed from the standard model or offered special facilities.

During the first half of the 1960's the range of Takumar and Super Takumar lenses expanded. Thanks to retrofocus design, ultra-wide-angle lenses could be made which did not interfere with the movement of the mirror and were put into production for the Asahi Pentax. The accessories also increased in number and variety. Studies in sensitometry led to the design of the Asahi Pentax Meter which used a CdS cell and coupled with the speed-setting dial of Asahi Pentax cameras. It remained in production after the arrival of the Spotmatics. It was manufactured up to the end of the 1960's, in its final form as the Asahi Pentax Meter SL.

In July 1963 the last Asahi Pentax of the generation preceding the Spotmatics was introduced. It was sold in Europe and Japan with the designation "SV", but

46

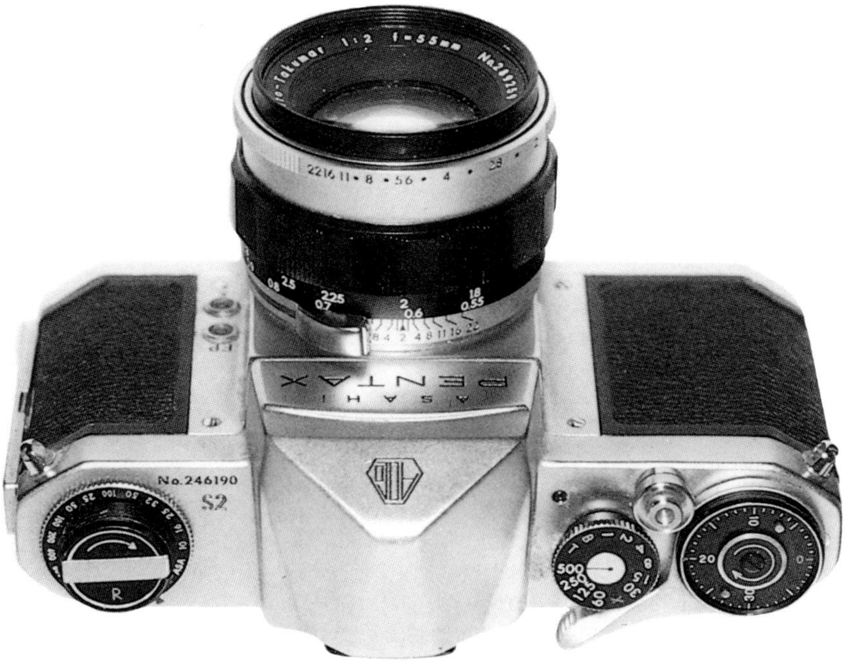

Asahi Pentax S2 with Auto Takumar 55mm,f/2. The first Asahi Pentax camera with a single shutter speed dial.

in the USA it was named the Honeywell Pentax H3v. The SV was the culmination of a fully matured photographic system. It was a sturdy, reliable camera with a comprehensive range of facilities. This and other SLR's of its generation were unjustly pushed aside by the pressing tide of TTL reflexes.

Between the end of the 1950's and the early 1960's many Japanese manufacturers had launched into SLR production. We saw the Canonflex and Petriflex, the Minolta SR and Topcon R. The most professional reflex of the time, the Nikon F, arrived in 1959. The rival reflexes possessed interesting features and often provided excellent facilities, but no camera managed to equal the Asahi Pentax cameras for compactness, lightness and elegance.

Asahi Pentax S2

The Asahi Pentax S2 replaced the Asahi Pentax K, with a number of design improvements. The separate slow speed dial disappeared from the front of the camera, and a single dial on the top plate controlled the full range of shutter speeds, and it did not revolve during shutter release.

The focusing screen comprised a Fresnel lens, with a central microprism disc and a fine-ground outer area. On the top plate of the camera, next to the shutter release, a tiny round window showed a red signal each time the shutter was rewound.

The range of shutter speeds was from 1 to $^1/500$ sec. and plus B and T. The $^1/1000$ sec. present on many reflexes of the period and on the Asahi Pentax K, was unaccountably omitted. Just as unaccountably, the standard lens was not the 55mm,f/1.8 Auto Takumar, which was supplied with the Asahi Pentax K, but a 55mm,f/2 Auto Takumar which was slower by half a stop.

The fastest shutter speed of $^1/500$ sec. and the relatively slow standard lens is most likely explained in terms of cost. The choice of a technologically advanced, but less expensive model was induced by competition from other Japanese producers. Nikon, Canon and Topcon aimed high by offering professionally ambitious, expensive models. Asahi Optical opted for the mass market.

In the United States, Asahi Optical was represented from the autumn of 1959 by the Honeywell Corporation, which distributed the cameras through its Heiland Division. The Asahi Pentax S2 cameras destined for the USA market adopted the designation "H2" in honour of its prestigious business partner, and the name was changed to Heiland Pentax. The Asahi Pentax logo, on top of the pentaprism was replaced by the H of Honeywell. The Heiland Pentax H2 was on sale at $179.50. The price was $70 lower in comparison with that of the 1958 Asahi Pentax K. The lower price, due to the simplified specification, helped to establish the Heiland Pentax brand on the market. Some cameras labelled H2 and marked Asahi Pentax as well as Heiland Pentax were imported into Europe alongside the Asahi Pentax S2. The sale price of the S2 and H2 was lower than that of the Asahi

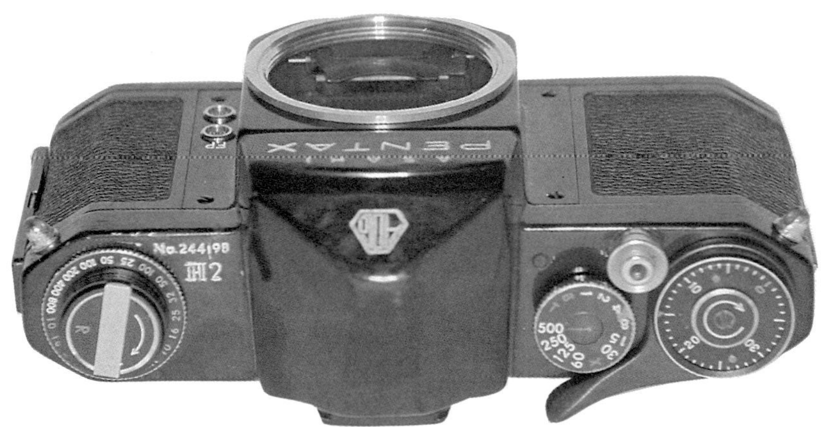

The S2 was designated H2 in the U.S.A. Subsequently the name Heiland replaced Asahi on the pentaprism.

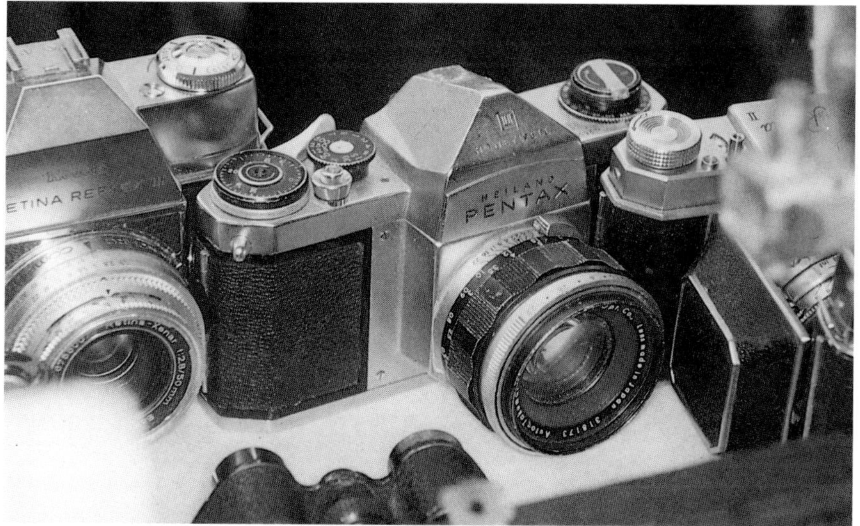

Heiland Pentax H2, photographed in shop window.

Pentax K on the European markets. From the S2 version onward the Asahi Pentax was available in black as well as chrome.

The range of Auto Takumar lenses was increased with the advent of the S2. Two 35mm lenses replaced the 35mm,f/4 Takumar. The faster one had an f/2.3 aperture, the other, particularly compact and light, was an f/3.5. There were also two medium telephoto lenses, a standard 85mm,f/1.8 portrait lens, and a 200mm,f/3.5 lens which was fairly fast in relation to the focal length.

Asahi Pentax S3

The cameras designated "S3" were presented at the 1960 Photokina. They were improved versions of the S2 and had a slightly superior specification, including a maximum shutter speed of $^1/1000$ sec. (but not on all models) and a 55mm, f/1.8 Auto Takumar lens as standard. The faster standard lens justified an increase in the list price. A few of the Asahi Pentax S3 cameras had the facility for mounting the separate Asahi Pentax Meter. Production of the S3 was sporadic and inconsistent. Cameras with even quite considerable differences had the designation S3.

Asahi Pentax S1

The Asahi Pentax S1 was introduced in 1961 as the poor relation of the S2 and S3. They were supplied with a 55mm,f/2 Auto Takumar lens or the slower 55mm, f/2.2 Takumar as standard. The maximum shutter speed was $^1/500$ sec. A notch

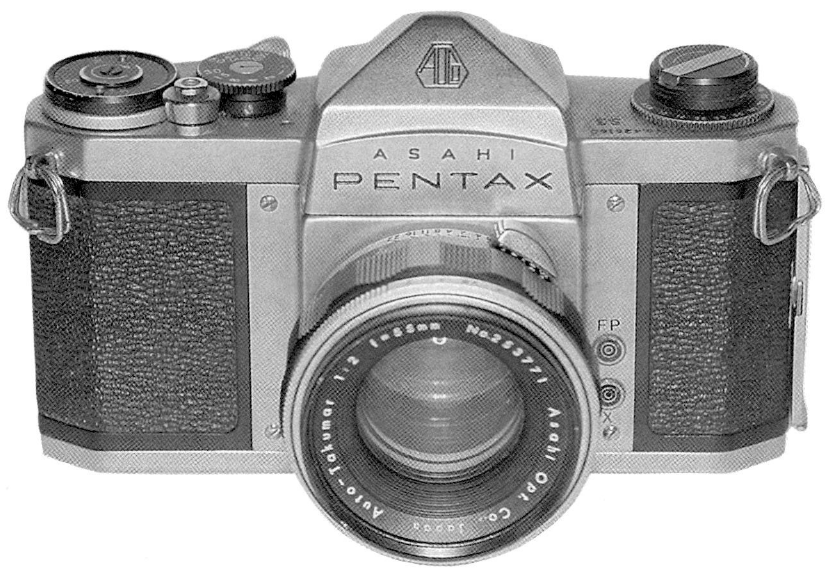

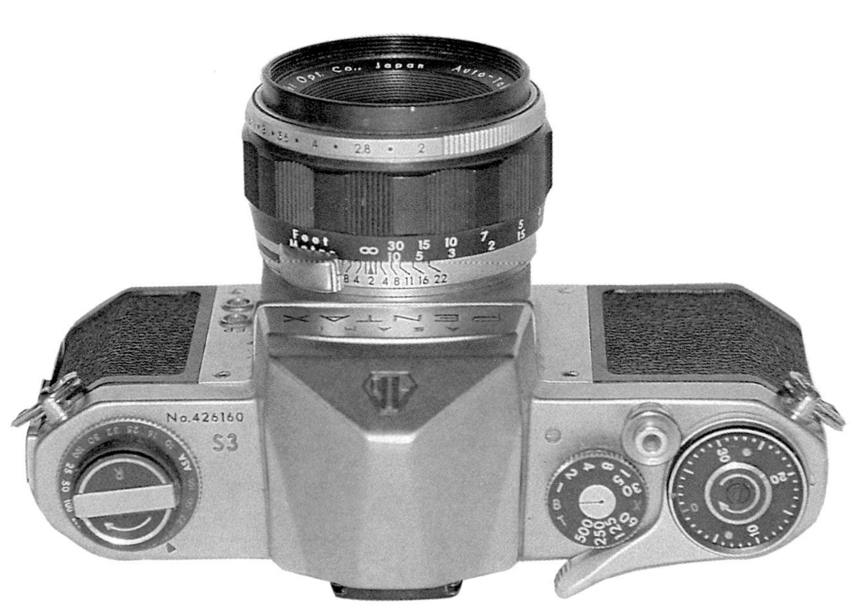

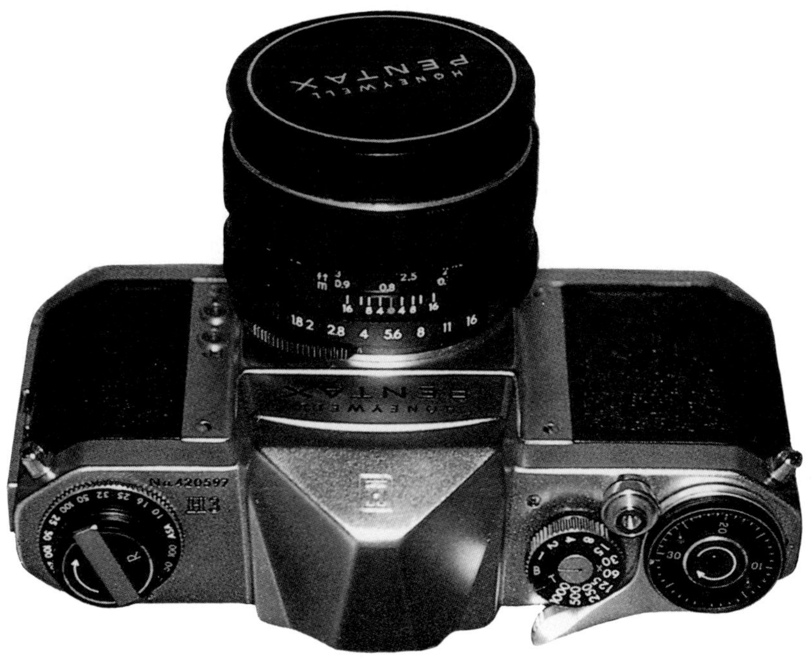

Honeywell Pentax H3 - the U.S. version of the S3.

on the shutter speed dial, corresponding to T, made it possible to couple with the separate Asahi Pentax Meter.

Although the speed dial on the Asahi Pentax S1 was only calibrated to $^1/500$ sec., by continuing to turn it beyond $^1/500$ one could locate a further stop. When set at this non-indicated value, the shutter of the Asahi Pentax S1 operated at a speed of $^1/1000$ sec. In order to offer the S1 at a lower price the figure on the speed dial was removed without modifying the shutter with a mechanical lock.

Equipping the same camera bodies with standard lenses of different maximum apertures, and identifying them with different designations to sell at different prices, formed part of a careful sales strategy. This had been the usual practice, in Europe from the end of the 1930's.

The S-family Asahi Pentax was sold as transition models between the original Asahi Pentax and the very successful Spotmatics to come. The role they played in the commercial success of the make was far from secondary however. In the early 1960's the Asahi Pentax stood out by its rational design, its lightness and

Left: The S3 was identical to the S2 but had a top speed of 1/1000 sec. Even so, some examples labelled S3 had a top speed of only 1/500 sec. Here with Auto-Takumar 55mm, f/2 lens.

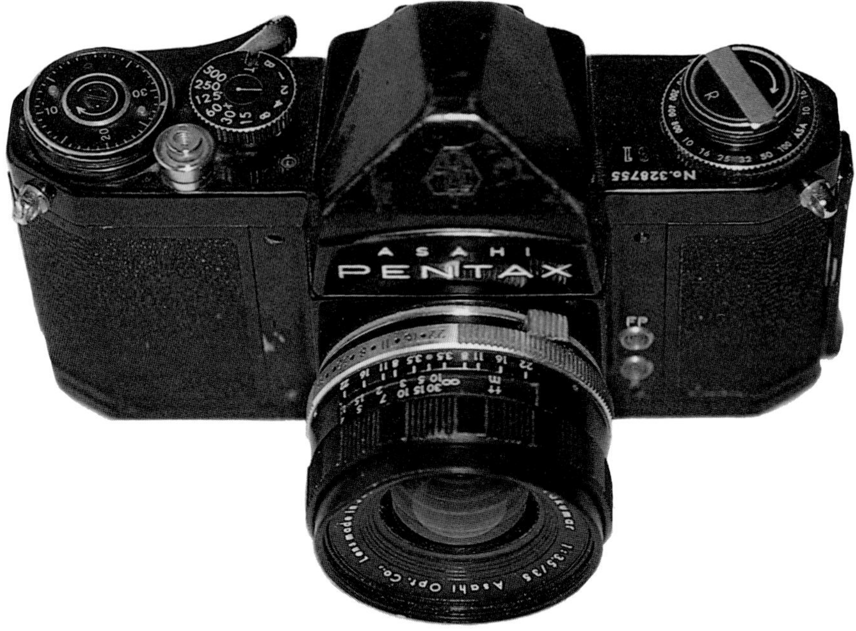

Asahi Pentax S1 in black finish.

compactness, as well as by a generally cleaner line. A few of the S-series were produced in black with white lettering, increasing the compact effect of the cameras.

Asahi Pentax SV

In 1963, a new model was brought out to replace the somewhat chaotic production of the previous years. The features which had marked the various Asahi Pentax models of the early 1960's were combined into a camera which was then subsequently improved. It was identified on the European and Japanese markets by the designation "SV". In the USA the Asahi Pentax SV was seen as a modified version of the Pentax H3, and called the H3v.

The Asahi Pentax SV became part of the Pentax tradition by incorporating a number of interesting features. It was fitted with a self-timer mechanism with the control located in a rather original position, and automatic control of the diaphragm. The standard SV lens was a fully automatic 55mm,f/1.8 Super Takumar. The Asahi Pentax SV replaced the previous range of S2 and S3 models and the Asahi Pentax S1a replaced the Asahi Pentax S1.

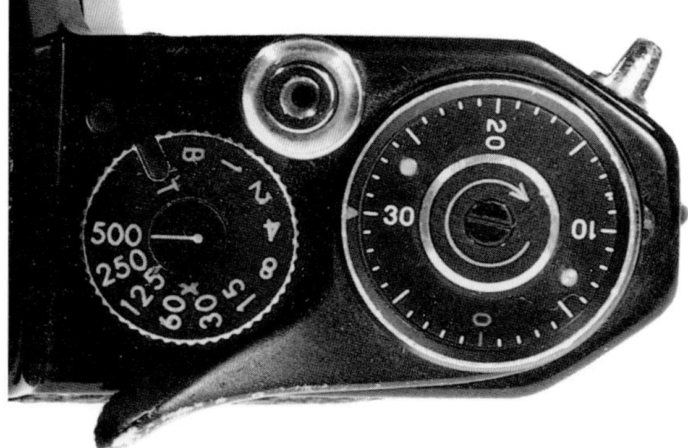

Note the notch in the shutter speed dial of the S1 for mechanically coupling the Asahi Pentax Meter.

The Asahi Pentax SV and S1a remainded in production for almost five years, up to 1967. Despite the success of the Spotmatics, they continued as cheaper alternatives. The three Pentax sisters were put on the market at the same time, at three different price levels, in accordance with the firm's marketing policy.

The Asahi Pentax SV represented the best of the Asahi Pentax generation without a built-in exposure meter. It was the culmination and natural evolution of the models which had preceded it. It continued to use the same body but with considerable improvements at the control and functional levels.

It had the full range of shutter speeds, from 1 to $^1/1000$ sec., including B and T. It utilized a standard design wind lever which incorporated the frame counter which automatically self-zeroed after the last exposure. The number of frames exposed could be read through a small window. The focusing screen was improved, with increased brightness and incorporating a microprism circle. The back door was opened by a vertical latch located on the camera body and not on the door, as with previous models. The latch fastened at two points and incorporated a spring.

The most interesting feature of the Asahi Pentax SV was a timing mechanism for delayed-action release. This self-timer was situated on the top plate. The large dial for winding the timer spring was coaxial with the film rewind knob. The only other reflex with a self-timer release mechanism located in a similar position was the Exakta, but that had its rewind knob on the base.

Winding of the self-timer was done by turning the knurled wheel clockwise. The timing train was set in motion by pressing a button situated on the top plate next to the pentaprism. This complicated solution was not followed up on subsequent Asahi Pentaxes, nor on any other reflex. It had been designed this way because it made it possible to incorporate the self-timer into existing bodies. The combination of the rewind knob and the self-timer meant that the film reminder disc had to be modified. This was divided into two sections, one for black-and-white film calibrated from ASA 25 to 1600 and the other for colour film, negative or slide, from ASA 12 to 400.

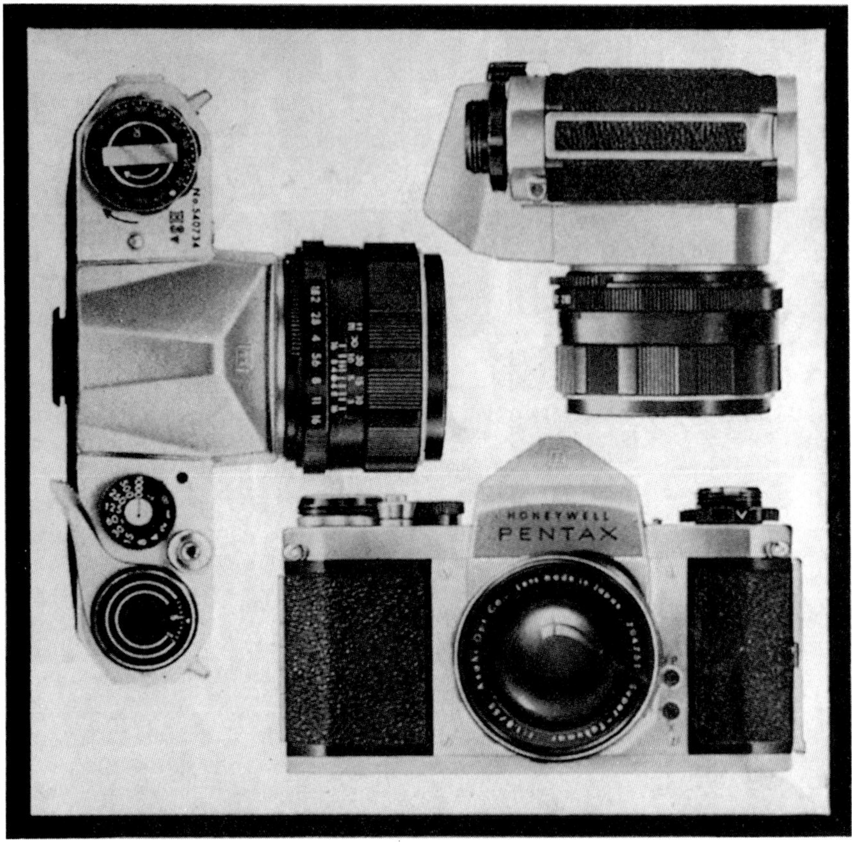

Advertisement for Honeywell Pentax H3v

In the USA, the Honeywell Pentax H3v was sold at $199.50 with the 55mm, f/1.8 Super Takumar lens. With the 55mm,f/2 Super Takumar, the price came down to $179.50. In 1965 the Asahi Pentax Spotmatics reached the mass market with the 50mm,f/1.4 lens. The Asahi Pentax SV and S1a were modified to accommodate the 50mm,f1.4 lens and the retrofocus wide-angle lenses. The last-generation Asahi Pentax SV and S1a were distinguished by a small "R" on the rewind knob being orange rather than green, and by the seven-digit serial number.

The system of interchangeable screw mount lenses with automatic diaphragm reached its zenith. German, Japanese and Russian manufacturers produced lenses compatible with the Pentax system. Alongside the standard 55mm lenses, Asahi Optical featured fourteen interchangeable lenses in its catalogue during the first half of the 1960's. Some lenses remained in the catalogue for years. Alongside these, Asahi Optical introduced many new lenses. The lenses planned or redesigned for the Asahi Pentax SV were the 18mm,f/11 fish-eye, the wide-angle 28mm,f/3.5 Super Takumar and 35mm,f/3.5 lenses and the 85mm,f/1.9, 105mm,f/2.9 and 135mm,f/3.5 short telephoto Super Takumar lenses. It was possible to mount onto the Asahi Pentax SV the existing Auto Takumar lenses, some of which remained in the catalogue. The Super Takumar lenses and more recent Auto Takumar models had the diaphragm ring next to the screw mounting, rather than on the front as in the previous Takumar and Auto Takumar generation. Many of the manual super telephoto lenses with focal lengths from 300 to 1000mm, for which automatic working of the diaphragm was scarcely relevant, remained unchanged in mount and function.

Asahi Pentax S1a

The basic companion of the Asahi Pentax SV was called the S1a and filled the position previously occupied by the cheaper S1 model. The Asahi Pentax S1a was sold on the American market under the name Honeywell Pentax H1a with the standard 55mm,f/2 lens. The H1a cost $149.50, $30 less than the H3v.

The Asahi Pentax S1a had an SV body without the costly self-timer mechanism. The fastest shutter speed shown on the speed dial corresponded to $^1/500$ sec. but in practice the shutter of the Asahi Pentax S1a did not differ from that of the Asahi Pentax SV. The mechanism was not modified and removal of the $^1/1000$ sec. was purely for psychological reasons in placing it in the market.

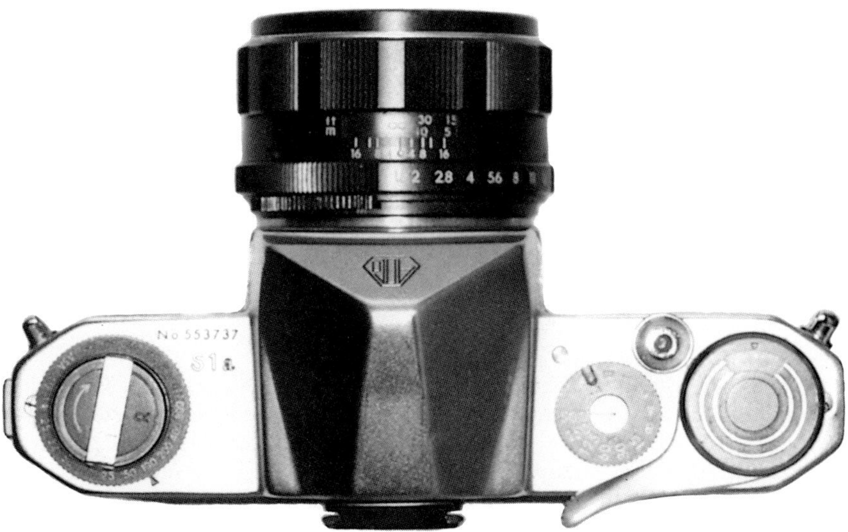

Asahi Pentax S1a - the simpler version of the SV, without self-timer and with maximum shutter speed 1/500 sec.

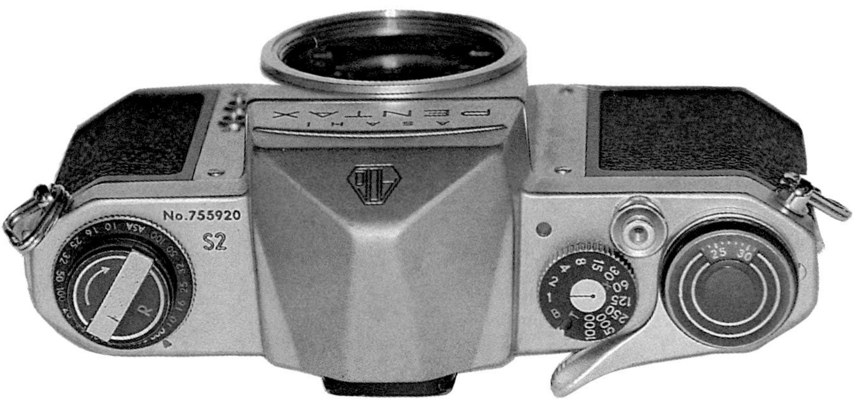

The Asahi Pentax S2 Super was produced only for the Japanese market. It differed from the S2 by having a top speed of 1/1000 and film advance lever with automatic film counter like the Asahi Pentax SV.

The trimmings of the Asahi Pentax S1a were a compromise between those of the Asahi Pentax SV and those of earlier models. The wind lever and frame counter were those of the SV, whilst the door mechanism on the back and the focusing screen were typical of the previous generation.

Asahi Pentax S2 Super

Alongside the cheap Asahi Pentax S1a, a number of cameras were built which were identical to the S1a but were marked with the $^1/1000$ sec. shutter speed. The S1a with the $^1/1000$ sec. was mainly sold in Japan with the designation S2, identical to that characterizing the initial 1959 production. These cameras gave up their position to the S1a and came out of production. In order to distinguish them from the first generation S2's, they were commonly known as the Asahi Pentax S2 Super, even if the word "Super" was not engraved on any part of the camera body.

Asahi Pentax Meter

In expectation of putting the Spotmatics into production Asahi Optical, at the beginning of the Sixties, brought out an accessory exposure meter for attaching to the pentaprism of the Asahi Pentax. It was mechanically coupled to a notch in the camera speed dial in the manner of the Leicameter. It was called the Asahi Pentax Meter and was fitted with a very sensitive CdS cell, powered by a tiny Mallory 625-type mercury battery.

The Sixties saw the mass adoption of colour photography by both amateurs and professionals. Colour films had a poor exposure latitude and demanded extremely accurate light metering.

Many other companies also produced clip-on coupling exposure meters. Minolta introduced the SR Meter for the SR1 and SR3 reflexes, equipped with a suitable side bracket, and Nikon brought out the Photomic viewfinder with external CdS cell for the Nikon F. On this type of exposure meter the photocell is permanently directed towards the subject and the metering angle is obviously fixed. An angle of 40^0 was chosen for the Asahi Pentax Meter. This metering angle was less than the field framed by the standard 55mm lens and enabled correct evaluation of the brightness at the scene. The performance of the clip-on meter was limited in the case of close-up shots or when using long telephoto lenses, but in general photography they proved to be a match for the situation. In order to read the light metering data it was necessary to remove the eye from the viewfinder and check the meter needle position from above.

The first Asahi Pentax meter model had an unusual shape, elongated and surmounted by the circular data scale. The data were visible through a crescent-shaped window. A large ring coaxial with the data scale acted as a switch. The central position of the switch corresponded to "OFF" and the side positions

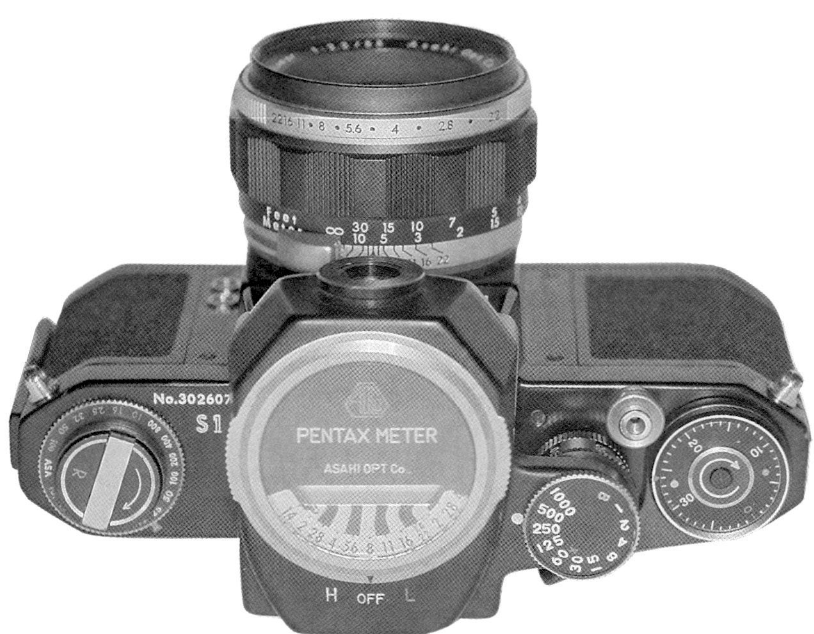

Asahi Pentax Meter in place on Asahi Pentax S1.

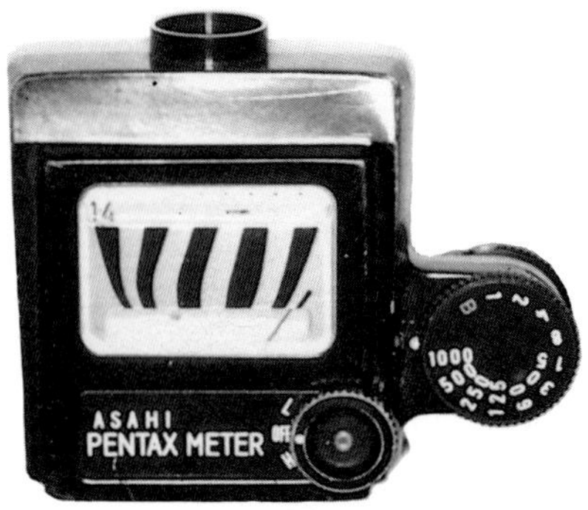

Asahi Pentax Meter SL.

corresponded to the measurement of high light levels "H", and low light levels "L". The dual metering scale went from f/1.4 to f/22, with a reference notch every half stop. The shutter speed dial corresponded to that of the camera, with speeds from 1 to $^1/1000$ sec. plus B setting. The film speed scale coaxial with the speed dial, was calibrated from ASA 6 to 1600. The cameras intended for coupling with the exposure meter were the S1, a few of the S3's, and all the S2 Supers, SV's and S1a models.

Asahi Pentax Meter SL

The Asahi Pentax Meter SL evolved from the first clip-on exposure meter. It was intended for the Asahi Pentax SL but could be used on all earlier models designed for the Asahi Pentax Meter. The Asahi Pentax Meter SL was equipped with a CdS cell with a 40^0 metering angle, exactly like the previous model. As with the previous model, it could be used with films of a sensitivity of between ASA 6 and 1600 and was calibrated from f/1.4 to f/22.

The main difference between the two models was in the body. The Asahi Pentax Meter SL was square-shaped. The large switch was situated on the rear part of the top plate and the data window was rectangular.

The Asahi Pentax Meter SL remained listed until the beginning of the Seventies. Although technologically surpassed by the very sophisticated Spotmatics, the Asahi Pentax Meter SL was justified as an economical alternative to the TTL system.

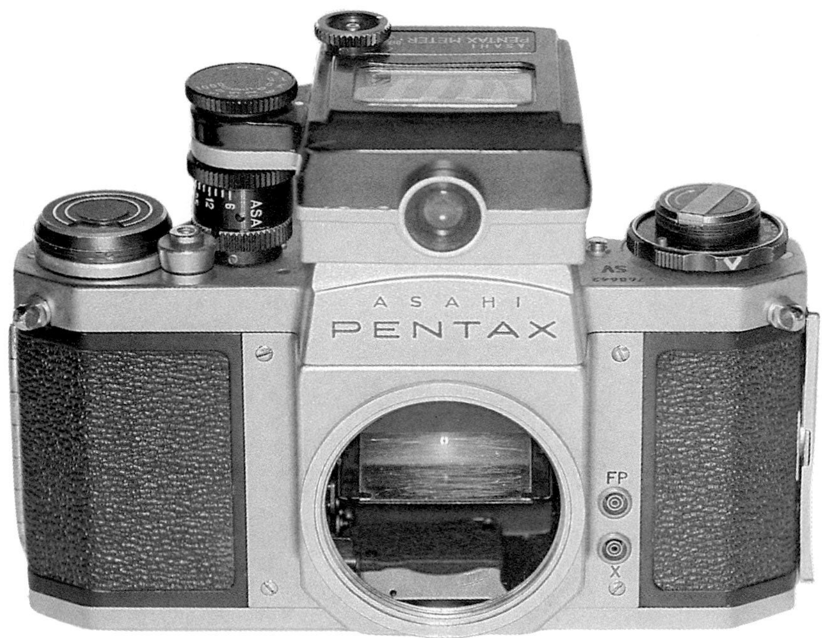

The Asahi Pentax SV was the improved model of the Asahi Pentax S-family. The top speed was 1/1000 sec. and it had a self-timer coaxial with the film rewind knob. This example with Asahi Pentax Meter SL attached.

CHAPTER 5

The Era of the Spotmatic

The prototype Asahi Pentax Spot-Matic was unofficially presented at the 1960 Photokina exhibition. Its conception caused a sensation in the world of the SLR. For the first time the photocell built into a camera was directed, not at the subject, but directly onto the ground glass on which the image was formed.

The metering of light on the image plane proved to be extremely accurate. The photocell measured the amount of light which effectively fell onto the focal plane. The exposure was determined by the effective speed of the lens used, independently of the theoretical speed. Therefore when extension tubes or filters were used for the shot there was no problem because the exposure meter measured the light after it had passed through them. Independently of the focal length of the lens, the photocell measured the brightness within the framed field and the amount of light at the scene. It took into account only the factors determining the image.

The data supplied by the built-in exposure meter with TTL metering were, in theory, free from error. In practice, as with any light metering method, the information needed to be interpreted by the photographer. The light metering data could be misleading in cases where illumination was not uniform and strong contrasts existed between the subject and its background. The metering carried out by the TTL system improved with time. Many initial defects were gradually ironed out until virtually perfect results and complete reliability were attained. Right from its inception, it was clear that the TTL method was considerably faster and more accurate than any other metering system used up until then.

The photocell in the prototype Spot-Matic was a cadmium suphide (CdS) cell. The most accurate and sensitive hand-exposure meter of the time, the Gossen Lunasix, employed the same kind of photocell and Asahi Optical used then in the Asahi Pentax Meter and their professional Spotmeter exposure meter.

On the 1960 Asahi Pentax Spot-Matic, the single photocell was mounted on an arm which moved into the frame area to make the reading. The reading took place over a very limited area of the framed field (SPOT) justifying its name Spot-Matic.

60

Asahi Optical's idea, however, needed five long years to go from prototype to mass production. The Spotmatic was exhibited to the press at the end of 1964 and a number of professional photographers were able to use the pre-production models at the Tokyo Olympics that year. Although not having spot metering, nor special automatic working, it preserved the name of the prototype - or nearly so. It was called Spotmatic instead of Spot-Matic. The Spotmatic was officially presented to the public at the New York IPEX in 1965. It had been completely rethought and improved and looked quite different from the original concept model. *Popular Photography* featured the Spotmatic in April 1965 and published a test on it in the September. It quickly become a success.

The light metering circuit now comprised two fixed cells, positioned at the sides of the pentprism and taking in almost all the image formed on the ground glass. By activating the switch of the exposure meter the aperture closed to the pre-set value. The image in the viewfinder darkened and became difficult to see with very small apertures. The switch automatically cut off after every shutter release. The image in the viewfinder became bright again and the exposure meter was switched off. For subsequent metering it was necessary to activate the switch again and once more darken the image in the viewfinder. This system of discontinuous metering limited the Spotmatic and fostered doubts as to the effectiveness and speed of the TTL system. History would show that the system could be improved and would be developed beyond imagination.

The years between 1965 and 1970 saw the Japanese and East and West German industries vying with each other in the production of accurate and sophisticated TTL models. The next generation SLR's made it possible to meter light at any aperture. They had fully automatic diaphragms, exposure compensation, cells hidden behind the mirror, complementary cells directed towards the eyepiece to read stray light, and other such devices.

The Spotmatics were simple and spartan but elegant and accurate. The inspired Spotmatic body design became the epitome of style and convenience. Thanks to their indisputable optical and mechanical qualities, the Spotmatics were accepted by the public and gained a large slice of the market. They were backed up by the SL model without a TTL exposure meter, and by a special motor-drive model. After seven successful years the Spotmatics were replaced by the Asahi Pentax Spotmatic II.

In 1973, the Spotmatic II gave way to the Spotmatic F. True to the original ideal, the Spotmatic F preserved the Asahi Pentax features of simplicity and light weight. The traditional features were augmented by a fully automatic diaphragm which ended the drawback of stop-down metering. With the SMC Takumar lenses, the Spotmatic F took meter readings with the diaphragm fully open. This last-born of the Spotmatic family, pioneering in its way, was still operationally limited to a certain extent. The Spotmatic F was only on the market for a relatively short period. At the end of 1975, in an unexpected move criticized on many sides, Asahi Optical stopped production of the Spotmatics and Electro

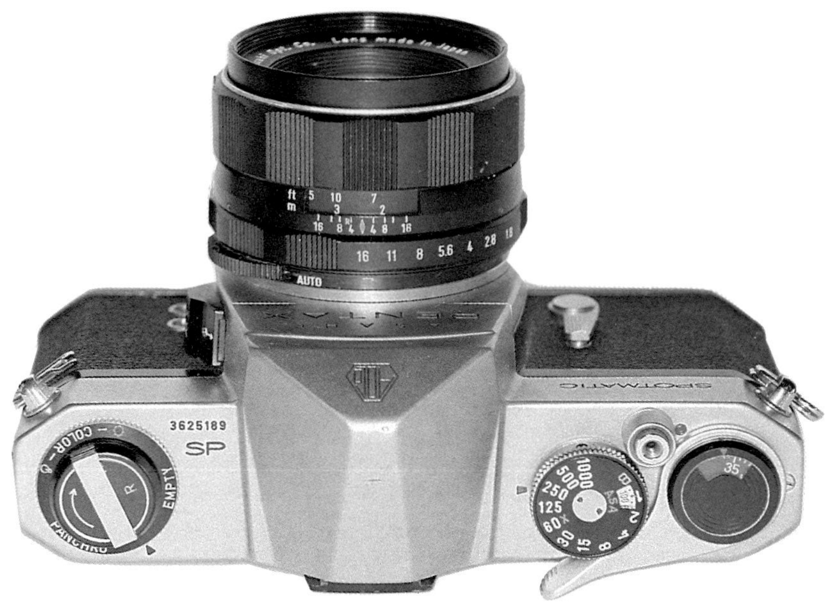

The Asahi Pentax Spotmatic was the first camera to have a TTL metering system. With Super Takumar 55mm, f/1.8.

Spotamtics and brought the long era of the screw mount Pentax cameras to a close.

Asahi Pentax Spotmatic

The Spotmatic body measured 143mm long, 73mm high, 92mm with penta-prism. Without lens, its depth was 43mm and its weight 665g. With these dimensions the Spotmatic for many years was the most compact and lightest weight 35mm SLR. It superficially resembled the traditional Asahi Pentax. The octago-nal body was almost unchanged and the shape of the pentaprism followed that of the original Asahi Pentax. But otherwise, the camera was completely rede-signed with regard to construction and mechanical details. Spotmatic promotion emphasized the importance of design and image in the marketing of industrial products.

The lens plate was widened at the base and rounded off below to the curve of the screw lens mount. The chrome strips which emphasized the mirror box in the pre-Spotmatic models had disappeared. The screw lens mount was made more robust, but the old generation lenses could still be used.

The body of the Spotmatic was slightly longer than that of the Asahi Pentax

SV, but the side latch for opening the back was no longer present, making the camera more compact. The height of the body had been increased by a few millimetres but the overall height of the camera remained unchanged, so the pentaprism protruded less above the top plate. The weight of the camera was a few grams less than that of an Asahi Pentax SV fitted with the Asahi Pentax Meter.

The wind-on lever on the Spotmatic was slightly modified and the frame counter was less bulky. The working of the lever was additive, meaning that it was possible to advance the film and rewind the shutter by means of several short strokes of the lever rather than with a single movement.

The shutter speed dial was redesigned and made bigger. It selected all shutter speeds, from 1 to $^1/1000$ sec. plus B. The T setting, useful in many photographic situations, was removed never to reappear on an Asahi Pentax reflex. By raising and turning the ring round the shutter speed dial the film speed was set, from ASA 20 to 1600. The selected value appeared in a small window by the 1 sec. marking.

The back was opened by raising the rewind knob. Around the knob was the usual film reminder ring. The film was identified as "PANCRO", for black and white or "COLOR". The word "COLOR" was situated between a symbol for the sun for daylight films and a bulb for artificial-light films. The reminder "EMPTY" was also provided. The shutter release was also redesigned, becoming more sensitive and less stiff.

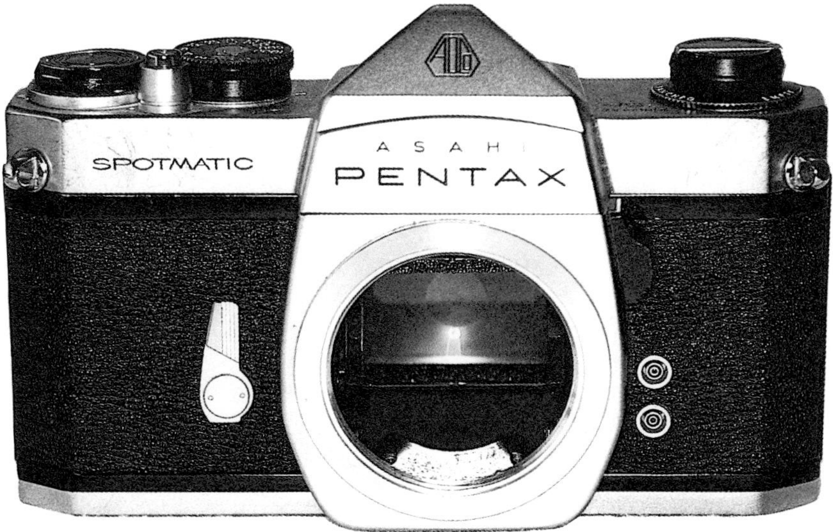

The Spotmatic had a more robust lens mount than previous Asahi Pentax cameras.

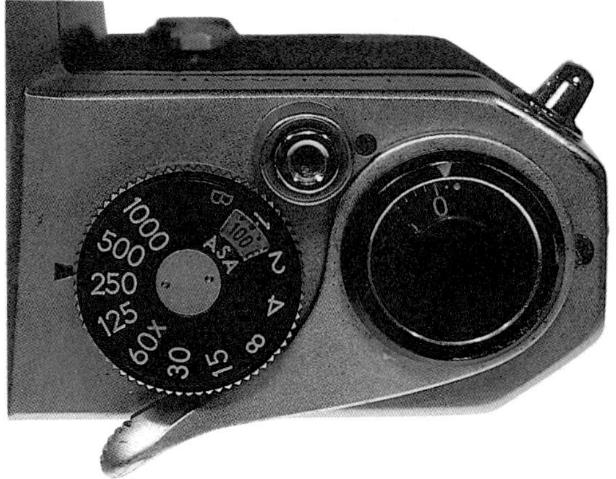

The ASA setting appeared in a small window in the shutter speed dial.

The Spotmatic had a self-timer mechanism. Its wind lever was situated on the front, to the right of the lens mounting, in the traditional position which it occupied on almost all reflexes of the time. The FP and X contacts were also on the front, to the left of the mounting.

The large exposure meter switch was situated close to the lens mounting, high up on the left-hand side. The meter was activated by pushing the switch up. The diaphragm of the lens mounted on the camera closed to the working value. The needle visible in the viewfinder moved between the signs + and -, which indicated over- or underexposure. In order to get perfectly exposed pictures it was necessary to centre the needle exactly. Intentional over- or underexposure was achieved by decentering the needle towards + or - as required. With practice, it was possible to control the degree of exposure by calculating the position of the needle.

The exposure meter was powered by a small 1.5 volt battery at the base of the camera. The preset aperture or shutter speed required was obtained by turning the shutter speed dial or the aperture ring. In practice, the shutter speed was selected and the aperture adjusted according to the exposure meter readings. Only when the aperture was off-scale was the speed adjusted.

The Spotmatic serial number was preceded by the letters SP; it remained in the traditional position and was increased to seven digits. Spotmatic numbering began with number 1,000,000. The Spotmatic was the first Asahi Pentax to have its model name engraved on the front, to the right of the lens mounting.

The technical specification of the Spotmatic was modest and interesting. Ease of operation prevailed over sophisticated facilities. The preset method for light metering proved for some years to be the soundest. Apart from its technical specification, clearly outstripped today, the factor which continues to fascinate about the Spotmatic is the extraordinary aesthetic result achieved by its design.

Exhibiting the greatest constructional and operational simplicity, the Spotmatic gained an international reputation for industrial design. A long-time heir of the Zen tradition, the Spotmatic was achieved by removing everything excessive and unnecessary, reducing it to very clean and basic contours. Spotmatic production placed Asahi Optical at the head of Japanese camera output and amongst the leaders in 35mm photography.

At the beginning of 1965 there were sixteen lenses of eleven focal lengths for the Spotmatic. The number rose rapidly to twenty-five Takumar and Super Takumar originals, covering a range of focal lengths from 17mm to 1000mm. The initial lens range for the Spotmatic corresponded to that of the Asahi Pentax SV, supplemented by the 50mm,f/1.4 and 35mm,f/2. The SV lenses included six Super Takumar automatic lenses: 28mm,f/3.5; 35mm,f/3.5; 85mm,f/1.9; 105mm, f/2.8 and 135mm,f/3.5. The other lenses available were the long-focus tele and special lenses without an automatic aperture. The Super Takumar name indicated that the aperture was fully automatic. Most striking within the the Takumar range of lenses were the 18mm,f/11 fish-eye, the 500mm,f/5 and the 1000mm, f/8.

During the Spotmatic years some very interesting lenses appeared. The 18mm,f/11 fish-eye was replaced by the 17mm,f/4 automatic, and the Super

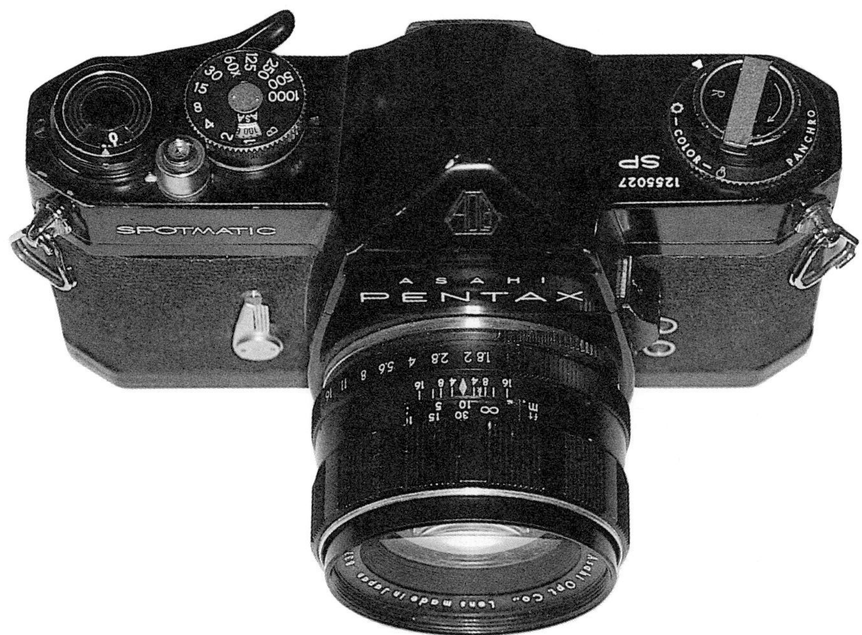

The Spotmatic looked even more elegant in black.

20mm,f/4.5 and Super 24mm,f/3.5 wide-angle lenses were introduced. Many non-automatic lenses were replaced by auto lenses of similar focal lengths, like the 200mm,f/4 and 300mm,f/4. The Super 50mm,f/4 Super Macro Takumar and an extremely compact, light-weight 150mm,f/4 were also built. At the end of the Sixties the Super Takumar family was completed by a 70-150mm,f/4.5 zoom and a 135mm,f/2.5 lens.

The sale price of the Asahi Pentax Spotmatics, renamed by the Americans the Honeywell Pentax Spotmatic, was set at $289.50 with the 50mm,f/4 Super Takumar lens, and at $249.50 with the 55mm,f/1.8 Super Takumar lens.

Asahi Pentax SL

In 1968 production on the Asahi Pentax SV and S1a closed and the Spotmatic became the only model in production. As marketing policy demanded a cheaper model, a simplified camera with a Spotmatic body but without an exposure meter was produced. This was called the Asahi Pentax SL. It was identical to the Spotmatic in all other respects, including the self-timer which was not usually put onto the cheaper models. The SL weighed a few grams less than the Spotmatic; and was sold for about 20% less than its older sister.

The Asahi Pentax SL could take a clip-on coupling Asahi Pentax Meter SL, but the combination could not match a real Spotmatic for price, weight and facilities.

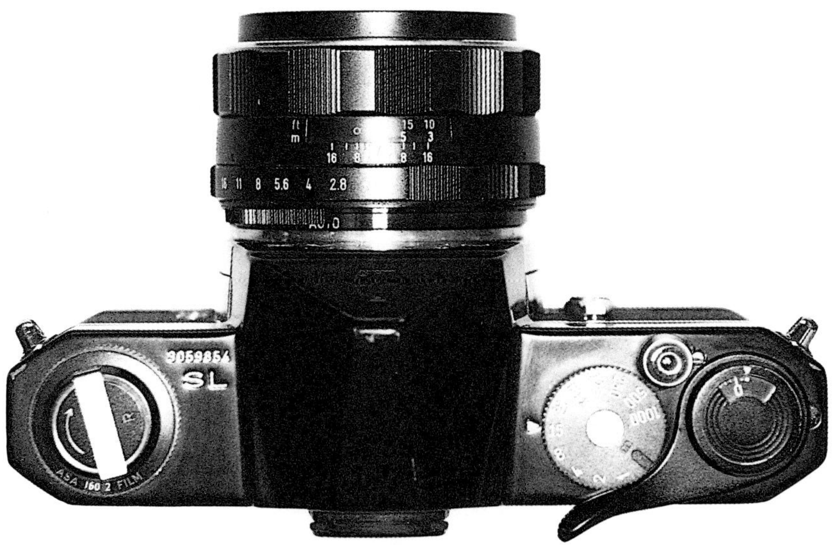

The Asahi Pentax SL replaced the SV and S1a in 1968 and was the last Asahi Pentax without TTL metering.

The Asahi Pentax Meter SL did not prove very successful. Reflexes without an exposure meter had rapidly become obsolete objects without a market. After three years the Asahi Pentax SL was replaced by the inexpensive SP 500 and SP 1000 models equipped with a TTL exposure meter.

Asahi Pentax Spotmatic Motor Drive

The Motor Drive version was the most important change in the basic Spotmatic model. The Asahi Pentax Spotmatic Motor Drive was presented at the 1966 Photokina and intended for professional use. The base of the camera was modified to take an accessory motor for fast winding of the film. Few Spotmatic Motor Drive cameras were produced, but modification of standard Spotmatics could be carried out at the factory or approved workshops.

The Spotmatic motor could reach a speed of three frames a second. Its features made it an interesting object and put the Spotmatic on the same professional plane as other famous reflexes such as the Nikon F and Topcon RE Super. The motor depended on batteries which were located in the large vertical hand-grip. Eight normal 1.5 volt dry cell batteries were needed to supply the requisite 12 volts. Alternatively, nickel-cadmium rechargeable batteries of the same voltage could be used. Mains current could also be used via an appropriate transformer.

As with motors of the time, the Spotmatic Motor Drive was a heavy, bulky and particularly expensive accessory. A Spotmatic equipped with a motor and without a lens weighed 1720g.

Many accessories were developed for the Spotmatic Motor Drive; radio controls, huge 250 frame backs, connection cords and intervalometers. The Spotmatic motor unit was introduced in the mid-Seventies for the last of the screw mount Asahi Pentaxes, the ES II and the Spotmatic F. The bayonet mount Pentax to come was designed with a completely different philosophy of motorization.

Asahi Pentax Spotmatic II, or SP II

At the beginning of the Seventies Asahi Optical felt the urgent need to restore the Spotmatic's image. The product had not changed for seven years and was beginning to show its age. The need to renew the product without affecting its nature was resolved by a compromise solution. The body was renewed by modifying the shape of the top plate. The minimum number of changes were introduced at a functional level.

The camera was given the same name, "Asahi Pentax Spotmatic", followed by "II" to indicate continuity. The introduction of the Spotmatic II came at a particular point in the company's life. It was done for purely marketing reasons and not because of technological advances. The Spotmatic II, abbreviated to SP

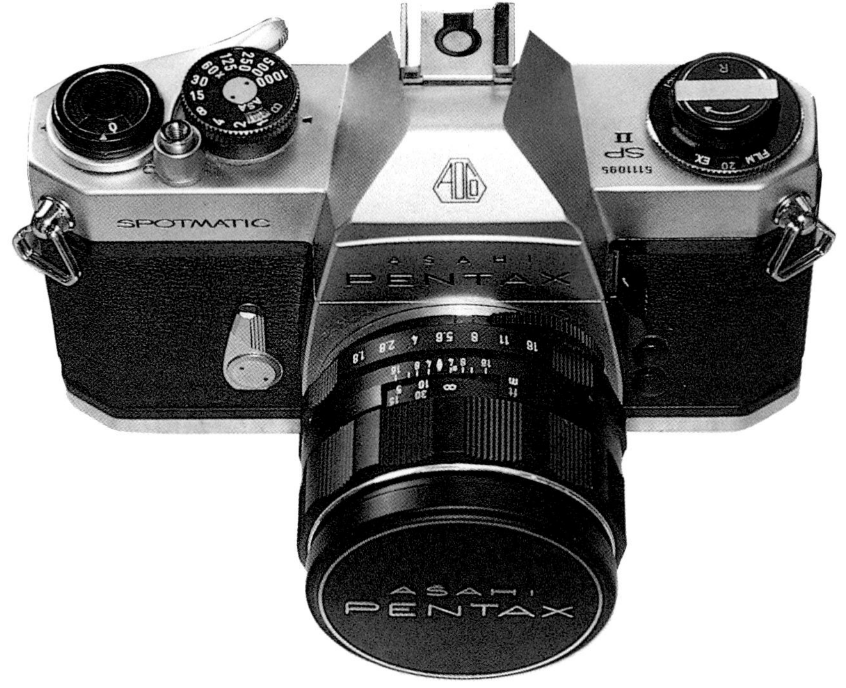

Asahi Pentax SPII

II, emphasized the continuity of the traditional Spotmatic without introducing substantial changes in facilities and product conception.

The SP II was launched in 1971. The competition were introducing technically advanced SLR's, reinforced by tough marketing promotion. There were dozens of imitation Spotmatics. Asahi Optical were working on ambitious projects still requiring time to come to fruition, so in the meantime the SP II was put onto the market as a compromise between tradition and innovation, conservatism and the avant-garde. The SP II exploited the success of the original Spotmatic for several years, but the peripheral changes introduced with the SP II were not of themselves sufficient to make it an interesting camera.

The body and basic structure of the Spotmatic was not altered at all. As already mentioned, the top-plate was modified and the shape of the pentaprism redesigned. The broader top of the pentaprism enabled a hot-shoe to be added, but it altered the distinctive face of the Spotmatic, making it awkward and impersonal. The pentaprism of the SP II had steep sides and it rose directly out of the top plate. The name Spotmatic remained on the front of the camera and the initials SP II were on the top plate, above the serial number. The sensitivity range of the exposure meter, was increased to ASA 3200.

The SP II's strong point was not the camera body, but the lenses. A new range of screw-mount Takumar lenses was brought out at the same time as the camera. The outer surfaces of the lenses were given a new multi-layer coating which reduced flare. They were called Super Multi Coated Takumar lens, abbreviated to SMC Takumar, and were designed for light metering at all apertures. Advertising for the SP II concentrated on the new lenses.

Asahi Pentax SP IIa

A modified version of the Asahi Pentax SP II was brought out for the American market. It had a built-in photocell which enabled automatic metering of the flash light reflected off the subject. This camera was called the Honeywell Pentax SP IIa and simplified the use of electronic flash, making it automatic on every occasion. This contrivance was not appreciated outside United States professional circles and was not followed up in other Asahi Optical cameras. Automatic electronic flashguns and TTL flash metering nipped this experiment in the bud.

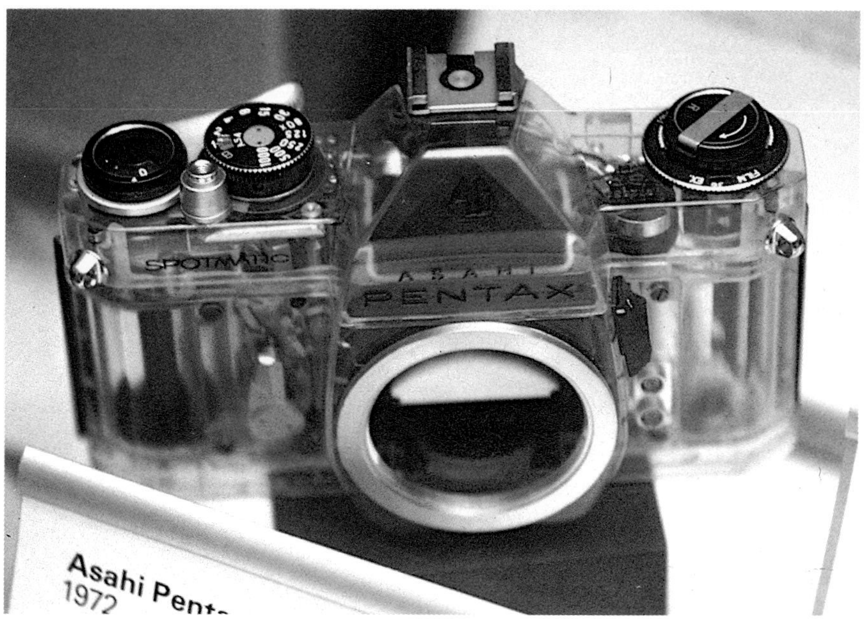

Spotmatic II in transparent shell (in Science Museum, London).

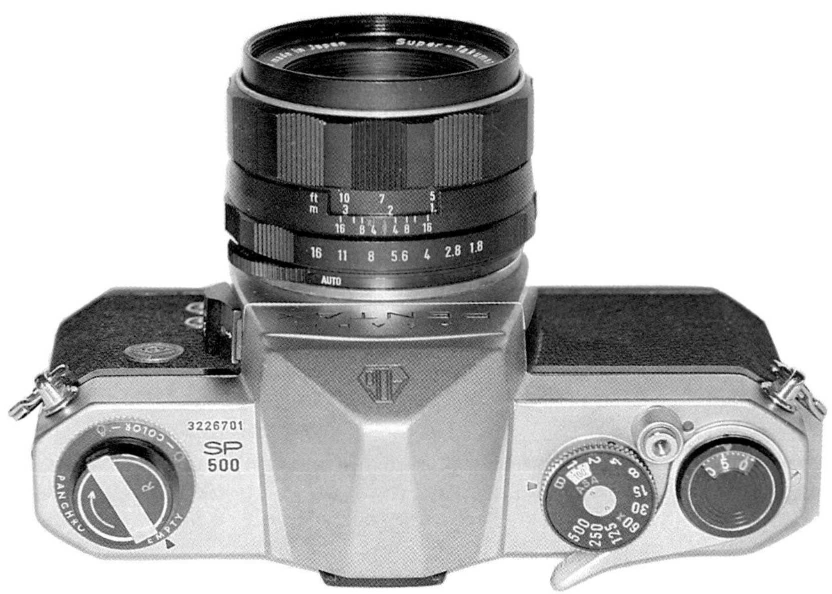

The Asahi Pentax SP 500 was the simplified version of the Spotmatic, with top speed of 1/500 and without self-timer.

Asahi Pentax SP 500

Along with the Asahi Pentax SP II, a cheap reflex, the SP 500, was brought out to replace the Asahi Pentax SL. It was simply a Spotmatic without the self-timer. Although the cheapest model from the Pentax stable, it had TTL metering.

In keeping with their old practice, however debatable, the SP 500's fastest shutter speed was restricted to $^1/500$ sec. This determined the name of the model. All other technical and aesthetic features of the SP 500 made it a typical Spotmatic.

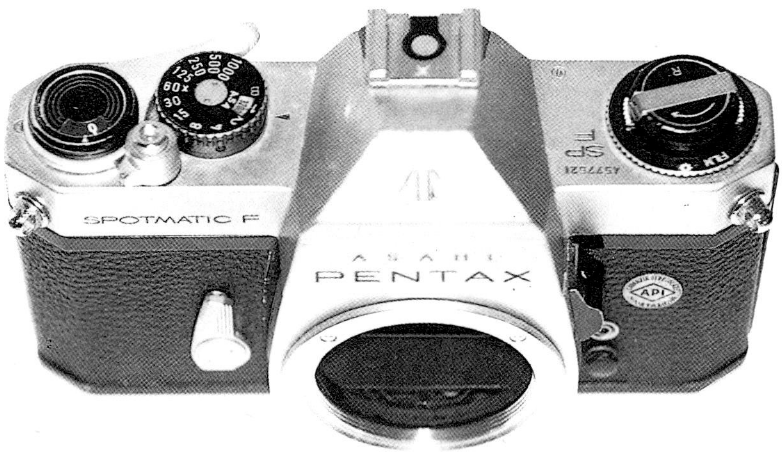

The Asahi Pentax Spotmatic F was the improved version of the SPII, with a diaphragm simulator for measuring light at full aperture. The SPF was the last Asahi Pentax produced in screw mount.

Asahi Pentax SPF

The introduction of the Electro Spotmatic with automatic shutter speeds and metering at any aperture with the SMC Takumar lenses aroused the expectation of a Spotmatic with the same type of metering. Heralded from the time of the Spotmatic II, the new Spotmatic F appeared in 1973 but was a bit of a disappointment.

Outwardly it was very similar to the SP II. Its facilities were not greatly superior to those of the standard Spotmatics. The external differences were limited to the presence of a safety lock around the shutter release placed so as to cover the shutter wind signal itself. The letter "F" was engraved on the front next to the name "Spotmatic". The letters SPF appeared on the top plate above the serial number, which still comprised seven digits.

Under the standard body the SPF incorporated a diaphragm simulator which brought it into line with contemporary developments. The main exposure meter switch was situated within the traditional screw lens mounting. By screwing a SMC Takumar lens into the Spotmatic F the exposure meter was automatically activated and could only be switched off again by removing the lens.

The meter was only activated by a properly seated SMC Takumar lens, and only with these lenses was metering available at any aperture. The external switch remained in its traditional position next to the lens mounting plate for use when Takumar and Super Takumar lenses, third party lenses, extension tubes, or bellows were mounted on the Spotmatic F.

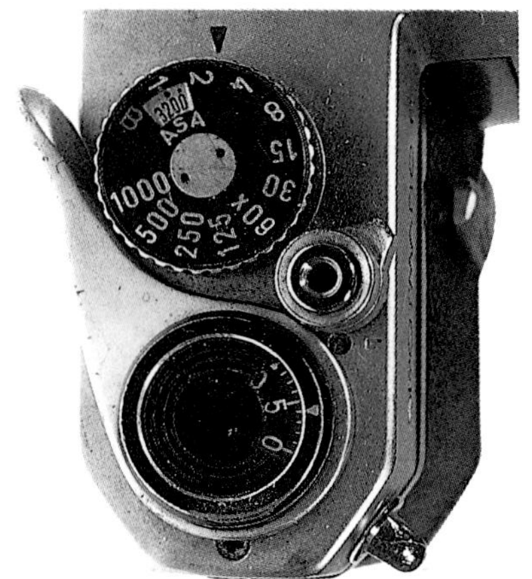

Detail of safety lock around the shutter release button on the SPF.

This secondary switch proved to be extremely useful for displaying the depth of field. When SMC Takumar lenses were mounted on the Spotmatic F the built-in button for closing the aperture manually locked and became unusable.

To all intents and purposes, the Spotmatic F replaced the Spotmatic II, whose body, weight and dimensions it preserved unchanged. Unenthusiastically received by the press, the SPF was sold in the United States at between $220 and $230 with the 55mm,f/1.8 lens. With the faster 50mm,f/1.4 lens, it cost some thirty dollars more.

Asahi Pentax Spotmatic 1000

As the Spotmatic F replaced the Spotmatic II, the SP 1000 replaced the SP 500 as the cheaper alternative to the top model. The SP 1000 was not a new camera. It was basically a Pentax Spotmatic, complete with metering and the full range of shutter speeds up to $^1/1000$ sec. and without the self-timer. The SP 1000 was the last chance for the purists to acquire a genuine Spotmatic without a hot shoe and unchanged in contour. For Asahi Optical it was the opportunity to use up the Spotmatic bodies and make use of the old production lines before the final closure of the era of screw-mount reflexes.

In the United States, the SP 1000 was sold with the 50mm,f/2 at less than 200 dollars.

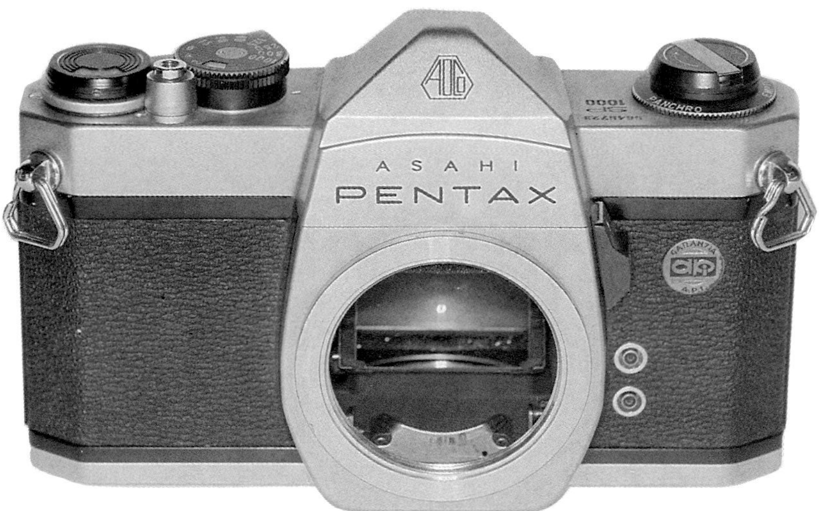

The Asahi Pentax SP 1000 was a Spotmatic without self-timer.

CHAPTER 6

Asahi Pentax and Electronics

The final chapter in the history of the screw mount Asahi Pentax camera was represented by the electronic models. Advances in electronics brought on the end of the screw mount and forced the change over to the K-bayonet.

Asahi Pentax Electro Spotmatic

The first Electro Spotmatics were sold in Japan from 20th October 1971. The cameras were considerably modified before being put on the international markets at the beginning of 1972. The design and marketing of an electronic reflex compatible with their traditional system of lenses showed that to the very end Asahi Optical had tried to remain faithful to its own image, its own philosophy, and to the screw mount.

By 1971 electronics were no longer novel in cameras. Electronically-controlled focal plane shutters were used on 35mm reflexes like the Zeiss Contarex SE and the Yashica TL Electro X. For some years Asahi Optical itself had been using an electronically-controlled focal plane shutter on its 6x7 reflex.

The revolutionary change introduced by the Electro Spotmatic was not the electronically-controlled shutter. The real revolution lay in the automatic setting of the shutter speed, which for the first time in history was applied to a reflex with a focal plane shutter. The shutter speed was automatically selected and set by a minicomputer which controlled the electronic shutter, depending on the light measurement and film speed.

Automatic working of the exposure meter was possible with any lens with either manual or automatic diaphragm. As the automatic working only depended on the shutter it was possible to use any non-automatic accessory, extension bellows or macro tube. Whatever the circumstances, the Electro Spotmatic computer read the intensity of the light on the ground glass and told the shutter to release at the most appropriate speed, uninterruptedly, from $^1/1000$ sec. to the slowest. The features of the Electro Spotmatic were unprecedented. The excitement caused by the announcement of automatic aperture priority was comparable to that caused by the original introduction of TTL.

Automatic reflexes belonging to the previous generation, like the Konica Autoreflex, the Miranda EE, and the Mamiya XTL, could work in automatic mode by means of servo-diaphragms activated by the exposure meter galvanometer. With these cameras the shutter speed had to be set manually by the photographer and it was necessary to use lenses set in advance.

With the Electro Spotmatic, under any shooting conditions the camera was able to set the appropriate speed automatically. It worked with mirror lenses without a diaphragm, with microscopes or telescopes, and in all special photographic applications even where standard lenses were not used.

The possibility of fully automatic shutter speeds opened unexpected avenues in camera design. Once more the makers found themselves forced to restructure their assembly lines and review their future plans so as not to risk being cut out of the market.

In imitation of Asahi Optical, Japanese and European manufactures rose to the electronic challenge. As ever, the Japanese were the quickest at adapting to prevailing trends. Nikon brought out its electronic Nikkormat EL reflex, followed by Minolta with its XM model. Canon opted for a joint solution with its first electronic EF model.

In spite of the incredible possibilities it offered, the Electro Spotmatic was far from being the perfect camera. It had a limited range of manually-selectable shutter speeds. It had to forego the self-timer mechanism in order to make room for the bulky batteries, and showed a certain unreliability in use. The electronic components had to be completely redesigned.

After the unofficial presentation the electronic Asahi Pentax was exhibited at the 1972 Japan Camera Show. At the end of the same year it was brought out again at the Cologne Photokina exhibition in its final version. The name was reduced to Asahi Pentax ES. The camera was finally ready to confront the American and European markets. In little more than a year, further improvements led to the Asahi Pentax ES II, the third model of Asahi Optical's electronic reflex. The ESII model, complete with self-timer, solved a number of problems outstanding on ES.

Asahi Pentax ES

The first version of the Electro Spotmatic was sold only in Japan by way of a market test. The model intended for export was called the Asahi Pentax ES and preserved unchanged the technical and aesthetic features of the Electro Spotmatic. The electronics, on the other hand, were replaced with more reliable circuits. The camera body showed many analogies with the traditional Asahi Pentax SP II. The upper part, the main controls and front of the camera, were only altered a little. The working of a number of controls was modified and adapted to the requirements of the by electronic technology.

The shutter speed dial was simplified. It lost the ring for setting the film speed and offered five manual settings, from $1/60$ to $1/1000$ sec. in addition to B. It also

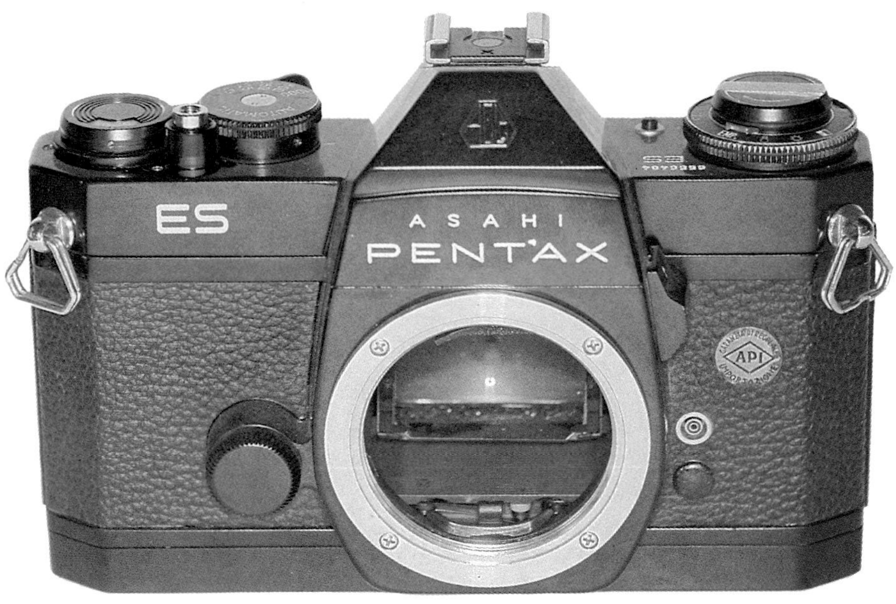

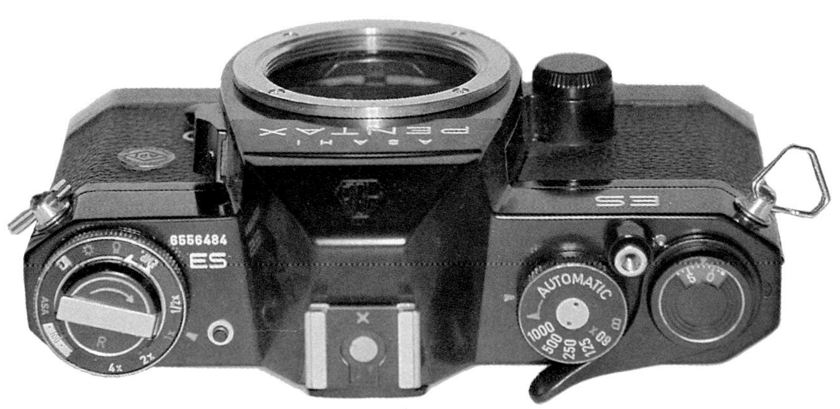

The Asahi Pentax ES was the first electronic automatic SLR in the world. This one carries a SMC Takumar 55mm, f/2 lens.

had an AUTOMATIC position. By setting this, one obtained uninterrupted automatic setting of the full possible range of shutter speeds from 8 to $^1/1000$ sec.

Coaxial to the film rewind button were the film speed ring and the ring for switching out the automatic working. The control unit was completed with the standard memo disc for showing the type of film being used.

The ES was a little taller than the SP II. It measured 98mm as against 93mm and was slightly heavier: 678g as against 642g. Its front was also slightly modified. The lens mount plate was lengthened and the large cover of the battery compartment took the place of the self-timer lever. The ES ran on a huge 6-volt battery which could not have been housed in the base.

The ES was bulkier in appearance than the Spotmatic. The numerous alterations made to the classic body over time had brought heaviness to the clean contours of the first Asahi Pentaxes. In the meantime other manufacturers had begun to introduce cameras styled by well-known designers.

From the technological point of view the ES was at the forefront. From the aesthetic point of view, by copying and distorting the outlines which had made the Spotmatic famous it carried little conviction. In spite of everything, the ES continued to be relatively light and lost none of the Spotmatic's ease of handling. It was produced exclusively in black in a style which soon became dominant. In the USA it was sold with the 50mm,f/1.4 lens at between $320 and $360. With the 55mm,f/1.8 lens it cost, as usual, some thirty dollars less.

The Asahi Pentax ES made use of the full range of Takumar lenses. With the latest-generation lenses, the SMC Takumars, it operated at any aperture. With the other screw mount lenses, it operated in stop-down mode without losing the automatic shutter speed working of the exposure meter.

In spite of recourse to more sophisticated electronics, the shutter of the ES was still of a standard type. It was electronically-controlled but the blinds were fabric, moving horizontally, with $^1/60$ sec. as maximum flash synch. speed.

In the ES viewfinder, a meter needle indicated the shutter speed selected by the computer. As the shutter control was electronic the ES could operate at any intermediate speed within the values shown on the scale. The automatic working of the camera depended entirely on the battery and a little button could be pressed to check the battery level. Without battery power, the ES could operate on its mechanical speeds but the TTL exposure meter was inoperative.

Asahi Pentax ES II

Two years on from the ES an improved, updated version appeared called ES II. The body remained practically unchanged. The self-timer lever was reinstated. The battery compartment returned to the base in a rather original position. Power was provided by four Eveready S76 or Mallory MS 76H silver oxide 1.5 volt batteries. Each battery had its own compartment and these were situated under the lens mount, which was now square.

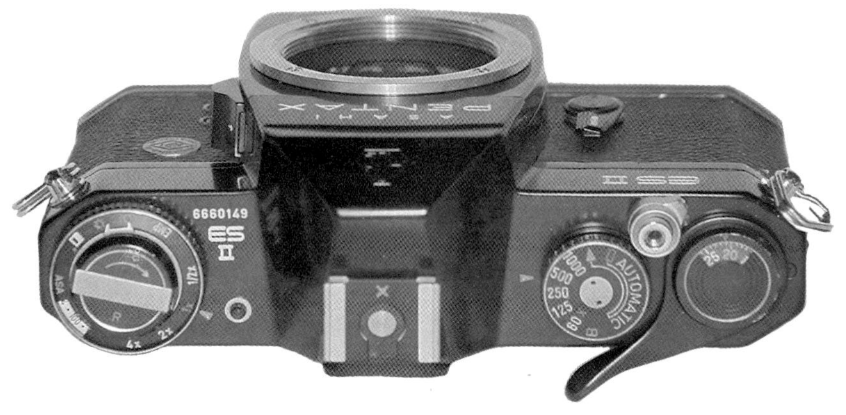

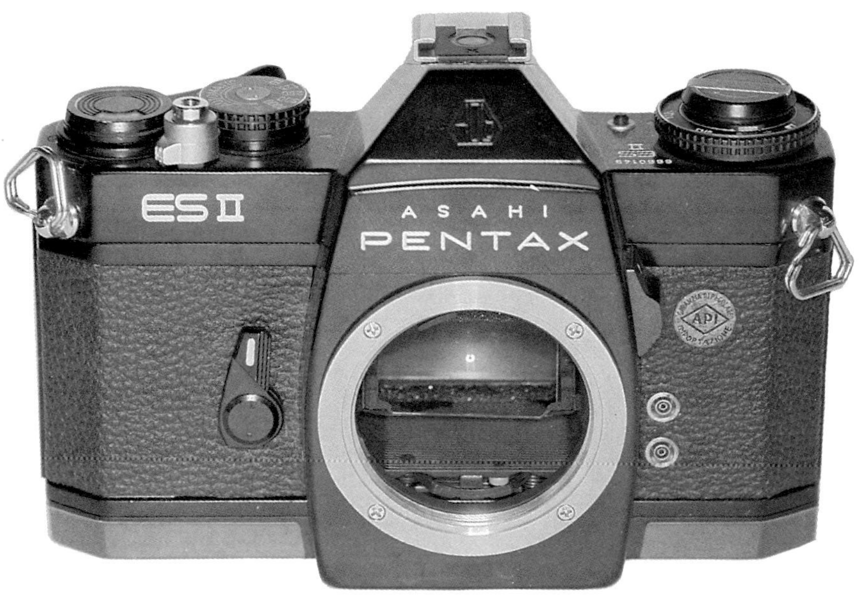

The Asahi Pentax ESII.

The eyepiece could be closed by a shutter for when the eye was not at the camera prevent light entering the eyepiece, with the self-timer for example. The release button was protected by a safety lock as on the SPF. It was a question of minor additions introduced to improve the working of the camera but also to justify the increase in price. In the USA, the ES II fluctuated between $340 and $390 with the 55mm,f/1.8 lens and reached $420 with the 50mm,f/1.4 SMC Takumar lens.

The sensitivity range of the exposure meter was increased to ASA 3200.

A motor drive version of the ES II was promised but it did not appear. Times were not ripe for an automatic, motor driven reflex. These were to become popular several years later.

With its aperture priority electronic models, Asahi Optical once again earned a place in the history of photography. Once again it claimed the virtue of having shown other reflex camera producers the road to follow.

CHAPTER 7

The Dreams of Asahi Pentax

At the 1960 Photokina exhibition the Asahi Optical stand excelled in the number of innovations on display. Various working prototypes were introduced which were not destined to go into production immediately. The most striking innovation was the Spot-Matic, but the other cameras displayed were also worthy of note. A few months later the same prototypes were on show at the Milan Fair. Asahi Optical brought out three reflex cameras with very different features. The S3 was a very traditional reflex and replicated the features of the well-known Asahi Pentax S2. The Spot-Matic, traditional on the outside hid a secret which qualified it as the world's first TTL reflex. A third reflex called the Asahi Pentax Metalica drew attention to itself with a bulky selenium photocell on the pentaprism. Two exposure meters, the Spotmeter and the Asahi Pentax Meter, were also brought out alongside the cameras.

The Asahi Pentax S3 and the clip-on CdS Asahi Pentax Meter were mass-produced and put on the market immediately. It was five years before the Spotmatic was mass-produced. The Metalica remained no more than a prototype. The Spotmeter exposure meter, was to be developed and improved for its specialisst field of use in the years that followed.

In spite of the varying fate of the projects displayed, the cameras and equipment introduced in 1960 were worthy of particular interest. Added to these prototypes in 1966 were the Asahi Pentax Metalica II, the world's first automatic TTL reflex, and the Asahi Pentax Nocta, an accessory which turned the Pentaxes into special cameras for shots in complete darkness.

Asahi Pentax Metalica

The Asahi Pentax Metalica was an interesting reflex, especially in relation to the period in which it was designed. The ingenious Spotmatic, which it resembled in its main structural features, nevertheless managed to eclipse it and focus the public's attention and the efforts of the designers onto itself.

For the first time in the Asahi stable, the Metalica had a Copal-type metallic focal plane shutter with vertical movement and with fastest flash synch. speed

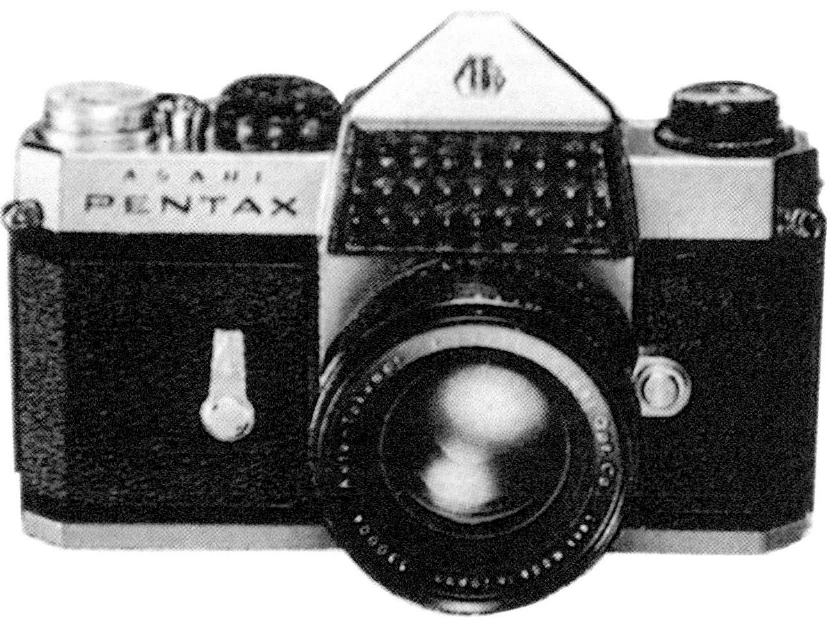

The Asahi Pentax Metalica had a bayonet mount and a built-in selenium meter with the cell on the pentaprism.

of $^1/125$ sec. and top speed of $^1/1000$ sec. The Metalica was also the first Pentax to be fitted with a built-in, coupled exposure meter. The exposure meter was of the selenium type and was outclassed by the emerging CdS exposure meters. The fact that the exposure meter was out-of-date meant the ditching of the Metalica project which did in itself include many positive features.

Its lens was a fully automatic bayonet-mount 55mm,f/1.8 Auto Takumar. Apart from the built-in exposure meter the other novel features of the Metalica were not used on any production Asahi Pentax for many years to come. The selenium exposure meter was abandoned in favour of the more accurate and sensitive CdS exposure meter, which made it possible to experiment with TTL metering. The metallic shutter did not appear on any mass-produced Asahi Pentax until the middle of the Seventies. The bayonet mount for the lenses had to wait another fifteen years. The features of the Asahi Pentax Metalica were perhaps too far ahead of their time, but history puts paid to prejudices.

The bodies of the Metalica and prototype Spot-Matic were similar to that of the mass-produced Asahi Pentax S2. The instrumentation was replaced by an unusually-shaped wind lever and shutter speed dial. The self-timer lever appeared for the first time on the front of the camera, together with the lens-release

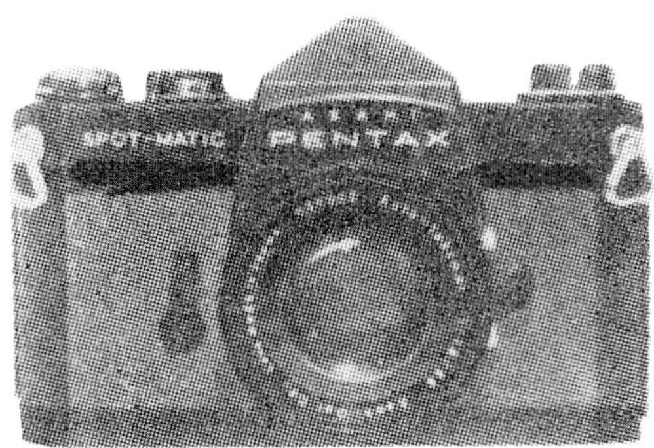

The Asahi Pentax Spot-Matic had a bayonet mount and the first TTL metering system. It only metered a restricted area of the image.

button. The metallic bands on the sides of the lens mount disappeared and the top plate was raised a few millimetres.

Some of the technical and aesthetic modifications displayed on the Metalica became fully fledged on the 1964 Spotmatic model. In particular the self-timer was built in and the vertical bands on the front were done away with. Such details made the Metalica a true forerunner of its type.

The front of the Asahi Pentax Metalica was distinguished by the wide window of the exposure meter, which took up the full lower part of the pentaprism. The name Asahi Pentax, traditionally engraved on the lower part of the pentaprism, was perforce displaced and found its place on the right-hand side of the front housing.

Asahi Pentax Spot-Matic (Prototype)

The 1960 prototype Spot-Matic used a modified S2 body, exactly like the Asahi Pentax Metalica. It included the same self-timer mechanism and the same lens-release button. Like the Metalica, it had a new metallic focal plane shutter. Synchronization with flash took place at $^1/125$ sec. and the fastest speed was brought up to $^1/2000$ sec.

The big exposure meter window on the pentaprism of the Metalica was absent from the Spot-Matic, which regained its customary appearance. Its extremely sensitive photocell, of the CdS type, was mounted on a moving arm located in relation to the ground glass. The power was provided by two batteries. One battery served to power the circuit for metering strong light, the other powered the low brightness circuit. Measurement of the exposure was extremely selective (spot method) and needed a good deal of ability and experience on the part of the photographer.

In spite of the prototype Spot-Matic's unusual features, Asahi Optical decided to take time and rethink its design. Many of the advanced solutions tried out on the Metalica and Spotmatic were shelved.

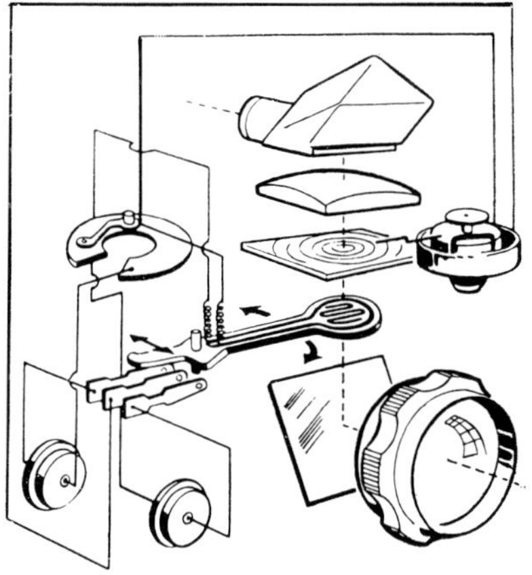

Asahi Pentax Spot-Matic meter scheme, with two batteries and the cell on a moving arm.

The screw mount was kept on for another fifteen years. The self-timer returned three years later on the Asahi Pentax SV in a solution which was not permanent and which was certainly more complicated than that tried out on the bayonet mount prototypes.

Of the noteworthy facilities and advanced features, the metal focal plane shutter was considered too demanding, not very reliable, and not sufficiently proven. The 1964 Spotmatic continued to mount the traditional shutter with horizontally moving blinds in rubberized silk which was also retained for the screw mount Asahi Pentaxes which followed the Spotmatic.

The remarkable achievement of the 1960 prototypes was worthy of note but remained an isolated fact. The fruits of the experiment would be harvested many years later.

Asahi Pentax Spotmeter

The selective light measuring exposure meter called the Spotmeter was brought out in conjunction with the Spotmatic. The prototype Spotmeter had a very unusual shape which distinguished it from the removable exposure meters produced up until then. It was built like a small single-lens reflex. A lens directed a beam of light towards the CdS photocell which measured its intensity. It was possible to direct the meter at the required point in the scene, as well as see the values indicated on the metering scale, through a vertical eyepiece similar to that of the Hasselblad viewfinder.

The Spotmeter was reintroduced a couple of years later, equipped with a practical hand-grip and a pentaprism for viewing the subject directly. The field of vision framed was 21^0 and the light metering angle was usually 3^0.

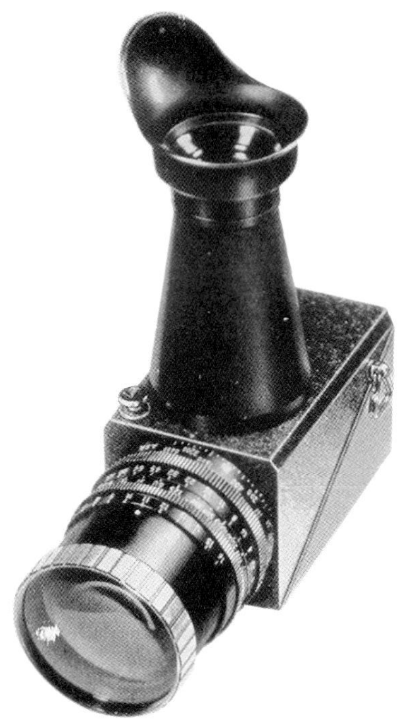

The Asahi Pentax Spotmeter was a very selective meter built on the principle of a SRL camera: for accurately directing the meter. The combination between the Spotmeter and an Asahi Pentax camera was the idea for the Spot-Matic.

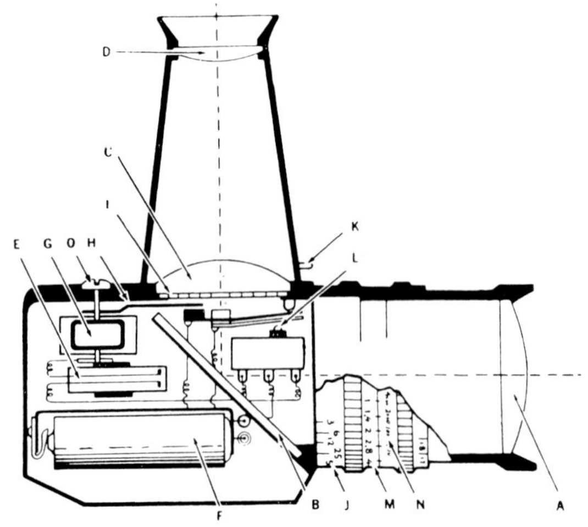

The Asahi Pentax Spotmeter

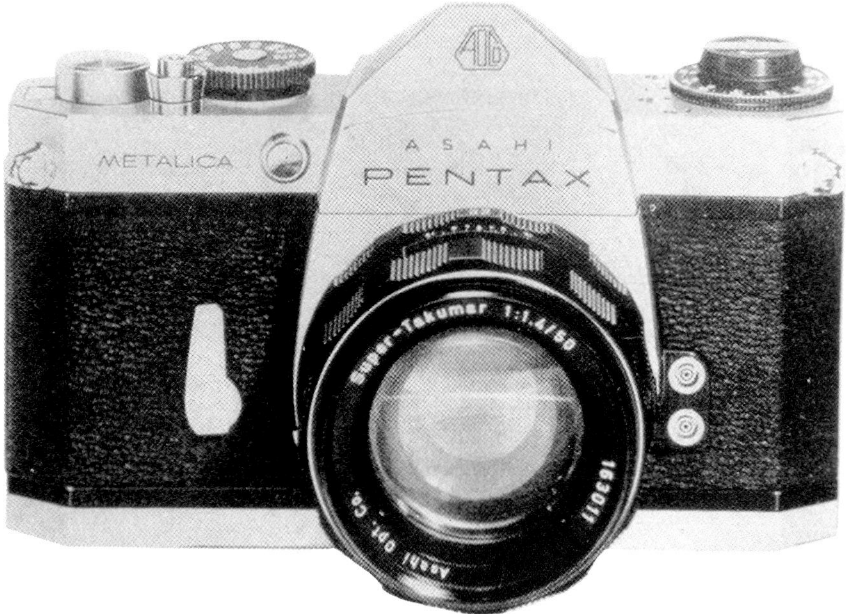

The Asahi Pentax Metalica II was an automatic SRL camera based on the Spotmatic body but with bayonet mount.

The Spotmeter III, some years later, adopted still more selective metering restricted to a single degree. It was followed by other models which became more and more sophisticated and sensitive. The last traditional Spotmeter model bore the number 5, had a silicon cell and was sensitive from EV 1 to EV 19. The V FL model gave light meter reading data in Lambert feet.

The traditional Spotmeter was backed up and then replaced in the second half of the Eighties by a model with digital display. It was sensitive from EV 1 to EV 20 and measured f/number differences with an accuracy of one-third EV.

The evolution of the light metering system from the Sixties onwards was inextricably tied into the evolution of the camera. Asahi Optical was one of the first companies to sense this phenomenon and to act accordingly.

Asahi Pentax Metalica II

After six years of lethargy, Asahi dusted off the idea of the metallic focal plane shutter. At the 1966 Photokina exhibition, a reflex of the Spotmatic line, called the Metalica II, was presented in the form of a prototype. The body of the Metalica II was almost identical to that of the standard Spotmatic. The innovations were all on the inside and were ten years ahead of the main features of the Asahi Pentax K2.

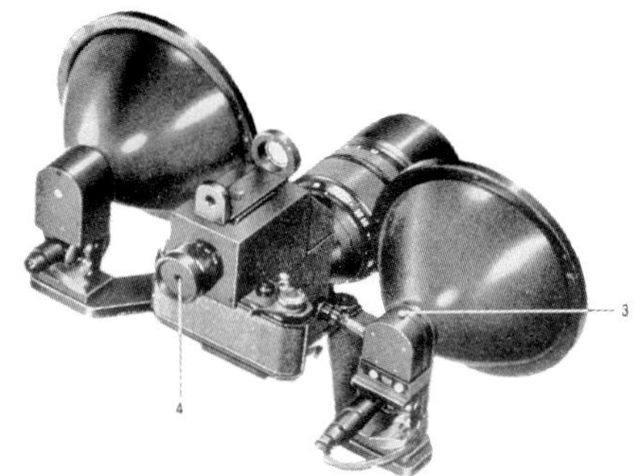

The Asahi Pentax Nocta was an accessory for shooting pictures in darkness.

The exposure meter switch was taken off the front. The wind lever was simplified and the frame counter sunk into the camera body. The wording Metalica towered over the wording Spotmatic. Alongside the wording was a button for manual closure of the diaphragm and direct observation of the depth of field.

The Metalica II was more innovative than the 1960 Metalica. It had a Copal Square metallic focal plane shutter, already used on many of the competition's reflexes. The meter reading circuit automatically controlled the shutter speed. The Metalica II was the first TTL in history to be equipped with an automatic exposure meter. The Konica Autoreflex T came onto the market in 1968, but in spite of its unquestionable priority, the Asahi Pentax Metalica never arrived on the market. The company decided that the project be completely revised. As with the Spotmatic the prototype predated mass-production by almost five years. The Electro Spotmatic derived from the Metalica, developing the concept of automatic working, but without the metallic focal plane shutter and bayonet mount. The Asahi Pentax Metalica II remained at the level of an idea and prototype on Asahi Optical's files.

Asahi Pentax Nocta

The Asahi Pentax Nocta was not a camera but a very special device which made it possible to take shots in complete darkness, using films sensitive to infrared rays. It could work in harness with any Asahi Pentax camera and was complemented by two hooded illuminators which emitted black light. The Asahi Pentax Nocta was not suitable for normal photography and was intended for highly specialized use. It stayed in the catalogues for some years without much public success. It was testimony to the fact that in the Sixties and Seventies Asahi Optical catered for photography at every level, including very highly specialized scientific work.

CHAPTER 8

Takumar-The Eyes of the Asahi Pentax

Asahi Optical originated in 1919 as an optical company. For many years their predominant activity related exclusively to the working, but not smelting, of optical glass. The cameras arrived thirty years later. Camera manufacture grew in parallel with glass working, going hand in hand with it and sometimes inseparably interacting with it.

When developing the Asahiflex camera the choice was made to adopt a screw lens mount. This was the 42x1 universal screw mount. Standardization of the mount made it possible and easy to fit German, Russian or Japanese lenses of different makes onto the Asahi Pentax reflexes. It might appear strange that a lens manufacturer did not try to ensure a reserved market by obliging the user of their cameras to purchase lenses of the same make. Most camera manufacturers produced bayonet mount lenses which were only compatible with their own cameras. When the first Asahi Pentax came out, Japanese production found itself subordinated to German. Nippon Kogaku built the rangefinder Nikon S, giving it a mount compatible with the Zeiss Contax. Canon produced its own cameras with a Leica-type screw mount. Most Japanese manufacturers followed the commonest European moves without too many problems. This was not in order to offer the possibility of using German lenses on Japanese cameras. The aim was to encourage users of German cameras to buy Japanese lenses, which were cheaper and good enough to withstand comparison. Another reason for adapting to European standards was the fact that the camera market was dominated by rangefinder models. Asahi Optical preferred to fit into a recent tradition rather than tackle completely unknown territory.

In Europe there was a fairly clear division in photographic production. Some companies specialized in making lenses, others in making cameras. Only companies like Leitz and Zeiss Ikon controlled both the optical and mechanical sectors. In general, lens producers found it difficult to build cameras well, and vice versa. The best known European lens producers, Schneider, Meyer, Angenieux, Zeiss Jena, Zeiss Ikon itself, etc., produced lenses with different mounts to order

87

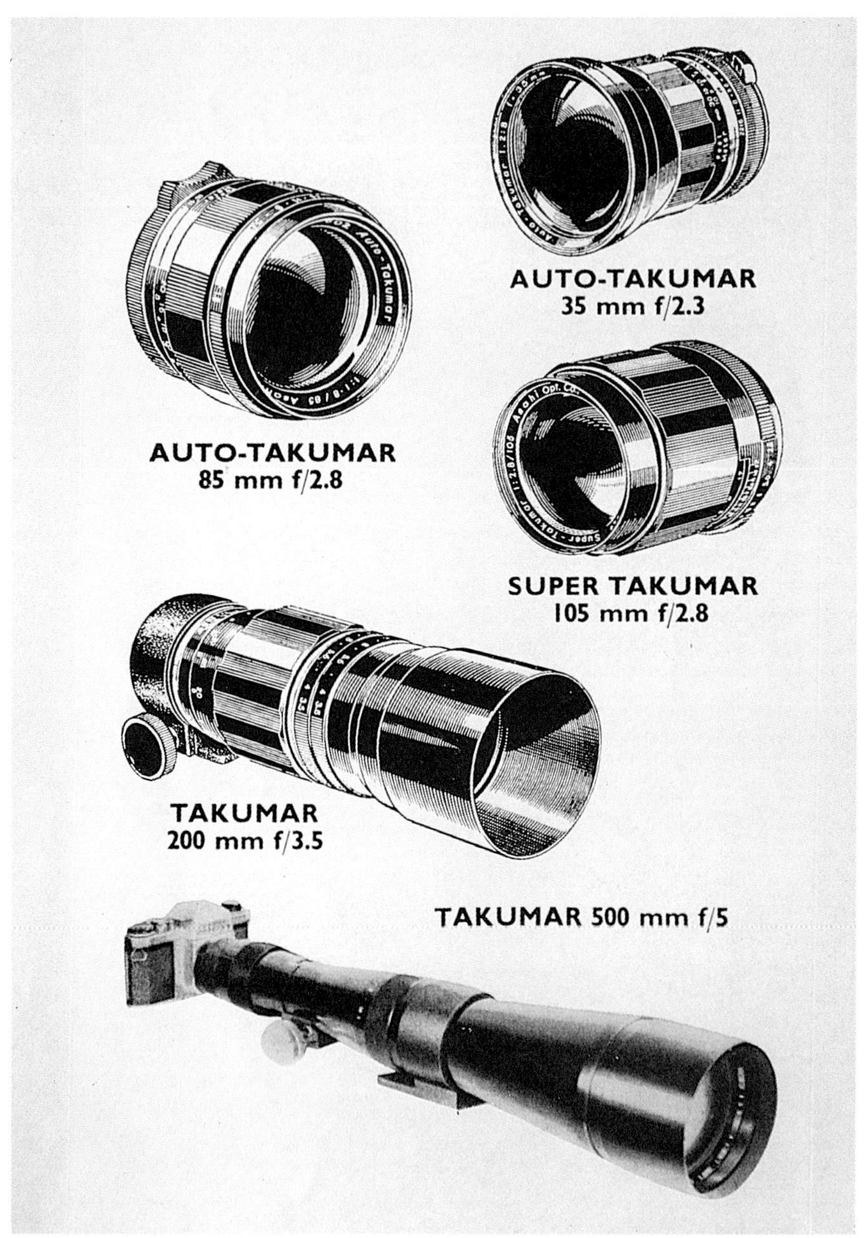

Takumar lens set at the end of the Fifties.

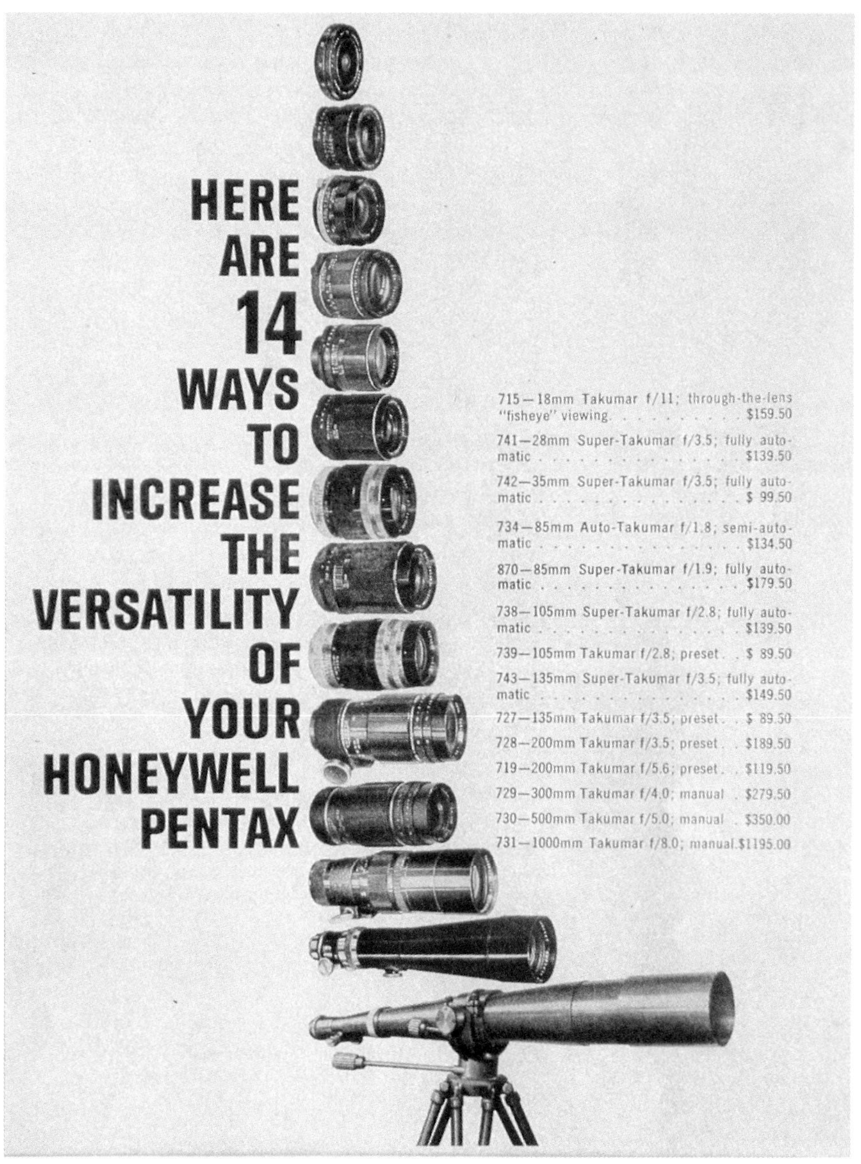

Takumar lens set of the middle Sixties.

from various customers. Zeiss Jena produced the same lens with an Exakta mount for Ihagee and with a screw mount for Pentacon. Zeiss Ikon supplied lenses to both Rollei and Hasselblad, besides Zeiss Ikon itself. Each camera manufacturer marketed and included in its own list lenses built by other companies.

In Japan, the manufacturing philosophy was different. Once the period of collaboration was over, in which Nikon sold its own lenses to Canon and Asahi Optical sold to Konishiroku, companies exhibited a tendency towards self-reliance. Nippon Kogaku essentially produced lenses for the Nikons. Canon began to produce its own lenses by itself, increasingly specializing in the treatment of optical glass. Each company adopted an exclusive mount and created a reserved market.

In the face of this tendency, many companies offered lenses with universal mounts, adaptable directly or by means of suitable adapters to the most popular cameras of the time. By developing a trend already started in Europe some Japanese manufacturers devised universal lenses with an interchangeable mount, that became very important in the amateur field. The list of makes would be a long one: Sun, Suntar, Sigma, Elicar, Soligor, Tamron and so on.

The original 39x1 Leica screw thread was too small for reflex cameras. It would cause vignetting in the viewfinder and was unsuitable for heavier telephoto lenses. A bigger, 42x1 thread had been adopted by Pentacon in Dresden for the Contax S, and it also appeared on the Pentacon F and the cheaper Praktica cameras. This became the international standard. After the early, non-standard Asahiflex models, Asahi Optical adopted the 42x1 mount so successfully that it came to be known as the Pentax mount.

The European screw mount lenses were cheap enough to compete with the Japanese ones. The market became divided fairly equally between the various manufacturers. Amongst the screw mount lenses in circulation in the Sixties, those most valued by photographers were undoubtedly the Zeiss Jena and Super Takumar makes.

Evolution of Automatic Working of Lenses

To reconstruct the history of the lenses produced by Asahi Optical in the Fifties and Sixties is to relive the evolution of an idea. The screw mount lenses underwent considerable changes, becoming increasingly reliable from a mechanical point of view, and offering improved facilities. The changes from the Takumars to Auto Takumars and from Super Takumars to SMC Takumars were significant in terms of facilities and features.

The first lenses put on the market with the Takumar name at the beginning of the Fifties were in bright metallic finish and were fitted with a completely manual diaphragm, like all photographic lenses of the time. After focusing the subject with the diaphragm at maximum aperture, in order to have the clearest possible view, it was necessary to close the diaphragm by hand before releasing the shutter. After the shot the diaphragm had to be reopened manually. These operations were quite inconvenient and exasperatingly slow. Hence, reflex photography was relegated to a few highly specialized areas where accuracy in framing and focusing were more important than speed of operation.

At the end of the Fifties, a number of lenses with presetting of the aperture came onto the market. A ring located next to the diaphragm ring made it possible to preset the selected aperture and introduce a stop corresponding to the selected value. At the instant of release, without needing to take one's eye from the viewfinder, one just had to rotate the aperture ring to a stop at the selected value. This process involved a rudimentary mechanism which successfully simplified the work of the photographer. The preset diaphragm simplified the problem but did not resolve it completely.

At the beginning of the Sixties, Asahi Optical introduced screw mount lenses fitted with the so-called automatic diaphragm. A spring built into the lens caused the diaphragm to close to the selected value precisely at the moment of release. This required a mechanical connection between the camera and lens. The diaphragm was reopened manually by pressing in a little lever located on the outside of the lens mounting itself. Lenses equipped with the automatic diaphragm were pretentiously called Auto Takumar. In fact, they were semi-automatic lenses which remained in production for a few years.

The semi-automatic diaphragm was then replaced by the fully automatic diaphragm for both closing and reopening. With the automatic diaphragm reopening, Asahi Optical adopted the Super Takumar name. Fully automatic working came about gradually and some Auto Takumar lenses, in spite of the name, incorporated a mechanism for spring-opening. A lever on the mount of the Super Takumar lenses made it possible to close the diaphragm manually otherwise it would always remain open in rest condition. Manual closing was necessary in order to be able to estimate the depth of field through the viewfinder. The lever was kept on the Super Takumars even after the arrival on the market of the Spotmatic, which had a special switch for controlling closure of the diaphragm. The facility for manual closing was even on the last generation of screw mount Takumars, the SMC Takumars, intended for connection with the diaphragm simulators on the Spotmatic F and Electro Spotmatic cameras.

Takumar Lenses

The Takumar series of lenses originated with the 1952 Asahiflex. The choice of the name Takumar was a tribute to the Japanese painter Takuma, a friend of the President of Asahi Optical.

50mm,f/3.5 Takumar The first lens produced by Asahi Optical for the Asahiflex cameras had a focal length of 50mm and a maximum aperture of f/3.5. It was probably derived from existing well-known optical layouts. The 50mm,f/3.5 Takumar was used as a standard lens for the Asahiflex I and Ia.

58mm,f/2.4 Takumar The first Asahiflex lens was replaced around 1954 by a faster one with a slightly longer focal length, the 58mm,f/2.4 Takumar, which became the standard lens for the Asahiflex II.

83mm,f/1.9 Takumar This was a typical portrait lens. It was the fastest Takumar lens with an Asahiflex mounting.

100mm,f/3.5 Takumar A short medium speed telephoto, later to be completely reworked in optical design and its speed increased.

135mm,f/3.5 Takumar This lens later carried the standard 42x1 thread and remained in the catalogue for many years.

500mm,f/5.0 Takumar The biggest "gun" in the Takumar family exploited the potential of the reflex cameras to the full and was kept in the catalogue for over a decade.

The series of non-standard, screw mount Takumar lenses went out of production at the end of 1957 with the introduction of the 42x1 screw mount Asahi Pentaxes. The choice of the universal mount on the latest Asahiflex IIa models justified the hypothesis that lenses with the 42x1 mount had preceded the Asahi Pentaxes by several months.

55mm,f/2.2 Takumar; 58mm,f/2.2 Takumar In order to equip the Asahi Pentaxes with a pentaprism viewfinder and 42x1 screw mount, Asahi Optical built modern-design standard lenses. The 58mm focal length on the early models was brought down to 55mm. The maximum aperture for both became f/2.2. These lenses were for the Asahi Pentax AP and Asahi Pentax S and were fitted with a front ring for presetting of the diaphragm. The optical layout comprised six elements and f/22 minimum aperture.

35mm,f/4.0 Takumar With the triumph of the Asahi Pentax line, the range of Takumar lenses increased. This six-element wide-angle lens with preset diaphragm was introduced, but Asahi Optical's first wide-angle lens was fairly short-lived and was followed by others will revised optical design.

105mm,f/2.8 Takumar At the beginning of the Sixties, the 100mm,f/3.5 was replaced by the faster four-element 105mm,f/2.8 with preset diaphragm.

135mm,f/3.5 Takumar This was the original five-element 135mm brought out with a preset diaphragm and 42x1 screw mount.

200mm,f/3.5 Takumar Telephoto lenses with a focal length greater than 135mm did not have the mechanism for semi-automatic presetting of the diaphragm. The first 200mm lens built at the end of the Fifties comprised three elements and had a completely manual diaphragm.

1000mm,f/8.0 Takumar At the beginning of the Sixties, Asahi Optical brought out an extraordinary lens, the three-element 1000mm,f/8. This lens, variously reworked, remained in the Asahi Optical catalogue throughout the period of the Asahi Pentax system.

Auto Takumar Lenses

The mechanism for automatic closure of the diaphragm with manual reopening was introduced in 1958 with the Asahi Pentax K. The lenses which used this mechanism were called Auto Takumar.

55mm,f/1.8 Auto Takumar   This six-element 55mm was introduced as the standard lens on the Asahi Pentax K and for many years was the fastest lens in the Takumar family. The aperture selection ring was located on the front of the lens. The 55mm, was later changed into a completely automatic model and for some years kept the Auto Takumar name. In 1965, together with the Spotmatic, the 50mm,f/1.4 was introduced and became the fastest lens in the system. Despite the appearance of the 50mm,f/1.4, the 55mm,f/1.8 lens remained in production until the end of the screw mount era, and was also brought out in a Super Multi Coated version.

55mm,f/2.0 Auto Takumar With the appearance of the Asahi Pentax S2 cameras, a standard 55mm,f/2 lens was put onto the market, remaining unchanged in optical structure for several years.

35mm,f/3.5 Auto Takumar   The adoption of the semi-automatic diaphragm implied expansion of the range of focal lengths and lenses. The 35mm,f/4 was replaced by the successful 35mm,f/3.5 Auto Takumar, which was extremely light and compact and the cheapest of Asahi Optical's interchangeable lenses, apart from the standard focal length, and was kept in the catalogue in various mountings until 1975. The five-element optical layout remained unchanged over this time.

35mm,f/2.3 Auto Takumar Less successful than the smaller aperture lens with the same focal length, the 35mm,f/2.3 was only in production for a few years and did not survive to the mid-Sixties.

85mm,f/1.8 Auto Takumar; 105mm,f/2.8 Auto Takumar   The 85mm,f/1.9 medium telephoto was replaced by the 85mm,f/1.8 Auto Takumar and the 105mm,f/2.8 was also introduced in the automatic diaphragm model.

200mm,f/5.6 Tele Takumar The range of non-automatic Tele Takumar telephoto lenses was expanded with a 200mm,f/5.6, lighter but slower than the earlier 200mm,f/3.5. The slower lens was kept in the catalogue the longest. The faster 200mm lens was replaced in the second half of the Sixties by a redesigned, more manageable lens.

300mm,f/4.0 Tele Takumar The 500mm telephoto lens was backed up by a three-element 300mm,f/4 without automatic diaphragm. Asahi Optical was most prolific in the field of focal lengths and introduced several alternatives.

The Auto Takumar lenses were gradually replaced by fully automatic Super Takumar lenses which made their appearance in the commonest focal lengths in the mid-Sixties, together with the Asahi Pentax Spotmatics.

Super Takumar Lenses

The Super Takumar lenses were distinguished by the lack of a visible lever for reopening the diaphragm. The lever was replaced by a small switch which selected the positions AUTO and MAN. On AUTO the lens, screwed onto the camera body or removed from its seat, presented the diaphragm fully open. In order to close the diaphragm it was necessary to press the pin on the back of the mounting. On MAN the lens kept the diaphragm closed at the value shown by the aperture scale. The aperture scale on the Auto Takumar lenses was rotated anti-clockwise for the closed values. On the Super Takumar lenses the scale changed direction. To close the diaphragm one had to rotate it clockwise.

50mm,f/1.4 Super Takumar This lens was brought out in 1965 as the standard lens for the Asahi Pentax Spotmatics. Slightly shorter than the 55mm lenses, the 50mm,f/1.4 projected back into the camera body and could pose a few incompatability problems for the previous-generation reflexes. The eight-element optical layout was subsequently modified to seven elements. The minimum aperture was f/16, like the majority of Super Takumar lenses.

35mm,f/3.5 Super Takumar The 35mm,f/3.5 Auto Takumar was replaced by the 35mm,f/3.5 Super Takumar, preserving the same optical layout and the same very compact dimensions.

85mm,f/1.9 Super Takumar This replaced the earlier lens of the same focal length, reducing the maximum aperture from f/1.8 to f/1.9. It had a five-element layout and 85cm minimum focusing distance.

105mm,f/2.8 Super Takumar The short 105mm,f/2.8 Auto Takumar telephoto was promoted as Super Takumar and preserved the same five-element optical layout.

135mm,f/3.5 Super Takumar The standard 135mm,f/3.5 Auto Takumar was replaced by the Super Takumar with the same four-element optical head.

28mm,f/3.5 Super Takumar In the mid-Sixties, the 28mm,f/3.5 Super Takumar was added to Asahi Optical's wide-angle lens family. Its retrofocus construction incorporated seven elements. Despite its special optical construction, the external diameter remained compact and it could take a 49mm filter like the majority of the Super Takumar lenses.

18mm,f/11 Takumar Fish-Eye Without an automatic diaphragm, the extraordinary 18mm,f/11 fish-eye offered unusual facilities.

500mm,f/4.5 Tele Takumar The 500mm,f/5 telephoto was replaced by a more modern 500mm,f/4.5 Tele Takumar. It weighed 3.5 kilos. The 49mm filter-holder was next to the rear element.

35mm,f/2.0 Super Takumar Some interesting lenses were introduced with the Spotmatic, like the fast 35mm,f/2.0 Super Takumar, which became one of the fastest wide-angle lenses of the period. It had an eight-element optical layout and f/16 minimum aperture.

100mm,f/4.0 Bellows Takumar In 1965, two special lenses for close-up photography were introduced. The 100mm,f/4 Bellows Takumar was not automatic and was intended for use with the extension bellows for macro photography.

50mm,f/4.0 Macro Takumar This special lens was a four-element design, specially adjusted for close-up focusing, like the famous Macro Kilar. It was only in the catalogue for a short time before being replaced by the model with an automatic diaphragm.

50mm,f/4.0 Super Macro Takumar This lens had an automatic diaphragm with the same optical unit as the Macro Takumar. The minimum focusing distance, without extension tubes, was 23cm.

24mm,f/3.5 Super Takumar In Europe, Angenieux had devised the retrofocus system for wide-angle lenses for reflex cameras. Asahi Optical soon set great store by the European experiment. In around four years some very interesting wide-angle lenses were appearing on the market. The 24mm,f/3.5 Super Takumar was introduced at the end of the Sixties. Its optical layout comprised nine elements. The wide diameter of its front element necessitated the use of 59mm diameter filters.

20mm,f/4.5 Super Takumar At the end of the Sixties, Asahi Optical brought out its 20mm,f/4.5 Super Takumar ultra wide-angle lens, which covered the whole format without distortion. The optical layout had eleven elements. The diameter of the filters was 77mm, and the minimum focusing distance, 20cm. The minimum aperture was f/22, with a depth of field from infinity to a few centimetres.

17mm,f/4.0 Super Takumar Fish-Eye The old 18mm Takumar Fish-eye was replaced by the fantastic eleven-element 17mm,f/4, which produced a frame-filling image and covered an angle of view of 180^0. The enormous barrel distortion produced by such lens became a fashionable stylistic feature in photography in the early Seventies.

135mm,f/2.5 Super Takumar There were some interesting innovations in telephoto lenses. Alongside the 135mm,f/3.5 a five-element 135mm,f/2.5 Super Takumar was introduced. It was faster by almost a stop and 100g heavier. Like the slower 135mm lens, the minimum aperture was f/22 and it focused to 1.5 metres.

200mm,f/4.0 Super Takumar Alongside the existing 200mm,f/5.6, a lighter, more manageable lens with the same focal length and a fully automatic diaphragm was brought out. It had an eight-element optical layout. It weighed little more than half a kilo and focused down to 2.5 metres.

300mm,f/4.0 Super Takumar Without immediately replacing the preselection 300mm lens already in the catalogue, a 300mm,f/4 fully automatic Super Takumar lens was brought out at the beginning of the Seventies. It had a five-element layout, weighed nearly one kilo and focused down to less than five metres.

150mm,f/4.0 Super Takumar Amongst the medium telephoto lenses produced by Asahi Optical, one of the most noteworthy was the 150mm,f/4.0; a tele lens as light and compact as the 135mm,f/3.5.

70-150mm,f/4.5 Zoom Takumar The Super Takumar range was completed by a rather heavy and bulky 70-150mm,f/4.5 zoom.

300mm,f/6.3 Tele Takumar; 400mm,f/5.6 Tele Takumar During the era of the Super Takumars, some long focal length lenses were produced without an automatic diaphragm. In order to distinguish them easily from the automatic Super Takumars, they bore the name Tele Takumar. The already well-known 200mm,f/5.6; 300mm,f/6.3; and 400mm,f/5.6 telephoto lenses existed alongside their fellows equipped with automatic working. The typical operating slowness of long telephoto lenses made the lack of an automatic diaphragm less serious.

In 1971, with the introduction of the Spotmatic II, the Super Takumar lenses were replaced by the Super Multi Coated Takumars. The lenses making up the SMC series were treated with a multi-coating which had the double aim of making the lenses less subject to flare and of greatly reducing the loss of light through the many air-to-glass surfaces.

Super Multi Coated, SMC Takumar Lenses

All the Super Takumar lenses produced from 1971 to 1975, from the 17mm to the 1000mm, benefitted from the multi-coating treatment. Only the 55mm,f/2 lens, mass produced for the cheap SP 500 reflex, was excluded from the SMC treatment. The abbreviation SMC indicated, apart from the new lens treatment, that the mount was designed for connection to the diaphragm simulator on the Spotmatic F and Electro Spotmatic. The abbreviation was incorrectly placed on the long telephoto lenses; the 400mm,f/5.6, the 500mm,f/4.5 and the 1000mm, f/8, which did not have an automatic diaphragm. The Bellows Takumar became the SMC Bellows, but clearly remained a preset-type lens. The SMC Takumar lenses were designed for coupling with the diaphragm simulator. The bulky presence of the coupling to the simulator on the mount created serious problems with the cameras brought out before 1965. The barrel of some SMC Takumar lenses produced after 1973 had a chequered rubber casing. Almost all the SMC Takumar lenses used the same optical layout as the equivalent Super Takumars.

17mm,f/4.0 SMC Takumar Fish-Eye With eleven elements and f/22 minimum aperture, the Fish-eye only had the SMC treatment in more recent times. It had built-in filters.

20mm,f/4.5 SMC Takumar With eleven elements and f/22 minimum aperture, this lens only had the SMC treatment in more recent times. Filters 77mm.

24mm,f/3.5 SMC Takumar Nine elements and f/16 minimum aperture. Filters 58mm.

28mm,f/3.5 SMC Takumar Seven elements and f/16 minimum aperture. Filters 49mm.

35mm,f/2.0 SMC Takumar Eight elements and f/16 minimum aperture. Filters 49mm.

35mm,f/3.5 SMC Takumar Five elements and f/16 minimum aperture. Filters 49mm.

50mm,f/1.4 SMC Takumar Seven elements and f/16 minimum aperture. Filters 49mm.

50mm,f/1.8 SMC Takumar Six elements and f/16 minimum aperture. Filters 49mm.

85mm,f/1.8 SMC Takumar Five elements and f/16 minimum aperture. Filters 58mm. Maximum aperture increased to f/1.8.

105mm,f/2.8 SMC Takumar Five elements and f/16 minimum aperture. Filters 49mm.

135mm,f/2.5 SMC Takumar Five elements, f/22 minimum aperture. Filters 58mm.

135mm,f/3.5 SMC Takumar Four elements, f/22 minimum aperture. Filters 49mm.

150mm,f/4.0 SMC Takumar Five elements, f/22 minimum aperture. Filters 49mm.

200mm,f/4.0 SMC Takumar Five elements, f/22 minimum aperture. Filters 58mm.

300mm,f/4.0 SMC Takumar Five elements, f/22 minimum aperture. Filters 77mm.

400mm,f/5.6 SMC Takumar Lens without automatic diaphragm comprising five elements, minimum aperture f/45. Filters 77mm.

500mm,f/4.5 SMC Takumar Lens without automatic diaphragm comprising four elements, minimum aperture f/45. Used 49mm filters on rear part of mounting.

50mm,f/4.0 SMC Macro Takumar Macro lens in normal focusing mount. Copied well-known optical layout. Filters 49mm.

100mm,f/4.0 SMC Bellows Takumar Special lens with manual diaphragm for use on bellows, like the non-treated 1965 Bellows Takumar.

85-210mm,f/4.5 SMC Zoom Takumar Comprising eleven elements, the 85-210mm SMC Zoom Takumar replaced the 70-150 Super Takumar with the same maximum aperture. The focal range was increased whilst the total weight of the lens was practically halved.

85mm,f/4.5 UA Takumar; 300mm,f/5.6 UA Takumar Two very special lenses, the 85mm,f/4.5 Takumar Ultra Acromatic and the 300mm,f/5.6 Ultra Acromatic, were brought out in parallel with the new-generation Takumars. They were very expensive lenses intended for special shots. Fluorite and quartz elements were used in their construction. The two lenses were corrected against chromatic aberration produced by ultraviolet and infrared light. Besides being used in normal light, they could also be used for photography in i.r. or u.v. light.

120mm,f/2.8 SMC Takumar An interesting medium focal length telephoto lens consisting of 5 elements in 4 groups.

45-125mm,f/4.0 SMC Zoom Takumar This 45-125mm,f/4.0 zoom with a weight of 600g was brought out at the 1972 Photokina exhibition.

15mm,f/3.5 SMC Takumar Beating the renowned 20mm Takumar by a good 5mm focal length, Asahi Optical introduced an ultra wide-angle lens with new features at the 1972 Photokina. The thirteen-element 15mm,f/3.5 lens provided an image free from barrel distortion. The new model weighed 570g and incorporated four colour and UV filters. The two lenses were again on show at the 1974 Photokina and represented the final act played by the Takumar family.

Alpa Takumar Lenses

The world renown of the Takumar lenses was such that some were produced with a special mounting for the very stylish Swiss Alpa Reflex camera, improperly called the Alpa Takumar. The above two lenses were offered in Alpa mounts.

CHAPTER 9

From Screw to Bayonet

In the mid-Seventies the Asahi Optical Company was generally considered as one of the most successful Japanese photographic enterprises. Asahi Optical's reputation was based on its success with the Spotmatics in the second half of the Sixties. This success continued into the early Seventies with the Electro Spotmatic automatic cameras. But the company appeared to rest on its laurels, whilst the rest of the photographic world was well into a phase of growth. The success of the screw mount Spotmatic could not last forever. The early Seventies were full of uncertainty which demanded that tough decisions be taken.

In mid-1975 Asahi Optical abandoned the screw mount with much to-do. Gainsaying a long tradition based on renewal through continuity, they simultaneously brought out three cameras with totally new features. These three 35mm reflexes had a unique bayonet mount called the K-mount.

The introduction of bayonet mount Asahi Pentax cameras caused a great sensation because it signified the inevitable end of the screw mount and the Spotmatic line. The screw mount cameras were out of production by the end of 1975 whilst their K-mount successors took a long time to come onto the market.

The three bayonet mount Asahi Pentax cameras were designated K2, KX, and KM. They were introduced together as a single family. From the operating point of view they afforded a range of quite different facilities. In dimensions and general structure they closely resembled the Spotmatic models, from which they continued to draw their inspiration. Despite their common mould, the bayonet mount cameras were clearly distinguishable from the standard Spotmatic line.

The controls and styling of the new cameras were completely redesigned with many concessions to the aesthetic trends of the Seventies. The lettering was heavily modified and altered. The result was a series of cameras with a quite appealing and aggressive outline, perhaps less personal that that of the Spotmatic, but equally persuasive.

The cheapest model in the series, the KM, was a completely traditional mechanical reflex. It had a very well-proven CdS exposure meter with metering at any aperture and an equally proven fabric-blind shutter. It was a revised

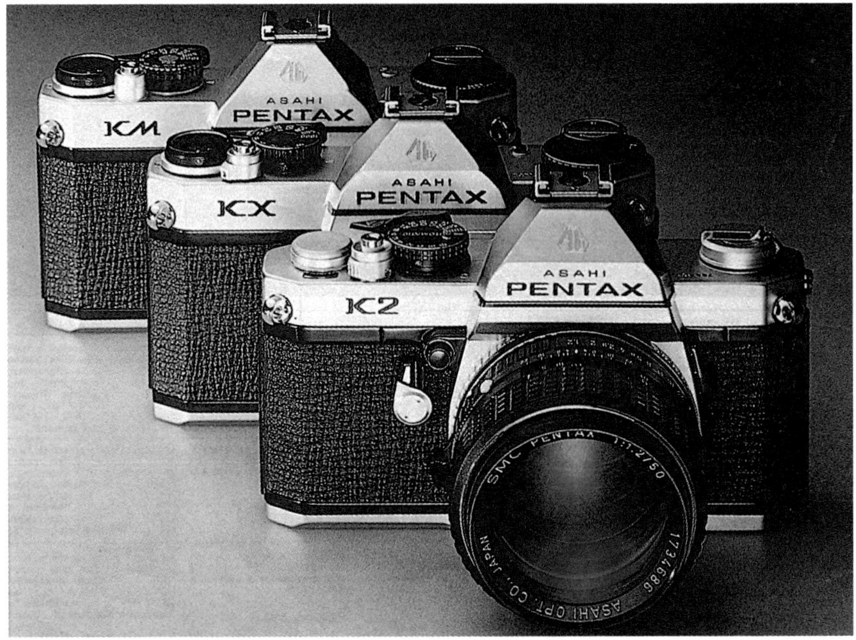

In 1975 Asahi Optical Company introduced three cameras simultaneously with bayonet lens mounts - the K-mount.

version of the Spotmatic F, the main controls and features of which it preserved almost unaltered, together with all its qualities and defects.

The Asahi Pentax KX was more advanced. It had a modern, sensitive silicon photocell and a match-needle light metering system. It was possible to see the value of the set aperture in the viewfinder through a little window at the base of the pentaprism. Like all the Asahi Pentax models which had preceded it, the KX continued to use the standard focal plane shutter. The Asahi Pentax KX was promised a motor and a data-back which in fact never made it onto the market.

The Asahi Pentax K2 was the spearhead model. This was a reflex with automatic and manual exposure and many structural innovations. For the first time on a standard Asahi Pentax the K2 did not have the normal shutter with fabric blinds. Instead it had a metal-blind Seiko MF with vertical movement and synchronization at $^1/125$ sec.

The K2 was an aperture-priority automatic reflex, based on the same principles as the Electro Spotmatic. All shutter speeds could be set manually, from 8 to $^1/1000$ sec.

By means of an intermediate ring, the K-family cameras, could take all existing Takumar lenses, although they had to forego metering at any aperture and

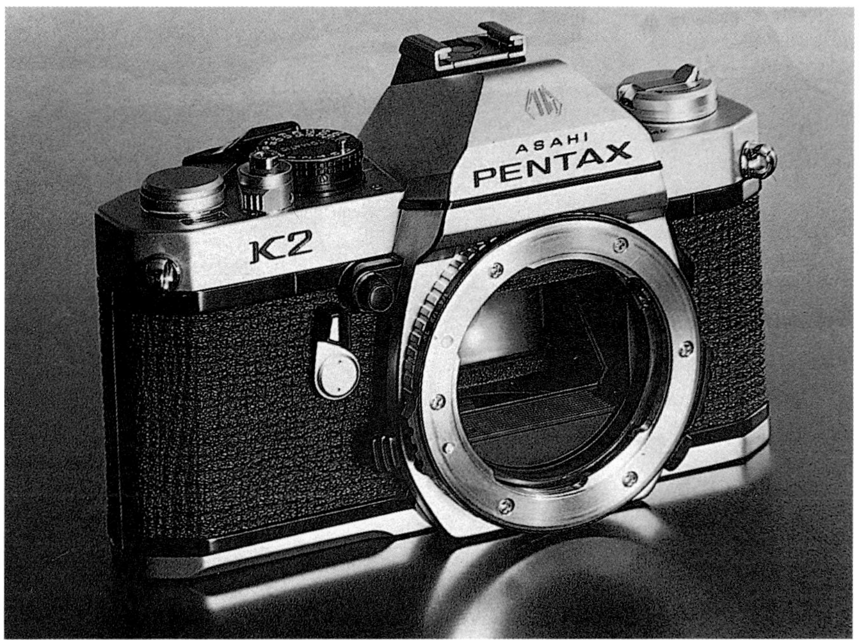

The new K-bayonet

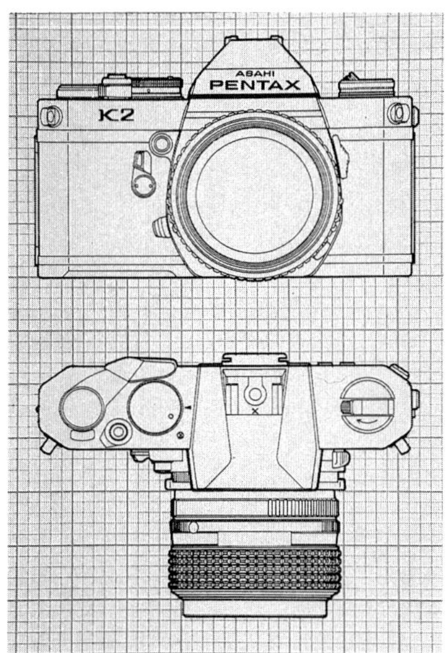

The controls and styling of the new cameras were completely redesigned. The result was a series of cameras with quite appealing and agressive outlines.

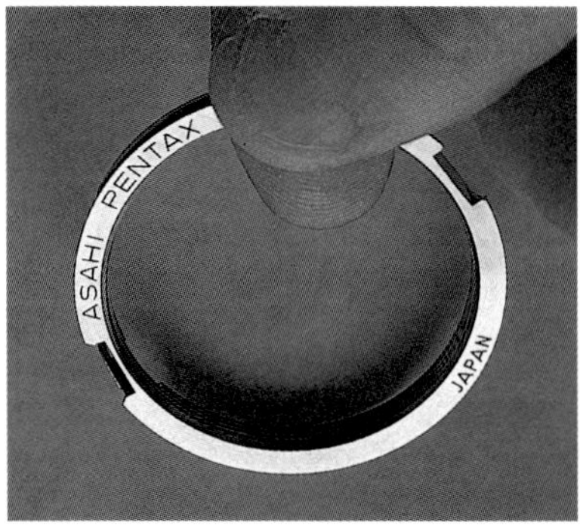

The K adapter ring permitted use of Takumar lenses on K-mount cameras.

automatic working of the diaphragm. In order to benefit fully from the features of the K-mount, one had to use the new bayonet mount lenses. They bore the name "SMC Pentax K", and had the same optical designs as the equivalent SMC Takumar lenses. They had a chequered rubber outer finish. Metering was possible at all apertures.

The bayonet mount designed by the Pentax technicians was very spacious and completely original. Pursuing a policy calling for maximum exploitation of its own patents, Asahi Pentax licensed right of use of the K-mount to several other Japanese firms. Cameras came out from Cosina and Ricoh and equipped with the K-mount, followed by the Petri and the latest Topcon model, and from 1984 on the Russian Zenit and Almaz cameras too.

The extension of the K-mount to cameras other than the Asahi's own was the last attempt, touching in some respects, to establish a universal bayonet mount. This attempt at standardization was intended to encourage interchangeability between cameras and lenses of different makes, returning the mechanical automatic workings and without recourse to tiresome intermediate rings. The attempt, however liberal, was unsuccessful.

The illusion of a universal bayonet, capable in some way of reviving the auspicious era of the screw mount, finally vanished with the introduction of programmed automatic reflexes. The need for exchange of greater amounts of information between camera and lens generated many different solutions, even between the same users of the K-bayonet mount. The multiplicity of solutions proposed ended up by frustrating the alleged universal application of the K-mount, without affecting the basic soundness of the proposal.

A year after the introduction of the three bayonet mount Asahi Pentax models, the group was completed by a fourth musketeer: the Pentax K1000. As the KM corresponded to the Spotmatic F, so the K1000 corresponded to the fondly-remembered SP 1000. Derived from the inexpensive KM, the Asahi Pentax K1000 was subsequently simplified, relieved of a number of costly optional extras such as the self-timer, and put on sale at extremely competitive prices. Sturdy and very cheap, the K1000 found its own slot in the market and has proved to be much more long-lived than its travelling companions, the KX and KM, which were out of production by the end of 1976. It is still on the market today.

After the arrival of the K1000, Asahi Optical introduced an improved version of the flagship K2, which was called K2 DMD. The camera was designed with the facility for motorization and was something more than just a K2 with a modified base. The K2 DMD was the first of Asahi Optical's electronic reflexes capable of being motorized. In order to make it more professional an optional arrangement was added for direct viewfinder observation of the set aperture. A similar arrangement had been successfully used on the Asahi Pentax KX. The K2 DMD was equipped with a device for printing data on the frame and underwent a few other minor internal improvements. Thus modified, the K2 survived until the end of the Seventies.

Asahi Optical's adoption of the bayonet mount represented freedom from the constraints imposed by the screw mount. This strategic move coincided with independence from its American distributor, Honeywell. Towards the end of 1976 the company established a direct sales network in the United States.

The word "Pentax" simultaneously assumed greater significance. The cameras bore the name "Asahi Pentax" on their pentaprisms, but the word Asahi became increasingly smaller and less evident.

The heydays of the Asahi Pentax K cameras, apart from the K1000, proved short-lived and served as a transition towards increasingly ambitious lenses made possible with the adoption of the bayonet-mount. At the 1976 Photokina, two reflexes were brought out which were destined to radically change the world of 35mm photography as well as the fortunes of Asahi Optical.

Confronted with cameras like the Canon AE1, the Olympus OM2 and other compact electronic SLR cameras with a wide range of facilities, Asahi Optical reacted by putting two very compact reflexes called MX and ME onto the market. These caused astonishment with their very small dimensions and once again Asahi had the world's smallest 35mm reflexes. They were even more compact than the Olympus OM1, which had caused such amazement at Photokina in 1972.

Apart from their size the two little Asahi Pentaxes proved to be big in the facilities they offered. The MX was a mechanical reflex with nothing traditional or predictable about it. The light metering circuit was based on a new gallium phosphoarsenide photocell, more sensitive and accurate than CdS or even silicon photocells. Data in the viewfinder was displayed by LEDs instead of the usual needle.

The MX was the first Asahi Pentax reflex designed from the start to use a film wind-on motor. The MX could be equipped with two different types of motors. A proper professional motor offered fast sequences of up to 5 fps. Alternatively, a very compact and cheap winder offered sequences of 2 fps. Light and very sturdy, the MX inherited all the qualities of the old Spotmatic.

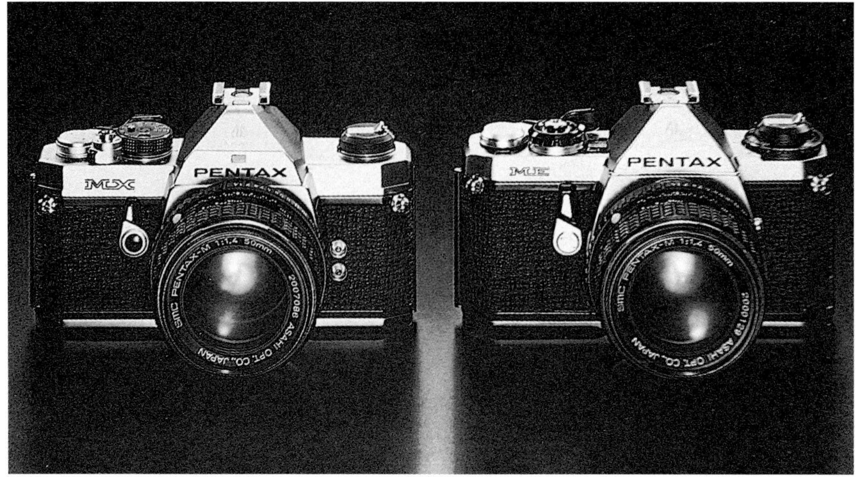

In 1976 Asahi Optical introduced the compact MX and ME. Similar in design, the cameras had different specifications.

The ME was more compact than the MX and was an electronic camera that could not be operated manually. It was designed for coupling with a compact winder, very like the one on the MX, but not interchangeable with it. The ME was improved and developed in many different forms giving rise to a truly authentic family of electronic, automated cameras.

An extremely interesting series of lenses, called SMC Pentax M, was brought out together with the compact reflexes. Particularly compact and light, the M-series lenses were completely revised as far as their optical design was concerned. They completed the range of K-mount Pentax lenses and replaced many of the existing focal lengths.

The introduction of the two little Pentax SLR's led to the premature retirement of the KX and KM manual reflexes. The ME electronic Asahi Pentax supplemented the K2 professional electronic reflex, whilst the MX manual reflex was several rungs above the spartan K1000.

The production needs of the two little reflexes brought about a reorganisation in the company. Asahi Optical's main factory, in Mashiko Park, did not have the capacity. Two new factories were added, one in Tokyo and the other in Saitama. The SMC Pentax lenses and MX reflexes were produced at the Mashiko factory, at the rate of 15,000 cameras a month. 25,000 Pentax ME's a month were produced and assembled at Saitama and Tokyo. At the beginning of 1977 total production was 40,000 cameras a month, but Asahi Optical aimed to reach at least 47,000. They exceeded this target. 50,000 a month were produced during the first months of 1978. With this expansion, Asahi Optical's production was now comparable with that of other Japanese companies. During the same period

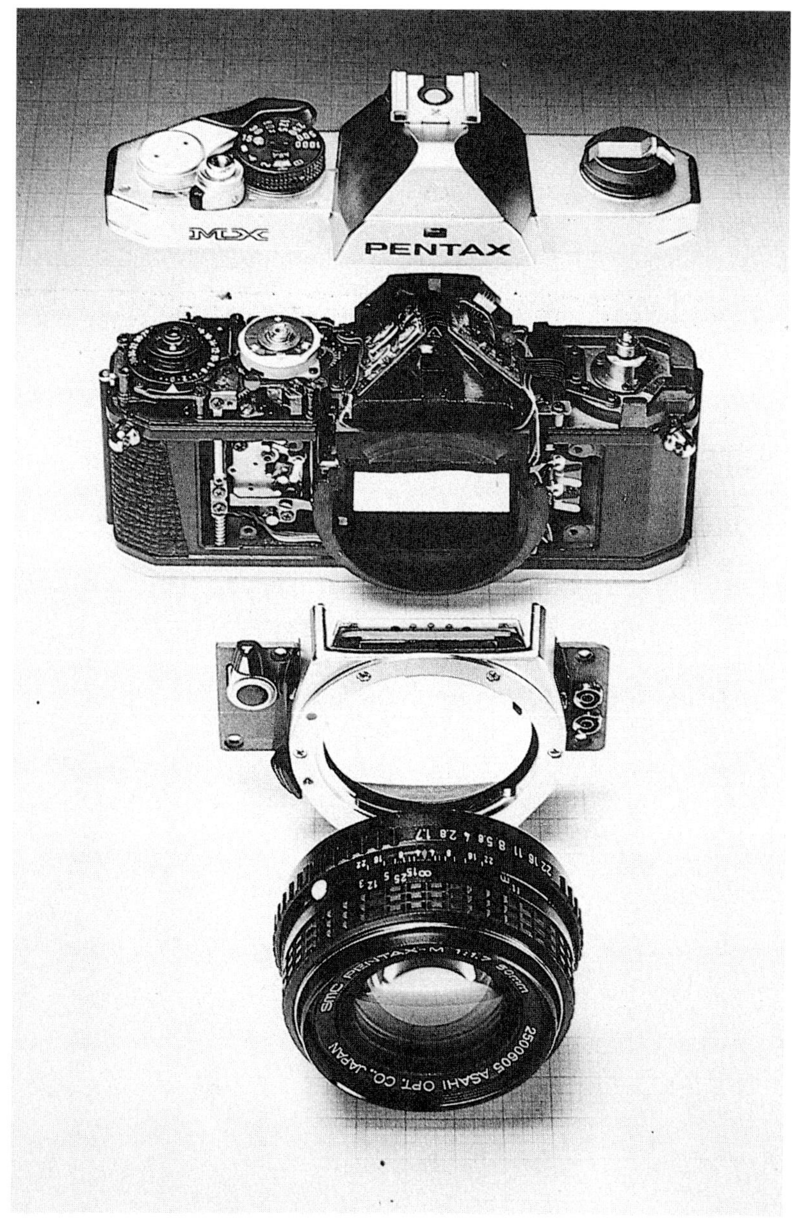

The MX was a full mechanical camera, motorised and reliable.

Canon, barely eighteen months after bringing out its AE1 model, celebrated the series' millionth camera. Competition between camera manufactures was fierce. Thanks to its efficiency, Asahi Optical managed to reduce the price of the ME, whilst increasing the volume of sales still further.

At the 1978 Photokina exhibition Asahi Optical introduced an unusual reflex camera. Unimaginably miniturized and compact, the world's smallest reflex did not use the 35mm format but the popular 110 size. It was a miniature version of the 35mm SLR's. The controls included a traditional wind-on lever. It had TTL metering and an electronic shutter. The equipment included all the accessories worthy of a professional reflex. Three tiny interchangeable lenses with bayonet mount were offered. The accessories included a small dedicated flash and a clip-

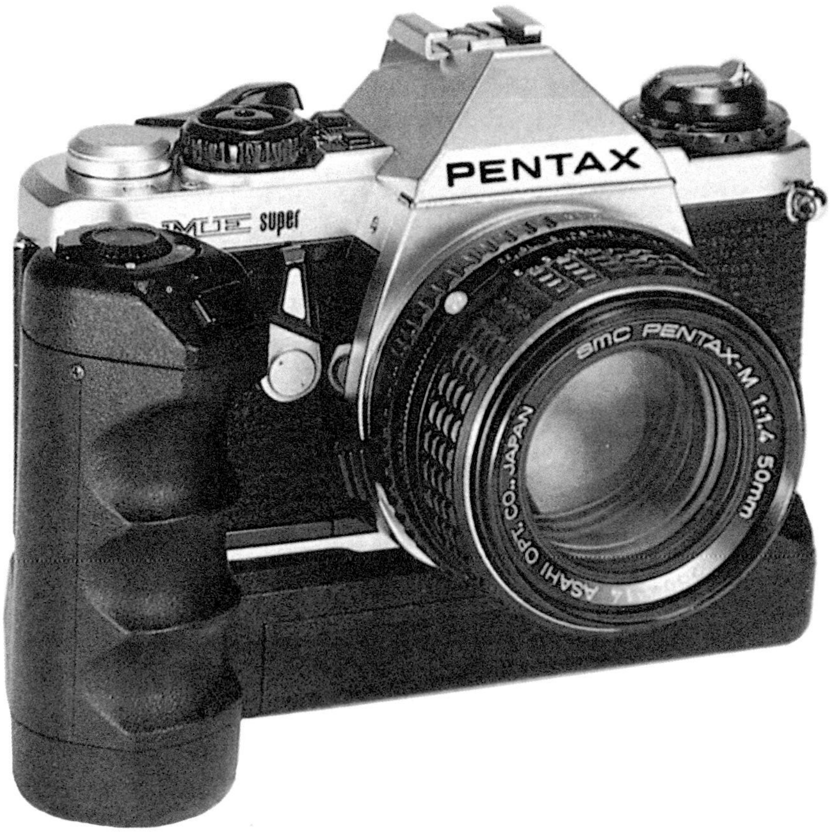

The ME Super was the improved model of the Asahi Pentax ME, easy to use automatically and manually. It took the improved winder MEII.

on winder. This mini reflex was called Pentax Auto 110 and was the only one of its kind. Other manufacturers had reflex cameras for the 110 format in their catalogues, but laid out differently and with non-interchangeable zoom lenses. The technological feat represented by the Auto 110 was perhaps excessive and out of proportion for a format like 110, but it repaid Asahi Optical hugely in terms of publicity.

Having brilliantly demonstrated its mastery over electronics and the most sophisticated miniturization techniques, Asahi Optical decided to aim higher. It developed very ambitious projects. In the best informed circles people began to talk of a professional Asahi Pentax, capable of competing on a level with the professional models from Nikon and Canon.

At the beginning of 1980 they brought out two reflexes based on the ME and intended to replace it. They were called the MV and ME Super. The Pentax ME Super was a more advanced version of the ME, preserving its general structure and very small dimensions. The ME Super had an automatic exposure meter but could also be used manually. The reflex, for the first time in history, had a series of small push-buttons which replaced the shutter speed dial for when the camera was being used in manual. The Pentax ME Super used the same winder as the ME, which was improved and renamed Winder ME II.

By making use of electronic components which were for the most part miniturized and sophisticated, the ME Super renewed and followed up the success of the compact ME, gaining equal sales acclaim.

The second reflex based on the Asahi Pentax ME was called MV. The Pentax MV was a reflex with simplified action. The automatic working of the exposure meter could not be turned off and the camera was not designed for motorization. The Pentax MV was aimed at the mass of photographers wanting acceptable results without having to solve technical problems. Although the camera was targeted at a less sophisticated public, mass acceptance of the MV was seriously handicapped by the fact that it was impossible to fit the winder. In an increasingly demanding market, electronic reflexes without a motor were unable to assert themselves forcibly enough. For this reason the Pentax MV was replaced by the MV1, identical to the earlier one and designed to take the ME-series winders.

The Pentax ME Super was an excellent reflex and offered better facilities than the other automatic electronic cameras on the market at the time. It was a reflex designed for a sophisticated public but was not aimed at professionals. The ME offered either automatic or manual working but professional requirements demanded far more than just these facilities.

In a surprise move, and some months ahead of the 1980 Photokina exhibition, Asahi Optical brought out an exquisite professional reflex, the Pentax LX.

The LX stood out from Asahi Optical's typical production standards. It was a completely different camera in shape, structure and price. The corners of the body were atypically rounded. For the first time an Asahi reflex had an interchangeable viewfinder and the camera was designed to stand up to the most

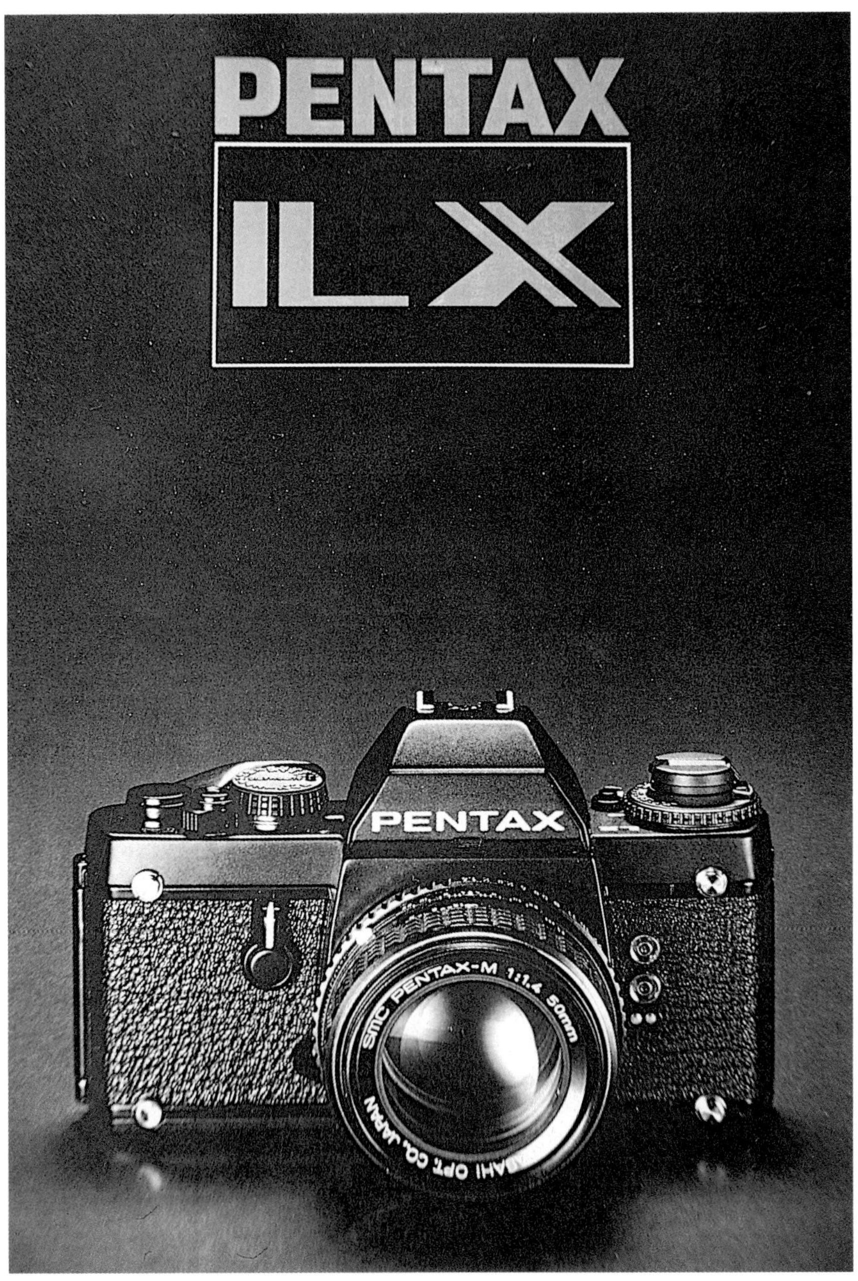
PENTAX
LX
PENTAX
SMC PENTAX-M 1:1.4 50mm
ASAHI OPT. CO. JAPAN

demanding conditions for a considerable period of time. It was dust- and waterproof, sturdy, bulky, and only available in black. Despite its features and more massive construction of some parts, the Pentax LX was no bigger or heavier than the illustrious old Spotmatic. It fell into a decidedly high price bracket. Only four or five rival reflexes were in the same category, all of them big-name cameras with professional facilities.

The very appearance of the Pentax LX overturned a number of preconceived ideas. It showed that a company like Asahi Optical, from always concentrating on medium-class reflexes, could cultivate professional ambitions. It showed that a professional reflex did not have to be exclusively mechanical with manual working. Together with the professional Nikon F3, Canon F1 New, and Leica R4, all built around 1980, the Pentax LX belonged to a class of automatic electronic reflexes which could also be used manually.

Like any decent professional reflex, the Pentax LX was provided with dozens of accessories: interchangeable viewfinders, winders, motors, data-backs, flashes and hand-grips. The Pentax LX introduced a number of curious details like three attaching points for the strap, which made it possible for it to be hung vertically as well as horizontally.

With the Pentax LX the name Asahi finally disappeared, giving way to "Pentax" which stood out in white on the black background of the pentaprism. The LX replaced the Asahi Pentax K2 in the catalogues. Thus at the beginning of the Eighties Asahi Optical fully covered the range with its own reflexes, from the simple and cheap K1000 to the stylish, electronic, exclusive and expensive Pentax LX.

Asahi Optical's ambitions did not stop here. At the end of 1981, almost simultaneously with its rival Canon, Asahi Optical brought out a so-called autofocus electronic reflex. This was the umpteenth reworking of the ME, on this occasion renamed MEF. The Pentax MEF was a special version of the ME Super to which had been added an electronic focusing control. A series of LEDs visible in the viewfinder gave information on correct or incorrect focusing. The Pentax MEF was the first reflex with assisted focusing. The camera was incorrectly called autofocus.

The Pentax MEF only focused automatically when fitted with a special 35-70mm,f/2.8 SMC Pentax AF zoom lens. The AF lens was equipped with a small motor which shifted the lens groups until they reached the focusing set by the computer. With the Pentax MEF, Asahi Optical had taken its first steps into the difficult realm of autofocus. The Pentax MEF was equipped with strange accessories such as an audible alarm. It met a lukewarm reception. At the beginning of the Eighties autofocus was little more than a publicity gimmick and only served to focus attention on the Pentax name. Despite the commercial failure of the Pentax MEF, it opened the road towards automatic focusing which would be profitably explored in the coming years, with surprising results.

The Pentax ME generation still kept going after the Pentax MEF. The cheap MV1 Pentax was replaced quietly in mid-1972 by the MG model. The Pentax MG was an automatic-only reflex with just a few improvements in comparison to the previous model.

No new Pentax reflexes were shown at the 1982 Photokina exhibition, but instead a 35mm automatic compact camera appeared on Asahi Optical's stand, designed to take a motor, equipped with a 35mm, f/2.8 lens and bearing the name "Pentax". This was a completely new departure for Asahi Optical. The full name of the new compact camera was PC35AF but it was very soon renamed Viva. The pocket camera represented a not insignificant revolution and was a sign that the world was changing. The Viva was the first non-reflex camera to be engraved with the Pentax trade mark. A few months later other manufacturers followed the example. Nippon Kogaku, highly specialized in reflex cameras, brought out a compact camera bearing the name Nikon L35AF. Yashica/Zeiss introduced an extravagant compact camera under the Contax name.

A reflex was introduced at the 1983 Milan Sicof which again broke with tradition. The Pentax Super A was the result of a technical advance comparable

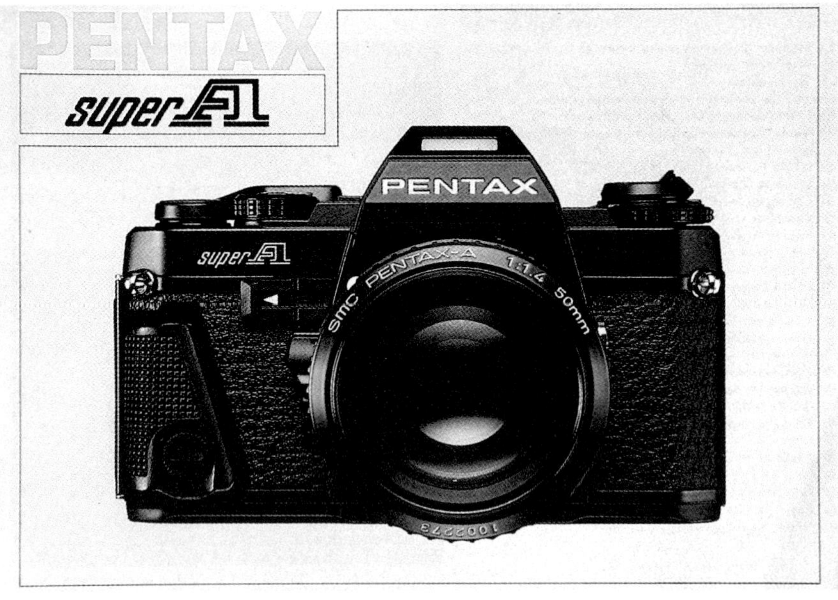

The Pentax Super A was the first program SLR camera produced by Asahi Optical Company. To have programmed exposure the Super A needed SMC Pentax A lenses.

to that of the K-family replacing the screw mount Pentaxes. The appearance on the market of programmed electronic SLR's, with automatic working of the exposure meter for dual priority - shutter and aperture - was the new challenge. Photographers appreciated the possibility of automatic working, even on professional cameras. The Pentax Super A was Asahi Optical's reply to these demands. It was a very advanced electronic reflex. Although compatible with the ME series winders, it represented a completely new chapter in the growth of the Pentax family.

The Pentax Super A built on the experience of the ME Super, and it had the usual buttons for manual control. With shutter, aperture, or programmed automatic working, the Super A fitted into the automatic Pentax range between the LX and the ME Super. In order to enable aperture priority automatic working and hybrid automatic working, the K-bayonet mount was provided with numerous electrical contacts and assumed the designation KA. The lenses designed to interact with the Pentax Super A were abbreviated SMC Pentax A.

Besides programmed automatic working, the Super A afforded a number of new and interesting features. It was equipped with a fast motor called Motor Drive A, compatible with the ME family reflexes. Light metering data was exhibited not by LED but on a digital display.

The SMC Pentax A-series lenses gradually replaced the earlier lenses. In putting the new lenses into production, priority was given to the long focal lengths, which were revised optically. There were many zoom lenses in the Pentax A-series and they came to challenge the predominance of the fixed focal lengths.

Exactly one year after its introduction, the Super A was supplemented by a slightly simplified cheaper model called Program A. This had the same operational layout as the Super A but did not allow shutter priority. With this sole limitation, and very little cosmetic change, the Program A occupied the space between the sophisticated Super A and the eternal ME Super. The ME Super stayed in production for a few more years having become a classic of the Pentax family.

A few months after bringing out the Program A, Asahi Optical introduced its first compact video camera, the PCK1200. This represented an even bigger revolution for the company than the 35mm compact.

All the Japanese makers were travelling video road in the mid-Eighties, against the day when the traditional silver-based photography might no longer dominate the mass market. But its entrance into video did not divert Asahi Optical from photography. In May 1984, a medium format SLR was brought out with much flourish for the professional market. The 645 was a programmed and motorized electronic reflex, designed quite differently from a 35mm or the standard reflexes. The camera was longer, the motor was built in, and the body had a wide hand-grip on the side. The automatic working reflected the systems tested on the small format Super A.

The camera had a large diameter bayonet lens mount, full of electrical contacts, and operated with SMC Pentax A 645 lenses. Asahi Optical demonstrated with the 645 that the technology developed on the small format reflexes could easily be adapted to bigger formats.

Having entered the field of bigger formats, Asahi Optical returned to 35mm. A number of compact cameras were introduced at the 1984 Photokina exhibition. The Viva was presented in different versions, some of which had the motor built-in and were fitted with the date back. The Pino 35 was brought out alongside the Viva, and was a cheap camera with fixed focus lens and automatic exposure meter. In 1985, the Pentax Sport came out, a motorized autofocus compact camera with DX-coding facility for reading the sensitivity of the film and other features making it simple and reliable to use.

Compact cameras continued their relentless advance at the 1986 Photokina exhibition. Asahi Optical introduced a number of reworked versions of the fixed focus Pino family and two sophisticated compact cameras called PC333 and PC555. Both were of the autofocus type, were motorized and had a programmed exposure meter. Two years later, they were followed by the Pentax PC303. In 1986, Asahi Optical brought out the Pentax Zoom 70, a camera which gained enormous success. The Pentax Zoom 70 was the first non-reflex camera with a motorized zoom lens, covering all focal lengths between 35mm and 70mm. The Pentax Zoom 70 was a step ahead of the competition's two-lens compact cameras and opened a new chapter in the history of photography. A million Zoom 70's were sold, to be followed by the improved versions Zoom 70S and Zoom 60.

Despite its success in sophisticated compact cameras, Asahi Optical maintained its presence in the 35mm SLR market and at the beginning of 1985 introduced the first Pentax 35mm reflex with a built-in motor. The Pentax A3 was an automatic, program only camera. Similar in function to a compact camera, the A3 had DX-coding for setting the film speed. By manually selecting the value of the aperture or using lenses prior to the A-series, the operation of the programmed automatic exposure became automatic aperture priority exposure. However, the camera was not a success and was shortly replaced.

Autumn 1985 saw the introduction of the Pentax P30, an electronic reflex with programmed and manual exposure. Compact and black, the P30 could not be motorized. One year later it was supplemented by the more sophisticated Pentax P50. Both compact and light, weighing little more than 500g, the two P-family reflexes had a very similar body and varied in facilities.

The Pentax P30 had programmed automatic working similar to that of the Super A. It was manually controllable by means of the shutter speed dial and was the cheapest electronic reflex in the series.

The Pentax P50 was much more sophisticated. It was designed to take the same motors as the ME and Super A and had two different programs which could be selected with a push-button. The fast program was similar to that of the P30, whilst the other program favoured depth of field. The Pentax P50 could be

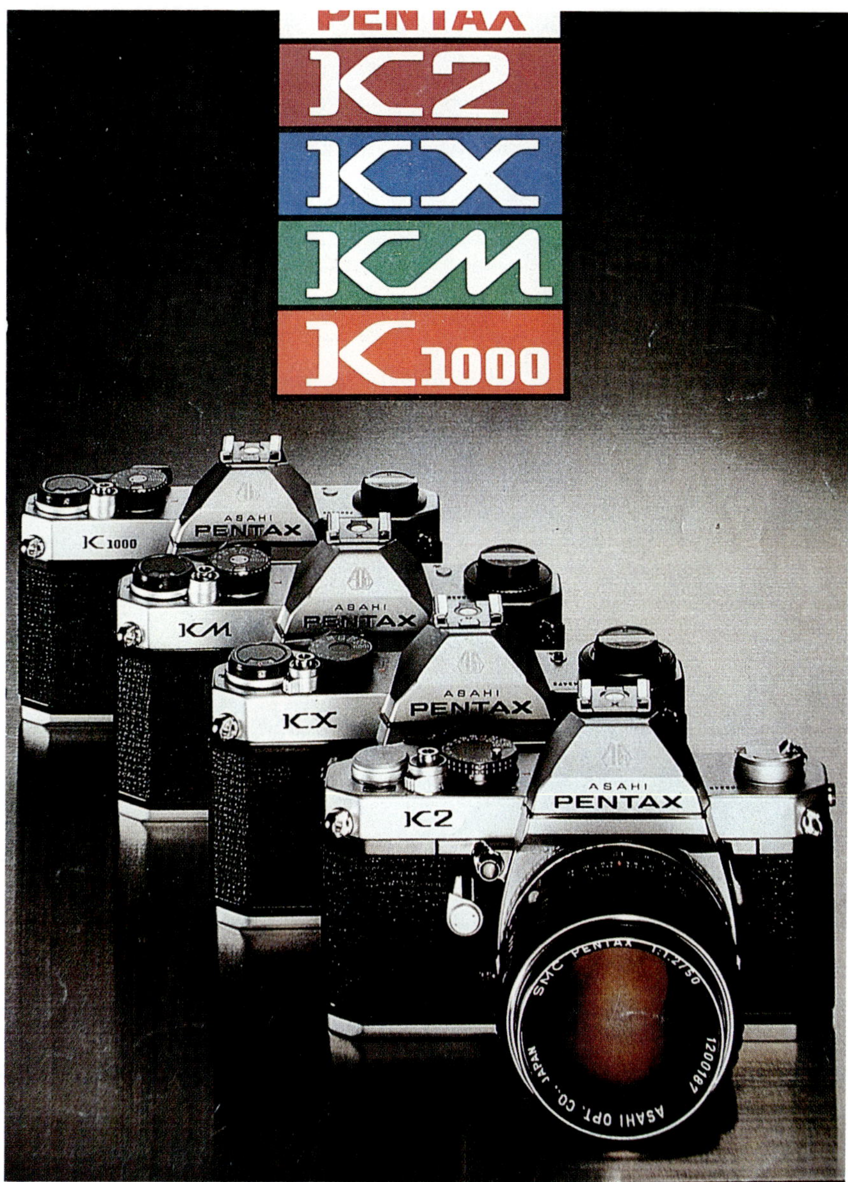

In 1975 Asahi Optical Co abandoned the screw mount and introduced a trio of bayonet-mount cameras. The K-family was completed one year later by the K1000, which is still in production.

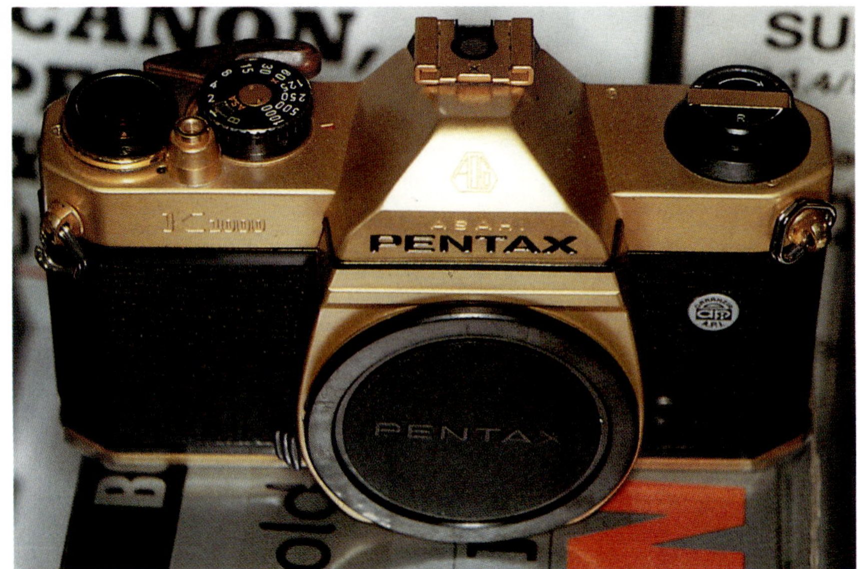

A rare K1000 in gold finish.

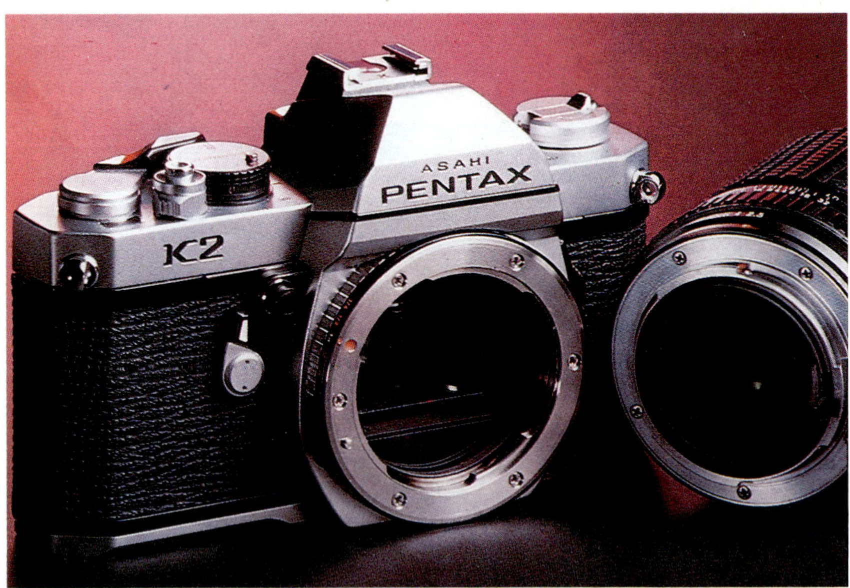

The new K-bayonet lens mount.

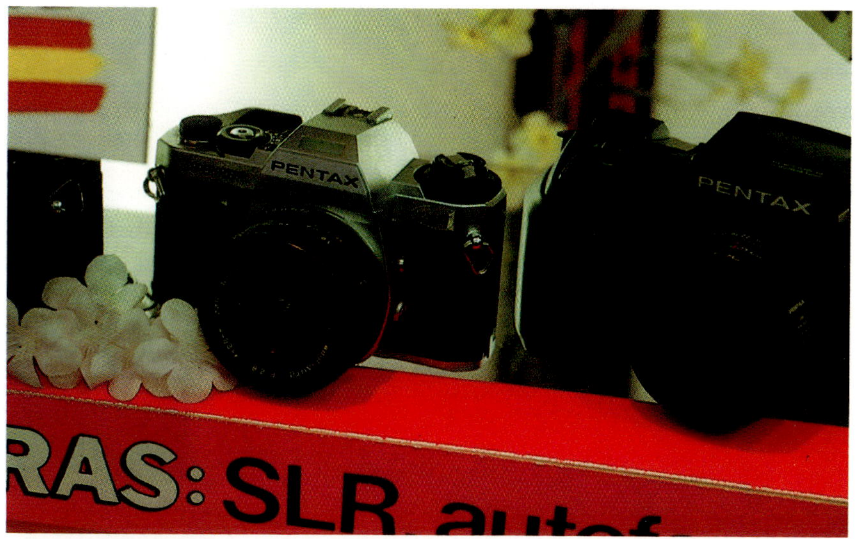

In the U.S.A. the Pentax Super A was the Pentax Super Program. This one in chrome finish was photographed through a shop window.

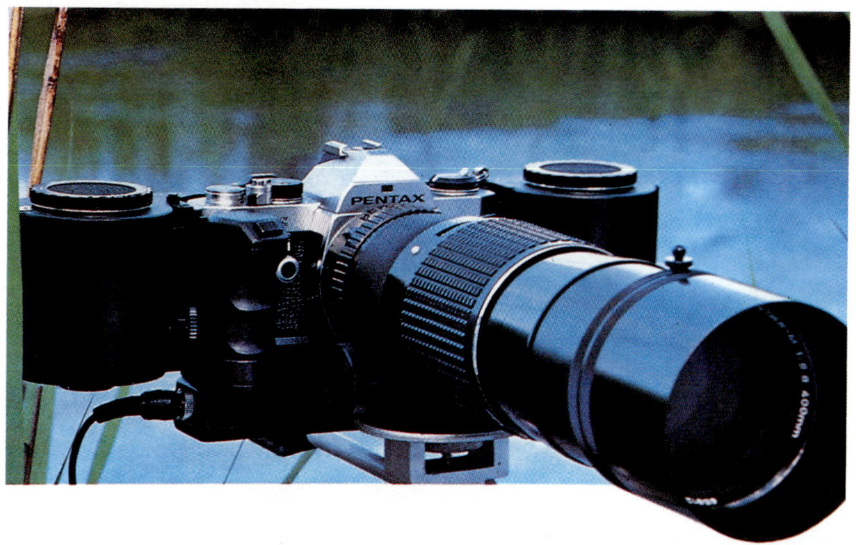

Asahi Pentax MX with Motor Drive and 250-frame back. The MX was a very versatile, elegant, and compact mechanical camera with interchangeable focusing screens. The first Pentax designed for a motor drive.

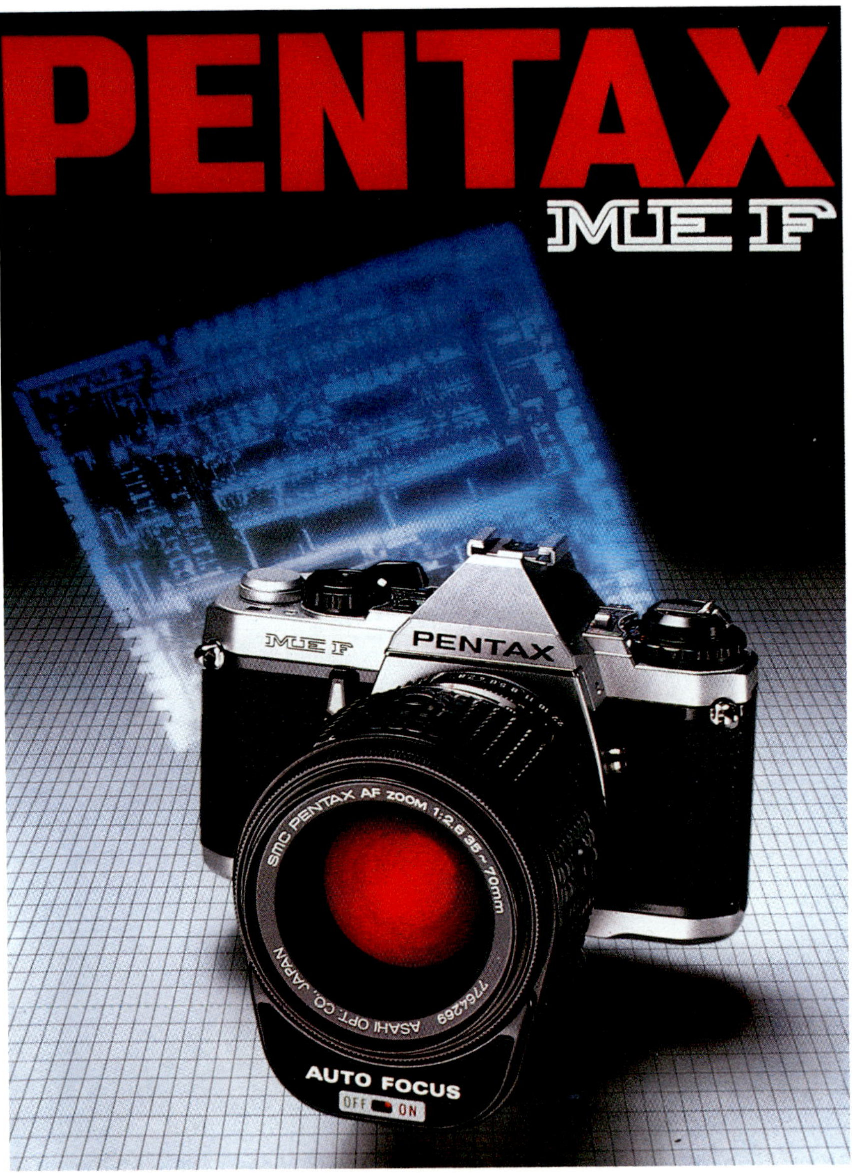

The first Pentax attempt at an autofocus SLR was the MEF of 1982. The autofocus control mechanism was primitive compared to what was to come later with the SFX. It was supplied with a special 35-70mm lens with built-in motor.

manually controlled by means of two press-buttons similar to those on the ME Super. On the top plate of the P50, a wide display indicated the type of pre-selected automatic working and the speed set, automatically or manually. The two P-family reflexes were aimed at a general public looking for a balance between facilities and price. Asahi Optical's marketing policy appeared to return to its traditional position, offering good standard products at moderate prices. The Pentax P50 remained in production for almost three years, whilst the P30 was replaced by the modified P30n version.

At the beginning of 1985, at the Milan Sicof, Minolta threw down a technological challenge to the competition. Minolta's new camera was an entirely motorized autofocus SLR of completely original design. With its arrival on the market, all existing SLR autofocus systems, from the Pentax MEF to the Nikon F3/AF, from the Olympus OM30 to the Canon T80, suddenly became out-of-date and obsolete.

The concept of Minolta's autofocus forced other makers to compete on the same ground. The Japanese firms took up the challenge and and within two years many high class autofocus reflexes had come onto the market.

Marketing and design strategies on autofocus differed among the various makers. Canon and Minolta chose to start from scratch, using entirely new bayonet mounts. Nippon Kogaku and Asahi Optical chose a less drastic solution and restricted themselves to modifying their traditional bayonet mounts, by adding the coupling clutch to the autofocus drive motor which was in the camera body. Autofocus working led to the birth of a generation of lenses with new features. Asahi Optical's autofocus lenses were called SMC Pentax F and were compatible with the A-series lenses. By means of a 1.7x focal length extender, it was possible to use SMC Pentax A lenses with full autofocus automatic working provided they had a maximum aperture of at least f/2.8.

Asahi Optical's autofocus reflex was called SFX, or SF1 in North America. The automatic focusing mechanism was very fast and operated even in complete darkness up to a distance of four metres. The pentaprism had a distinctive shape, broad and flattened, and it hid a small built-in flash. The built-in flash was powerful enough to be used as the main source of lighting in an emergency. It was very useful for lightening the shadows in shots taken against the light. The flash could be used in TTL metering mode and was coupled to the camera's means of functioning in programmed automatic working. Alongside its autofocus function, the SFX had numerous automatic exposure modes. It used a built-in motor, DX-coding for automatically setting the sensitivity of the film, and a wide external liquid crystal display giving data on the functions set. Motorized, multiprogram and autofocus, the Pentax SFX ushered in a new era.

Less than two years later, the Pentax SFX was followed by the simplified SF7 model, known as SF10 in North America, which retained its main features. At the end of 1988, the SFX was replaced by the SFXN (SF1N in USA) offering a number of additional facilities.

Initially nine SMC Pentax F lenses were offered, four fixed-focus, and five zooms. For the first time with newly-introduced equipment, the number of zoom lenses exceeded the number of fixed-focus ones, confirming the tendency to favour zoom lenses on autofocus cameras.

CHAPTER 10

The K-Family

On one of those rare occasions in camera history, there was a multiple-birth. Usually, each model had a reasonably long gestation period and a definite date of birth. Each camera was the product of its own time and the product of history. When two or more models came out simultaneously, they were very similar. In the first half of 1975, Asahi Optical simultaneously brought out three totally new reflex cameras, signifying the abandonment of the screw mount used for more than twenty years.

The cheap Asahi Pentax KM was obviously based on the Spotmatic F. The Asahi Pentax KX had all the original features, but had links with the Spotmatic tradition. The beauty queen in the K-family was the Asahi Pentax K2, which introduced many original feature. The shutter priority automatic working was similar to that tried out on the Asahi Pentax ES and ES II, but the electronic circuits were much more reliable and sophisticated and the shutter involved a totally new design for an Asahi Pentax.

The cheap K1000 reflex came out a year after the first three Asahi Pentax K cameras. It had the same facilities as the spartan Spotmatic 1000.

The four bayonet-mount Asahi Pentaxes preserved some features of the Spotmatic line and represented a considerable effort as far as design and production were concerned. The fruit of much research, the K-family Asahi Pentax cameras originated from prototypes unofficially brought out in 1960 and 1966, but were children of their own time. The Seventies had brought rapid progress in sensitometry and electronics. The K cameras skilfully exploited the achievements in these fields. They did not revolutionize the world of the 35mm reflex cameras, but demonstrated Asahi Optical's will to recapture lost ground and enabled it to catch up with more modern design standards.

Putting all four K-cameras on the market together was risking everything. Their optical equipment was very sound but re-evaluated piece by piece according to what already existed. Perhaps because of this, their sales success was not commensurate with their significance or their back-up promotional campaign.

The K2 evolved into the motorized K2 DMD model and survived until the end of 1980. The spartan K1000 survived and prospered and now, simply called

Pentax K1000, is still the basic tool used in U.S. schools and colleges to teach photography. The other members of the K-family, however, did not come up the market requirements. Asahi Optical's strategists probably anticipated this. The bayonet mount Asahi Pentax SLRs arrived too late to contend the success of the competition's electronic reflexes. With regard to the technical capacities they afforded, they arrived too early to repeat the Spotmatic's market successes. The K-family Asahi Pentax really laid the way open for the MX and ME compact reflexes, two models destined to change the company's fortunes.

Asahi Pentax K2

The Asahi Pentax K2 was introduced in 1975. Electronic and up-to-date, the K2 was the flag-ship in the Asahi Pentax K fleet right up to 1980 when it was superceded by the professional Pentax LX.

The K2 did not have completely new features and was intended as the natural follow-on from the Electro Spotmatic introduced four years before. This period had not passed in vain and the K2 differed radically from the ES in shape, finish and facilities.

The K2 was an electronic camera with automatic shutter-priority. Unlike the ES, it allowed all shutter speeds to be set manually, from $^1/1000$ to 8 sec. plus B. Its measurements signified the return to Asahi Pentax standards: 144mm long by 92mm high. The body alone weighed 680g. In 1964, the same measurements had characterized the Spotmatic. In 1975, the market was able to offer much more compact 35mm reflexes. With its dimensions, the K2 was certainly not one of the smallest reflexes around, but its well-researched proportions still made it one of the most appealing and interesting reflexes.

Aesthetically, the K2 was stylish to a high degree. It was adorned with refinements in comparison with the classical screw mount Pentaxes. The frame counter disappeared from the top plate and was sunk into the camera body. The wind lever became slimmer and smarter with a black plastic covering on the end. The shutter release was supplemented with a safety device against accidental release. The shutter speed dial, in spite of the large amount of information it contained, was still very typical and elegant. The controls were in the same positions as on the Pentax cameras of twenty years earlier. The rewind crank lost its outer ring for memorizing data and appeared in all its simplicity. The serial number, still seven digits, was engraved on the top plate, in the usual place, but was no longer preceded by an identification abbreviation. The abbreviation K2 dominated the front panel instead.

If the top plate appeared simplified, with a slimmer wind lever and memory ring, the front panel became adorned with decorative and functional features. An ornamental black band elegantly but unmistakably emphasized the base of the pentaprism, which projected above the lens mount. The self-timer lever was slightly higher, in its usual place. The depth of field preview button was on the

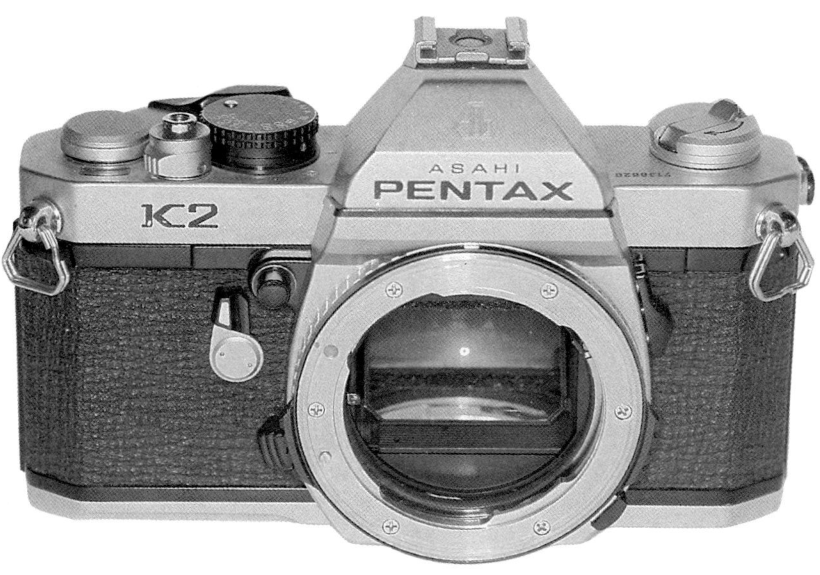

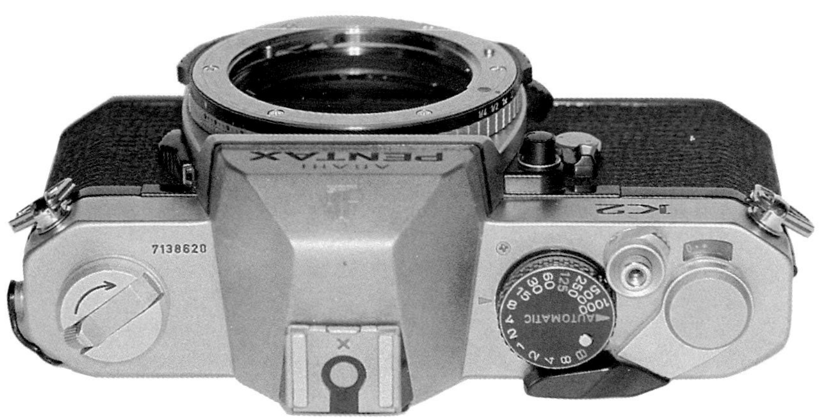

The Asahi Pentax K2 was the flagship of the K-family, electronic and automatic with a vertical metal focal plane shutter.

front panel above the self-timer lever. The bayonet mount lens release button was lower down, to the right of the lens mounting. The lever for manually locking the mirror in a raised position was on the left of the mounting. The K2 was the first Asahi Pentax reflex on which it was possible to lock the mirror in the up position. Coaxial with the lens mounting were two important controls, the ring for manually compensating the automatic exposure and the film sensitivity selector, calibrated from ASA 8 to 6400.

On the back of the camera was a slot for holding the top of the film box as a reminder. Next to the eyepiece, a warning light indicated the state of the batteries. The hot shoe was high over the pentaprism, as on all Asahi Pentax models after the Spotmatic II. The K2 also had the traditional FP and X contacts for synchronization with flashguns without hot shoe contacts or for off-camera flash. The flash terminals were on the left-hand side, next to the rewind lever.

To remove the lens, it had to be released and turned almost a quarter of a turn to the right. The bayonet mount was wide and sturdy, made up of three unequal sectors and had a diameter of 45mm. The lens mounting ring was fastened to the camera body by six strong screws. A large red marker indicated alignment of the lens, which had an identical mark engraved on its mount. It was possible to change lenses by touch alone in poor lighting conditions with the aid of a small raised white pip protruding from the mount. It was simple to align the little button with the release button and turn clockwise.

The K2 was an aesthetically pleasing camera and it had the family looks. A few revealing details betrayed its lineage from the screw mount Asahi Pentaxes. The shape of the body and pentaprism were not very dissimilar from the SP II. The layout of the controls was unchanged, in spite of a number of improvements. If the K2 remained tradition-bound on the outside, it was revolutionary on the inside. The K2 used a metal-blade shutter with vertical movement. This was not the Copal Square fitted on the medium-class reflexes ten years before. The K2 shutter was called Seiko MF and was a collaborative venture between Asahi Optical and the famous electronic company, Seiko. The shutter was electronically controlled and comprised five metal blades with a fan-like vertical movement. Although horizontally-running fabric shutters had been preferred in the past, Asahi Optical now abandoned any past reservations and chose a really unusual metal shutter for their leading reflex.

The K2's exposure meter made use of many very interesting elements. It had a silicon photodiode (SPD), which was fast-acting and almost insensitive to glare. Compared to the Asahi Pentax ES, which needed large batteries, the K2 was much more frugal. The light metering circuit was powered by two 1.5 volt Ever Ready S76E or Mallory MS76H-type silver oxide batteries. The same batteries powered the Asahi Pentax ES II. The K2 made do with two batteries, whereas the ES II needed four, to provide similar facilities.

The K2 viewfinder, like that of the ES, showed the full range of shutter speeds, including B setting and Auto position, on its right-hand side. On choosing automatic exposure, a small blue needle indicated Auto position. A second black needle showed the shutter speed chosen by the computer. By working in manual, the blue needle indicated the speed set by the photographer, and the black needle continued to show the computer-set value, leaving the photographer to choose which most fitted the information provided by the exposure meter.

Asahi Pentax KX

The Asahi Pentax KX was very similar to the K2, but only as far as general appearance was concerned. It differed from its electronic sister in its facilities and preserved much affinity with the screw mount models from the previous generation. The layout of the controls on the top plate was extremely simple and standard. Seen from above, the KX could be mistaken for one of the last Spotmatics. The wind lever incorporated the frame counter and had a design very similar to that of the SP II, with the exception of the black plastic covering which protected the end. The delayed-action release button and shutter release, with its safety lock, also preserved the classic Spotmatic design.

The rewind knob was encircled by the usual ring for remembering the film speed, rendered redundant now by the label slot on the back of the camera. Beside the rewind knob, a small button was added for checking the batteries.

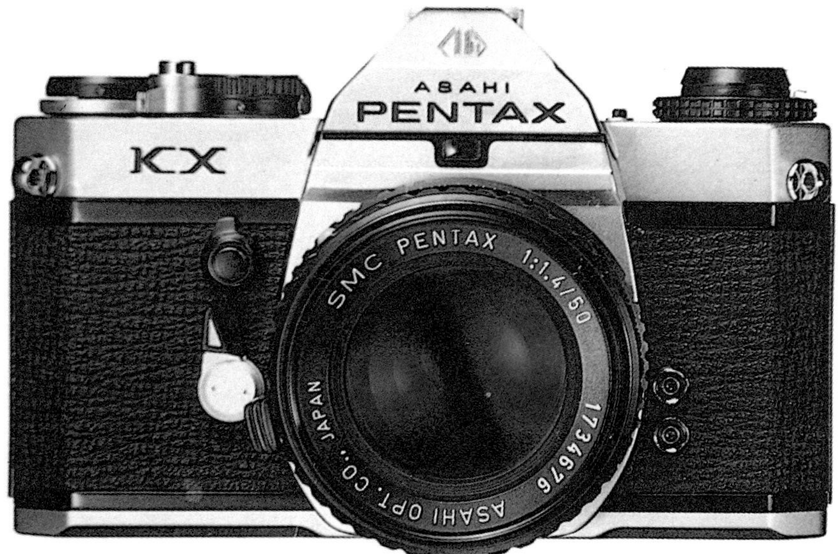

The Asahi Pentax KX was a mechanical camera, very reliable and beautifully made, here with a SMC Pentax 50mm, f/1.4 lens.

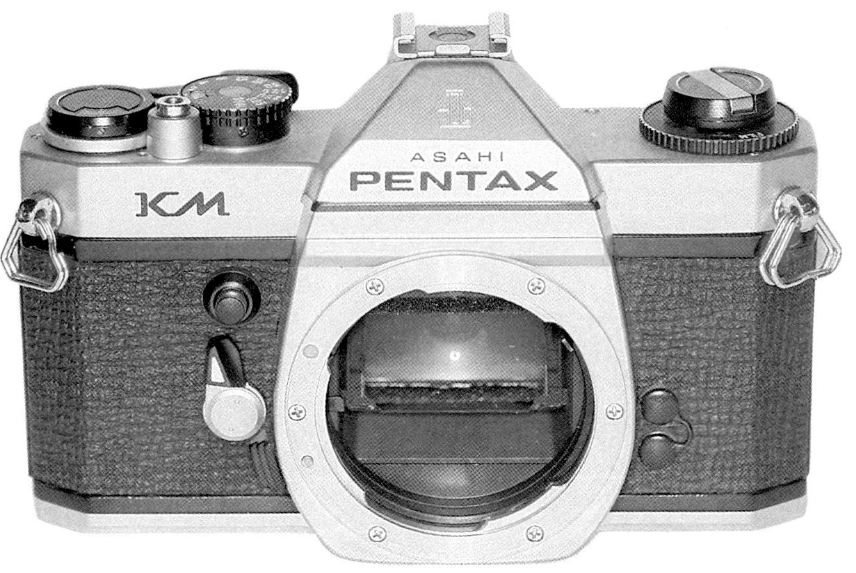

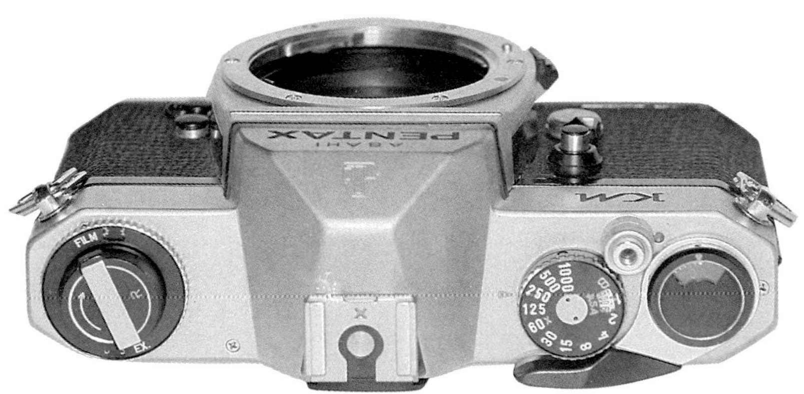

The Asahi Pentax KM was the bayonet version of the Asahi Pentax Spotmatic F.

The front panel of the KX was characterized by a window on the base of the pentaprism, enabling direct observation in the viewfinder of the set aperture value. This was not an original idea, but it was the first time that an Asahi Pentax had such a facility. The self-timer lever was in its customary place, but was redesigned and refinished with a black plastic cover, as on the K2 and KM. Above the self-timer lever, a large black button was used for manually closing the aperture and this was coaxial with the lever for locking the mirror. The button for releasing the lenses was next to the self-timer lever, in the same position as on all the other reflexes in the same family. The FP and X synchro contacts were still in their traditional position to the left of the lens mount.

The heart of the Asahi Pentax KX was made up of a silicon photocell light metering circuit, similar to the one on the prestigious K2. The shutter was completely mechanical and had rubberized silk blinds with speeds from $^1/1000$ to one second, plus B. The viewfinder gave fuller information than on the K2. Two needles, corresponding to the speed and aperture rings, covered the full range of speeds. By corresponding with one another, they indicated the correct exposure. A small window up above made it possible to observe the set aperture value. This could only be done on K2 models modified to take a motor.

The facilities on the KX were interesting but perhaps not developed to the full for fear of creating too great a wash for the K2 flagship. In spite of its operating limitations, the KX came in a special version, with the base modified to take a motor and with the facility for using a data-back. The modified KX Motor Drive version remained in the realm of intentions. The Asahi Pentax KX died prematurely, following the same fate as the SPF and ES. In its short life, it did not see the arrival of the motorized versions on the market. The KX and KM remained in production for a little more than a year. Having caused much gossip because of their bayonet mount, they were ousted with little regret by the MX mechanical reflex, which embodied a completely different production philosophy.

Asahi Pentax KM

The Asahi Pentax KM shared much with its KX sister. An uncertain fate, the same body, a traditional shutter and the problem of being too closely descended from the unfortunate Spotmatic F.

The KM was introduced as the cheapest model in the K-family. With the same aim, it was put on sale at 10% less than its KX sister. The difference in price was justified by the lack of any optional extras. It did not have the safety lock for the shutter release button or a mirror lock-up, the slot for the label, the button for checking the batteries or the little window for viewing the aperture value. Above all, it did not have the special Motor Drive and Data versions which made the KX a professionally over-ambitious reflex.

Compared to the Spotmatic F, the KM offered nothing more than the bayonet mount and a redesigned body. It had the same shutter and CdS cell light metering

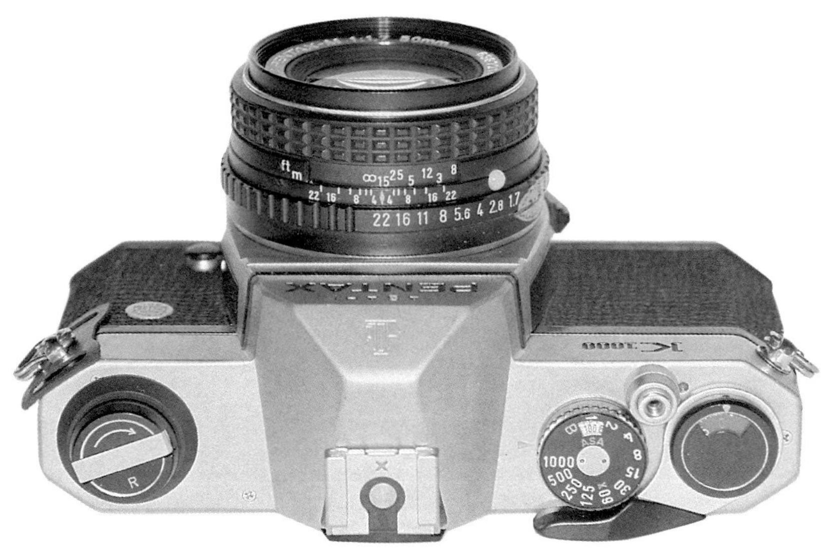

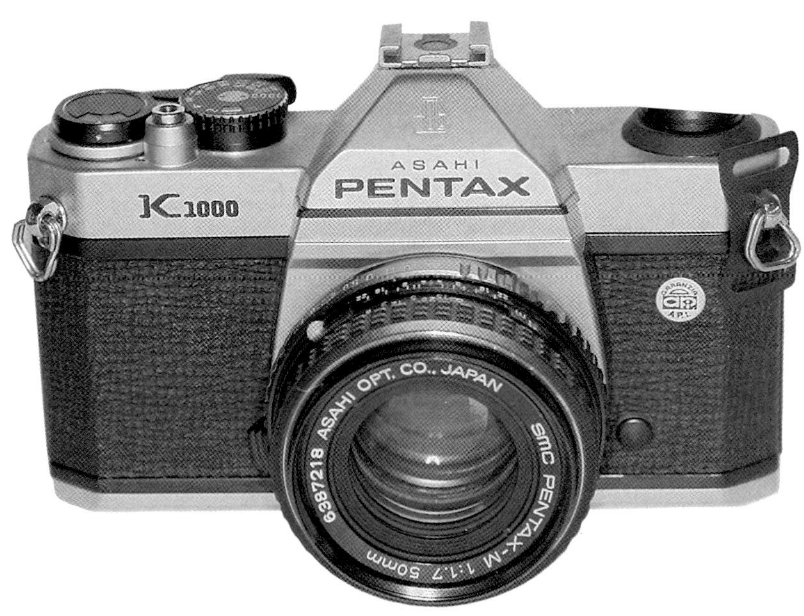

circuit. It had the same main controls, from the delayed-action release button to the wind lever and self-timer. The exposure meter switch was located within the lens mounting and could not be turned off, just as on the Spotmatic F.

The KM preserved almost completely unchanged the technical features which had distinguished the screw-mount cameras. Built without much effort as far as design was concerned, the KM was the connecting link between the Spotmatics and future generations. This transitional role was signified by the exceptionally short lifespan of the camera. Modest but unsuccessful, the Pentax KM was a hybrid between two generations of reflexes perhaps too far removed from one another.

Asahi Pentax K1000

Faithful to tradition, the K-family was supplemented in about 1976 by a decidedly cheap and spartan model. The Asahi Pentax K1000 originated from the body of the KM and was inspired by the same principles which had brought about the Spotmatic 1000 in 1973. It was in fact the bayonet mount version of the SP 1000, devoid of all extras which could be considered superfluous. It had no self-timer, depth of field button, the disc for memorizing the film used, nor a FP synchro contact. It came with the slowest of the standard lenses in production, the 55mm,f/2 SMC. Simplified in the extreme, the K1000 managed to assert itself on a market dominated by more sophisticated cameras. With a price less than half that of the K2, the K1000 afforded limited but reliable facilities.

The CdS exposure meter allowed metering at full aperture with the SMC Pentax K and compatible lenses. Information given in the viewfinder was sketchy but accurate. A single needle oscillated slowly between a positive and negative marker, indicating over- and underexposure. Compared with the viewfinders showing data relating to speeds and apertures, the K1000 finder was decidedly wanting. It gave exactly the same information as the screw mount Asahi Pentaxes, from the Spotmatic onwards. But the modest K1000 set off on a long career which still continues. With its extremely competitive price, it enabled many photographers to enter SLR-photography.

The K1000 was also produced in a slightly modified version, called K1000 SE. It was characterized by a diamond-embossed rubber outer casing and a split-image rangefinder at the centre of the ground glass screen. Only a small number of K1000 SE cameras were produced.

Amongst the special versions of the K1000, the K1000 Gold, in gold finish, was a shining example. The Pentax K1000 Gold was made up not by Asahi Optical,

---

Left: The Asahi Pentax K1000 was the bayonet version of the SP1000. Inexpensive and long-lived, the K1000 was introduced in 1976 and is still in production in 1990. This example with SMC Pentax-M, 50mm,f/1.7.

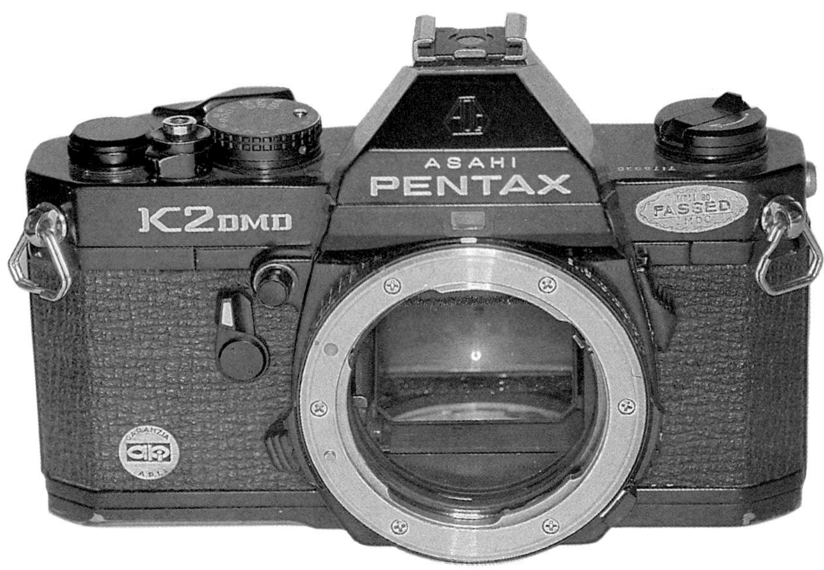

The Asahi Pentax K2 DMD was the improved version of the Asahi Pentax K2, arranged to accept the Motor Drive.

but by a private Florentine company. In 1982, twelve Asahi Pentax K1000 cameras were gilded, and sold to as many Italian dealers. Today, the Asahi Pentax K1000 Gold has become a valuable collector's item, and goes some way to compensate for the years during which plainest reflex in the K-family lived in the shadow of its fashionable sisters.

Asahi Pentax K2 DMD

The K-family was completed by a special version of the flagship K2, called K2 DMD (Data Motor Drive). This version of the K2 emphasized its over-ambitiousness as a professional reflex. The K2 DMD had a base modified to take a motor. The motor selected for the K2 was the same as that built for the Spotmatic Motor Drive and promised for motorization of the Spotmatic F, the Electro Spotmatic and the Asahi Pentax KX. It had limited facilities and was rather bulky, especially in comparison with the motors offered by the competition.

One interesting point about the K2 DMD was its little window just under the front of the pentaprism for direct viewing of the set aperture value. The same window had been tried out on the pentaprism of the KX. Photographers appreciated being able to check the value of the aperture in the viewfinder. The little window was fitted on high-class reflexes.

Another facility distinguishing the K2 DMD from the typical K2 was the

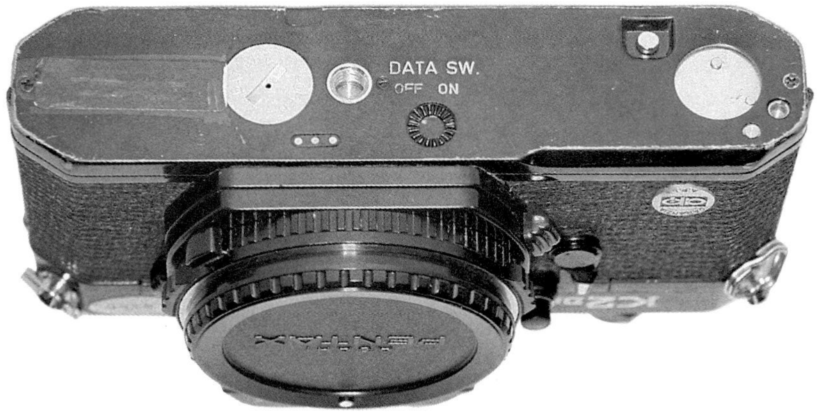

Base of the K2 DMD with Motor Drive connections.

possibility of printing data on the frames. This was useful in scientific photography to catalogue subjects and record dates. It proved all but useless for general and professional photography and had no value in the eyes of the mass of photographers at the time. Sophisticated reflexes retained the possibility of having data backs fitted, but only as an alternative.

The Asahi Pentax K2 DMD offered interesting facilities, but made no impact on the market. It was produced until 1980 as a professional alternative to the K2, without replacing the latter in the catalogues.

CHAPTER 11

Asahi Pentax MX, The Little Professional

The Asahi Pentax MX was introduced with its sister, ME, at the 1976 Photokina exhibition. The two cameras showed some similarities in shape and had very compact dimensions. Structurally, they were very different cameras, the products of different design choices, in many ways opposed. The ME was an electronic reflex with simplified automatic working. The MX was a traditional mechanical reflex.

With manual operation, a fabric shutter and a new, but not revolutionary design TTL exposure meter, the MX was Asahi Optical's last mechanical reflex. At first sight, it differed from the mechanical reflexes of the previous generation only in its small dimensions, but the MX hid unsuspected virtues under its traditional body, and was undeniably professional in inclination.

Its effect on the market was considerable. In a world inevitably heading towards total electronics, fully automatic working and photography becoming a commonplace activity, the MX stood out like the classic rare bird. In company with a few other high-class mechanical reflexes, such as the Nikon FM, the Asahi Pentax MX became associated with a certain type of photography.

The MX was a mechanical reflex offering advanced technical features. It was compact and reliable beyond bounds and embodied the dream of many traditionalist photographers. Tradition-bound, it was constructed along modern lines. Twelve years on, the MX restored the philosophy which had seen the Spotmatic arise and dominate, presenting itself as its worthy heir. Comparison with the Spotmatic was obligatory. Together with the reflexes of the K-family, with its very personal and definite features, it maintained a decisive role in the Pentax family for over ten years.

It would need an entire book to describe the many qualities of this big little reflex. Those who have used this tireless camera for many years and in all conditions can say that they truly know it and can fully appreciate its features.

The measurements of the MX body were very modest. From the moment of its appearance, its measurements had caused a sensation. It was 135.5mm long,

126

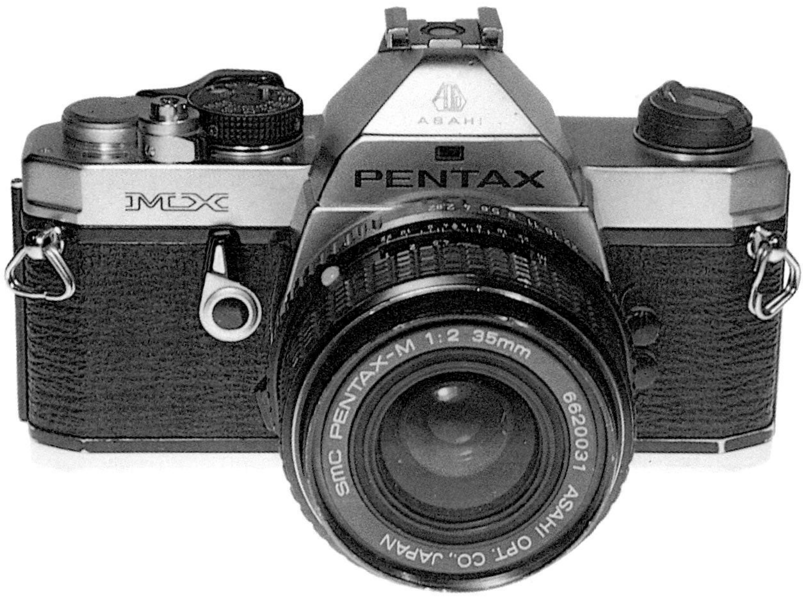

The Asahi Pentax MX was a full mechanical camera, produced without modification from 1976 to the late eighties, with interchangeable screens and with connections for winder and motor drive. Seen here with SMC Pentax-M 35mm, f/2 lens.

almost 6mm less than the Spotmatic. The body was 60mm high, 13mm less than the Spotmatic and fully 8mm less compared with the Asahi Pentax models preceding the Spotmatic. The body was 60.5mm high, and the total height including the pentaprism was 82.5mm. Altogether, the MX was almost 10mm shorter than the Spotmatic. The only measurement not reduced was the depth, which was almost 50mm. To reduce the depth would have created problems of incompatability with existing lenses. The weight of the body alone was less than 500g, in spite of the camera being built in die-cast metal.

With very few variants, the general structure of the MX replicated that proven on the Spotmatics for twenty years. The main control grouping, wind lever, shutter release and shutter speed dial were almost unchanged. The wind lever did not include the frame counter, which was sunk into the camera body as on the K2. The wind lever, like that of the K2, was adorned with a moulded plastic covering on the end. The shutter speed dial, as on the Spotmatic, selected speeds between $^1/1000$ and 1 sec. plus B. The same dial served to set the sensitivity of the film, expressed in ASA. To rotate the ASA selector, there was no need to raise the outer ring of the shutter speed dial, as on the Spotmatic, but a button on the top plate was pressed instead. It was virtually impossible to move the selector

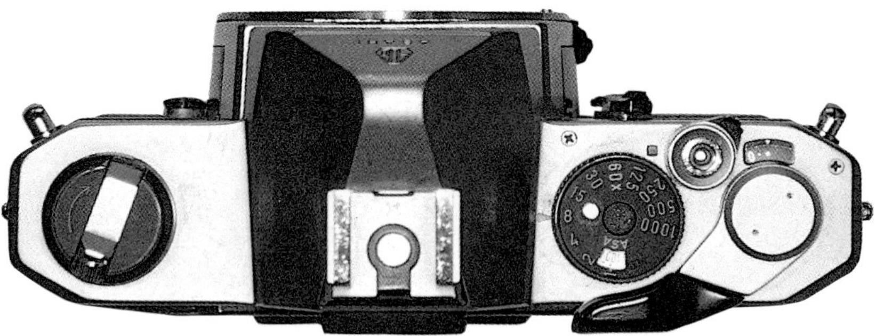

The controls and their layout on the MX were very similar to those of the Spotmatic, except that the frame counter was under a small window on the top plate by the wind lever.

accidentally. The shutter release was surrounded by a safety lock, which did not obscure vision of the shutter wind signal.

The FP and X synchro contacts were in their traditional position, protected by plastic caps. The pentaprism rose steeply above the top plate. It copied the shape of the Spotmatic pentaprism, by emphasizing its verticality. Its outline was not weighed down by the hot shoe. As on the K-family Asahi Pentaxes, the Asahi Optical mark and the wording Asahi was engraved on the upper part of the

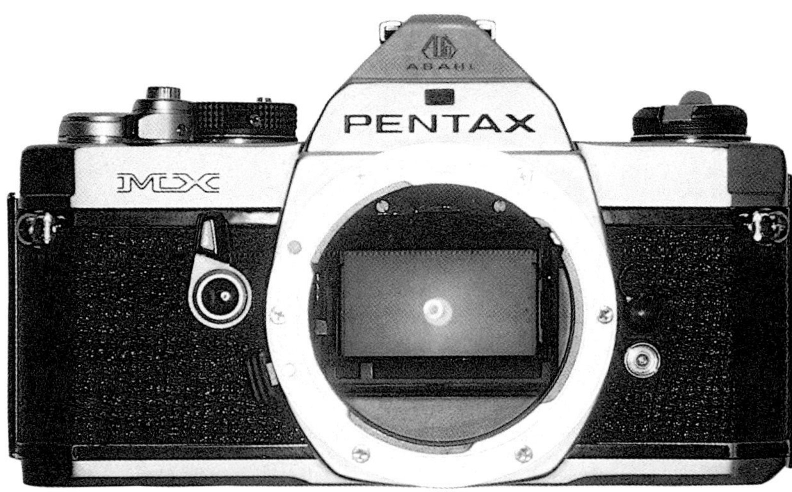

Slightly rounded corners and edge mouldings subtly emphasise the clean-cut, elegant lines of the MX. The size of the lens opening in relation to overall dimensions demonstrates the camera's truly compact design.

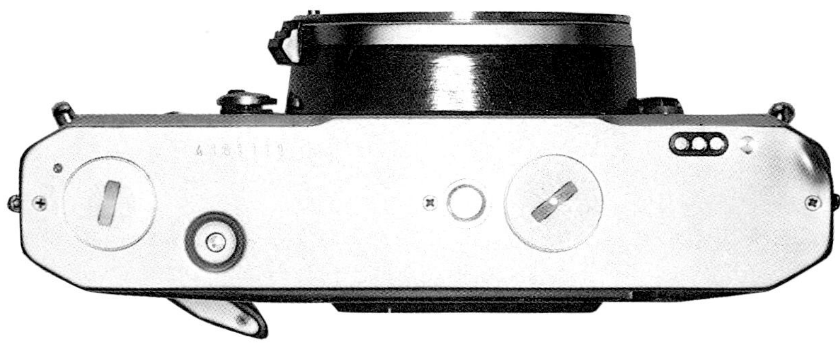

Baseplate details of the MX. The second screw cap at the left-hand end covered the mechanical coupling for the motor. The electrical contacts for the motor were at the other end.

pentaprism. The wording Pentax was engraved on the lower plate of the pentaprism, in huge black letters. On models finished in black, the wording was in white. Above the wording Pentax, the little window opened up for direct vision of the set aperture value.

The front panel of the MX was not straight like the Spotmatic, but equally clean-cut and elegant. The corners were slightly rounded and a number of mouldings subtly emphasized the corners and joints. By removing the lens, one could see how the wide lens mount took up most of the front panel, demonstrating the camera's truly reduced size.

The little miracle of reflex miniturization was made possible by a newly designed shutter. From the functional point of view, the MX shutter was in no way different from the Spotmatic's. It was a typical fabric-blind shutter with horizontal movement and speeds from $^1/1000$ to 1 sec. It was fully mechanical and absolutely traditional, but redesigned to reduce its height and bulk in the camera to a minimum.

There were the usual facilities on the base of the camera - the tripod socket, the rewind release button and the screw cap of the battery compartment. A second cap at the right end of the base hid the motor's mechanical coupling. The electrical contact panel for the motor was at the opposite end. The serial number was engraved on the base of the camera instead of the top.

Very compact, light and easy to handle, the MX reached the peak of refinement. The premises which had given rise to the Asahi Pentax and Spotmatic came to full fruition in the MX. No other camera managed the delicate balance between form and facilities, art and technique. In the same way as the Spotmatic was more than a Spotmatic, the MX embodied absolute perfection as far as cameras were concerned. Well-proportioned and reliable, none of its controls was out-of-place. The MX was the only one of Asahi Optical's reflexes which did not undergo further improvements and was not brought out in special or simplified versions.

It represented the peak of mechanical reflex development. A very stylish compromise between technology and tradition, the body of the MX showed evidence of extreme attention to detail and a high degree of refinement. In spite of its average price, it gave expression to out-of-the-ordinary features and facilities.

The MX exposure meter made use of a totally new photocell - a gallium photo diode (or GPD). These are based on Gallium phosphoarsenide, which is why they are also known as GaAsP cells. The features which led to preference of the GPD over the CdS and Silicon cells were its heightened sensitivity and the almost total lack of glare effect. After the success of the MX and the ME, Asahi Optical continued to use GPD photocells on reflex exposure meters for a great many years, right up until the most recent models.

A row of five coloured LEDs took up the right-hand side of the viewfinder. The LEDs were activated by the main camera switch. As on the K2, the exposure meter was activated automatically by slightly pulling the wind lever away from the camera body and putting it in the operational position. A few seconds after being activated, the exposure meter automatically turned itself off. To take further meterings, one just had to press the shutter release in halfway. The light metering circuit was switched off by returning the wind lever to rest position. When the exposure meter was thus deactivited, impromptu readings could be taken by pressing the shutter release in halfway, without the need to activate the wind lever.

By activating the exposure meter switch, one of the five LED's in the viewfinder lit up. The central green diode indicated the correct exposure,

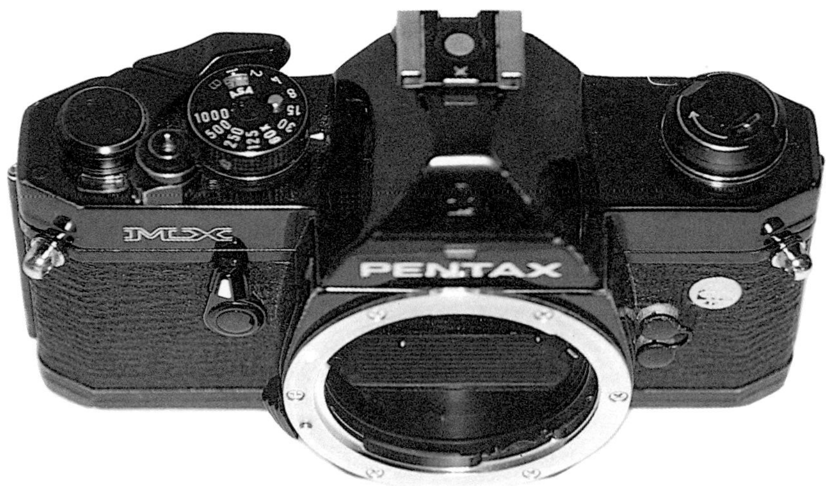

The MX was also available in a black finish.

corresponding to that selected by the camera. The two orange diodes next to the central one indicated half a stop over- and underexposure. The outer red diodes indicated incorrect exposure of one or more stops. The selected shutter speed indication corresponded with the central green diode.

The MX viewfinder gave full information on the light metering data, the aperture value and the shutter speed. The viewfinder was clear and bright, it was not overloaded with unneccessary signals making it possible to follow the course of the action in the frame without distraction. Despite the LED's, battery consumption was modest. The MX worked off two MS 76H-type 1.5 volt batteries, like the K2. Two new batteries had a life of over a year of intensive work.

The film speed scale on the MX could be set from ASA 25 to 1600. The selector indicated the values of ASA 32 64 100 200 400 800 and 1600. Intermediate values were shown. There was a very extensive metering range of light values, from EV 3 to EV 19. With an ASA 100 film, the MX meter could measure exposures of 1 sec. at f/1.4 to $^1/1000$ sec. at f/22.

The MX was the first Asahi Pentax with the facility of interchangeable focusing screens. The operation was accomplished through the lens mount, by means of special tweezers. The standard screen for the MX was a typical Fresnel lens with a split-image rangefinder and a microprism circle in the centre. The alternative screens offered other focusing systems. The simplest was the integral ground glass screen, with or without a central cross. The most elaborate were those with a graticule or graduated scale. There were also screens with just microprisms or a single stigmometer. In all eight screens were available.

The MX was the first Asahi Pentax designed for a motor (the K2 DMD had been a special version of the K2) and furthermore it accepted two different motors. The cheapest was a simple constant speed wind-on motor. It was light in weight and was powered by four 1.5 volt AA-size batteries. It screwed into the base of the camera and had a hand-grip with a built-in shutter release.

The switch was inaccessibly situated on the bottom at the back. It also acted as a function selector, with a choice of three positions, OFF, C and S. At OFF the MX could be operated with the manual release button. On S the MX released each time one pressed the button on the hand-grip and the motor wound the film on automatically. By selecting C and keeping the button on the hand-grip pressed in, the MX released in sequence at the rate of three frames a second.

To achieve higher speeds, one needed the Motor Drive MX instead. The Motor Drive consisted of two parts. The motor itself was like the winder in structure and size, complete with hand-grip, but did not have the function selector. The selector was on the power pack which had to be connected to the motor. There were two power packs, one was flat and contained rechargeable nickel cadmium batteries, the other was vertical and operated as an auxiliary hand-grip and housed twelve standard 1.5 volt batteries.

To take shots under normal conditions using the winder, 36 shots on a standard roll was enough. When using the high-speed Motor Drive, this length

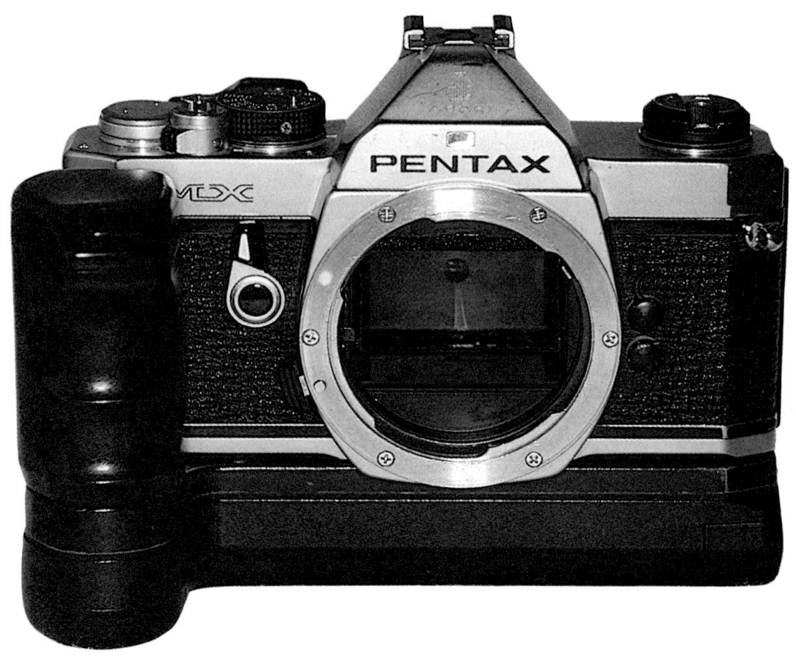

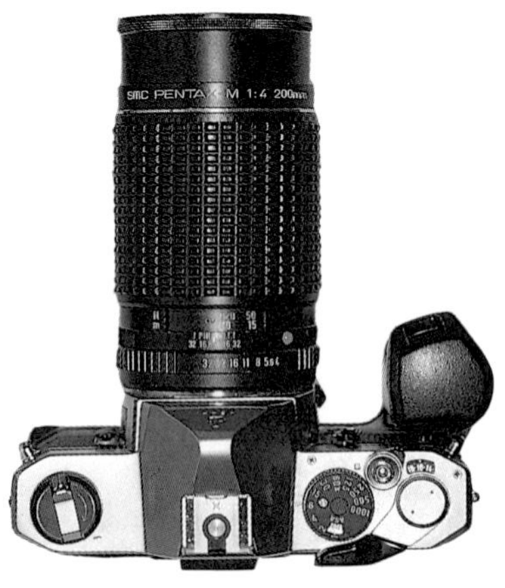

MX with Winder MX.

could prove wanting. Like every decent professional camera, the Pentax MX had a 250-frame cassette back, inspired by the Leica Reporter and the famous motorized cameras of the recent past.

The Data and MX Data backs were made available for the little MX.

A series of extremely lightweight compact lenses called SMC Pentax M were brought out for the Asahi Pentax MX and ME compact cameras. There were the first lenses, since the K-bayonet was adopted, to have a completely redesigned optical layout. They were perfectly compatible with the first-generation K lenses.

Many compact lenses replaced those of the same focal length in the existing range. The new optical designs did not always mean an increase in speed, but they were radically new, the number of elements was reduced, and they had improved resolution and constrast. Of the original SMC Pentax K equipment, the most recently introduced, like the 15 and 18mm ultra wide-angle lenses, were unchanged. The telephoto lenses with a focal length greater than 500mm and the special lenses also remained in production.

CHAPTER 12

The ME Family-The Electronic Challenge

The Asahi Pentax MX and its electronic sister, Asahi Pentax ME, were launched at the same time. The Asahi Pentax ME was slightly smaller than the very compact MX. There were some stylistic analogies between the two reflexes, but they had little in common technically. The Asahi Pentax ME was designed for motorization from the start, like the MX. It used a compact ME winder similar to the MX winder. It had SMC Pentax M compact lenses, like the MX. Other than these similarities, the two reflexes were poles apart conceptually.

The heart of the ME was electronic and its working was automatic only. There was no shutter speed dial and controls were reduced to the essentials. The MX mechanical reflex was intended for photographers who wanted a medium-priced reflex without giving up high-standard facilities. The ME was for less ambitious photographers who wanted a less sophisticated and less complex reflex. Asahi Optical made a winning choice. The ME flooded the markets and gained considerable commercial success. Once the market-launch phase was over, there was a slight reduction in price.

Thanks to the ME's success, Asahi Optical regained the position it had lost in the last years of the screw mount and early years of the K-bayonet. The devotees of the screw mount never forgave Asahi Optical for abandonning them. Many were unconvinced by the earliest bayonet-mount reflexes. With the Asahi Pentax ME, amateur enthusiasts flooded back to the Pentax make. The ME gained an overwhelming success. The "ME" abbreviation was widely used and ended up by identifying an entire generation of cameras.

When the time came to replace the Asahi Pentax ME with a later model, a unique choice was made. Two different models were derived from the ME. The more sophisticated model was called ME Super and was an automatic and manual reflex. The simplified model was completely automatic and called MV.

The division of the ME concept into two models was followed by rapid and contrasting evolution. The ME Super became the Pentax MEF and was given a rudimentary autofocus mechanism. The MV became first MV1 and then MG, maintaining the highest degree of functional simplicity. The application of electronics to photography was progressing rapidly and allowed increasingly complex possibilities. Electronic reflexes were destined to age prematurely, with rapid replacement of the models in production. The first programmed reflexes came out. Asahi Optical devised its first programmed reflex on the ME body, calling it Pentax Super A and ending the cycle of the ME family. The introduction of programming on reflexes opened the way for exciting experiments and increasing sophisticated automatic working.

Asahi Pentax ME

The Asahi Pentax ME was introduced in 1976 together with the MX and seemed like the electronic automatic *alter ego* of Asahi Optical's professional compact camera. In a body with extremely small dimensions, the ME proved to have well-defined features. The MX was more polished and better equipped. The ME was smaller and had more meagre controls and a plainer front panel. The actual dimensions of the ME did not differ greatly from those of the MX. Depth and height were the same but the body was 4mm shorter and this, together with superior design accentuated the appearance of compactness and set a record which no 35mm reflex managed to equal.

In controls, functions and facilities, the ME conspicuously stood out from its manual sister. The exposure meter of both reflexes was based on the same GPD cell and was one of the few things they had in common. The world's smallest reflex had a totally new shutter. This was a vertical Seiko MCF shutter with metallic blades. It was derived from the Seiko MC shutter which was fitted to the Asahi Pentax K2. The shutter was electronically controlled and allowed any speed, from $^1/1000$ to 8 sec. The camera's computer chose the most appropriate shutter speed and indicated the value selected in the viewfinder by LED.

The ME could not be controlled manually. The photographer was not able to set any speed other than that selected by the computer except by working within the restricted margins of the exposure compensation. The ME was conceptually derived from the Electro Spotmatic and Asahi Pentax K2. The operational simplicity of the ME was appreciated by the great mass of photographers, who preferred it to many electronic reflexes on the market.

The controls on the ME, greatly simplified, were grouped around the shutter release. A large switch coaxial with the shutter release selected the positions L (off), AUTO (automatic working), 100 X (flash synchro) and B (time exposure). The wind lever was similar to that on the MX and had a black plastic covering. As on the MX, the frame counter was sunk into the camera body.

There were two coaxial discs around the rewind lever. The inner disc was used for setting the film speed. The outer one was for manually adjusting the exposure. Adjustments were possible from two stops overexposure (4x) to two stops underexposure ($^1/4$x).

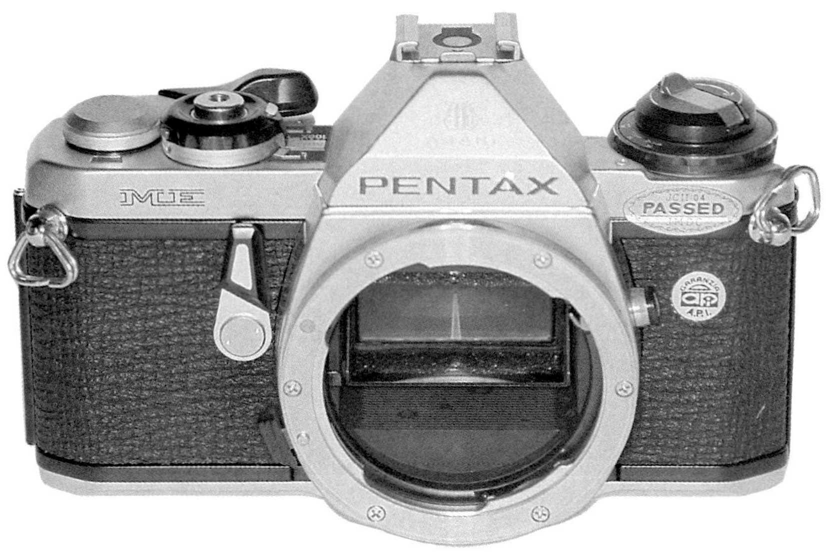

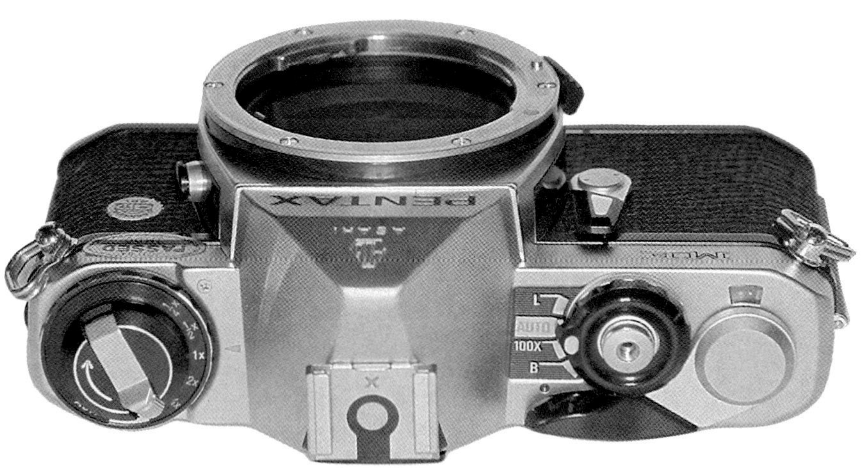

The Asahi Pentax ME, introduced in 1976, was the smallest SLR camera ever made arranged for a simple winder.

The self-timer lever was located on the front panel. The mechanism was of the standard timing type. The only flash contact, other than the hot shoe, was located on the left-hand side of the lens mount.

Electronically very advanced, the Asahi Pentax ME suffered from a number of design limitations. There was no depth of field preview. This was not justified by the camera's cost. A second limitation was the fixed focusing screen. True, it was not possible to replace the ground glass on any of the earlier Asahi Pentax models, only the MX afforded this facility which was appreciated by professional photographers. The screen for the ME was the same as that normally fitted to the MX with a microprism centre and horizontal split-image rangefinder.

The Asahi Pentax ME was a reliable and extremely advanced camera. It was designed with the greatest attention to detail and with recourse to the most developed technologies. In spite of its apparent operational simplicity, it adopted interesting and intelligent technical solutions.

The power was supplied by two single 1.5 volt silver oxide batteries. Consumption was minimal in spite of the numerous electrical circuits controlling the functions of the camera. A circuit for checking the batteries made a battery-check button unnecessary. A hold circuit stopped the LED flickering in the viewfinder when the mirror swung up. A stabilizing circuit prevented the LED from flashing while the exposure was being measured. The light metering circuit did not need special switches because it was activated by the shutter release and the wind lever. On the back of the camera was a film label slot and a little window so that one could check that the film was winding through smoothly.

The viewfinder gave indications on the left-hand rather than the right-hand side like the MX and the other Asahi Pentaxes. LED's oscillated over a scale of values from $^1/1000$ to 8 sec., coming to rest on the value closest to the one selected. The shutter's electronic control allowed intermediate release speeds between the conventionally indicated values. In extreme cases where the exposure meter went out of the shutter's operative range, the LED indicated OVER or UNDER.

The Asahi Pentax ME could be motorized with an ME compact winder. The only drawback with the ME winder was that it could not be coupled to the MX. In order to motorize two Asahi Pentaxes, an MX and an ME, one needed to have two different winders.

With its original features, the ME overturned the concept of automatic working in photography. Automatic exposure was not offered as an operational possibility, but as the strong point of an entire extremely sophisticated and developed system. The choice of automatic exposure did not take place at the time of release, but when buying the camera.

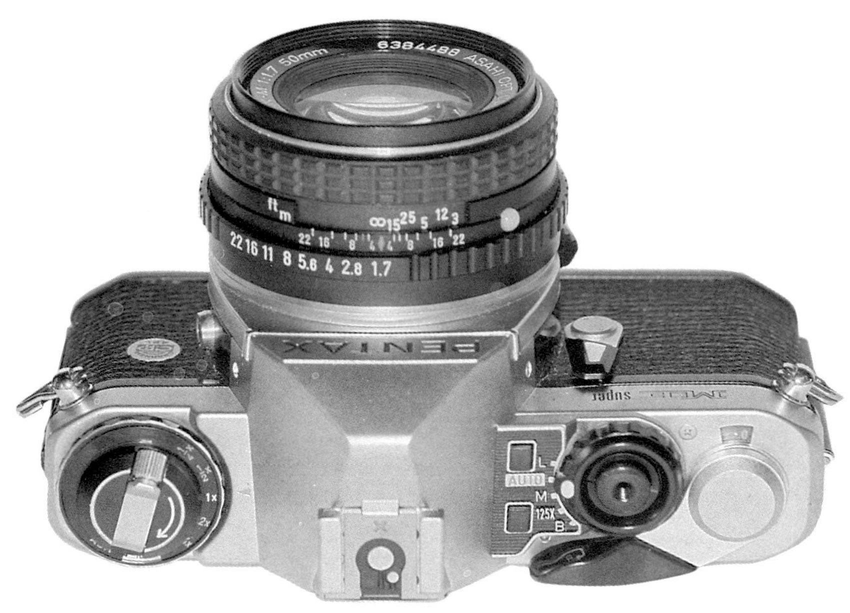

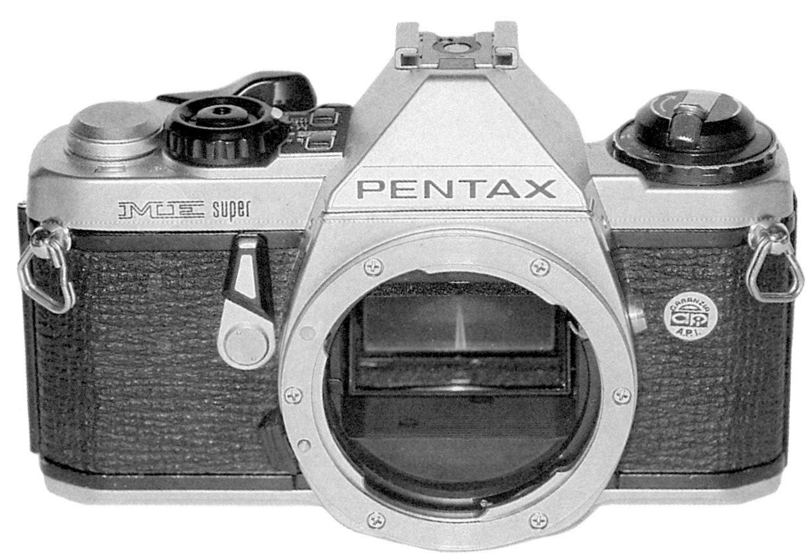

Pentax ME Super

Four years after the birth of the ME, two sister cameras were introduced. The Pentax MV and ME Super replicated the basic concepts of the ME, developing and extending them.

The abbreviation ME Super indicated continuity with the previous model, plus more developed facilities. The ME Super was no longer called "Asahi Pentax" but simply "Pentax". The body of the ME Super was similar in every way to that of the ME. The cameras differed from the previous model in that the shutter was faster and the function selector more comprehensive.

The ME Super had a Seiko MFC E2 shutter with speeds from $^1/2000$ to 4 sec. Flash synchronization occurred at $^1/125$ sec. The shutter could be controlled both automatically and manually. The substantial difference between the ME Super and the ME was that the former could be operated manually.

The control selector was coaxial with the shutter release and besides the L, AUTO, 125x and B functions, offered M for manual use. There was no shutter speed dial, but in its place a pair of small push-buttons were used to select the desired speed. The speed selected, was indicated in the viewfinder.

The viewfinder afforded a full series of data. The shutter speed scale went from $^1/2000$ to 4 sec., plus OVER and UNDER. Above the wording OVER, the markers M and EF indicated manual selection of the shutter speed and manual adjustment of the automatic exposure. When working in automatic, an LED indicated the value selected by the computer. Speeds slower than $^1/30$ sec. were shown by a yellow LED. The EF marker lit up in the event of manual adjustment of the exposure. The M signal lit up in the event of manual functions being selected.

In addition to the M signal, the value of the speed selected also lit up in manual. If this did not coincide with the speed selected by the computer, one of the OVER or UNDER signs came on. By pressing the delayed-action release buttons, one could compensate the exposure until the incorrect exposure signal went out. It was also possible to get the correct exposure by adjusting the aperture ring. The long row of illuminated LEDs in the viewfinder was a fascinating sight which threatened to distract the photographer.

Finding the correct exposure with an automatic reflex like the ME Super could seem like a complicated procedure. In practice, the operation was simple and instinctive. The ME Super was conceived and designed for the demanding photographer who normally worked in automatic but on particular occasions wanted to be able to control the automatic working at will.

Like the ME, the ME Super could be motorized with the ME and ME II winders. The ME II winder offered the same facilities as its predecessor but

---

Left: The Pentax ME Super was the improved version of the Asahi Pentax ME. The name Asahi was dropped and the AOC logo removed. Here with SMC Pentax-M 50mm, f/1.7.

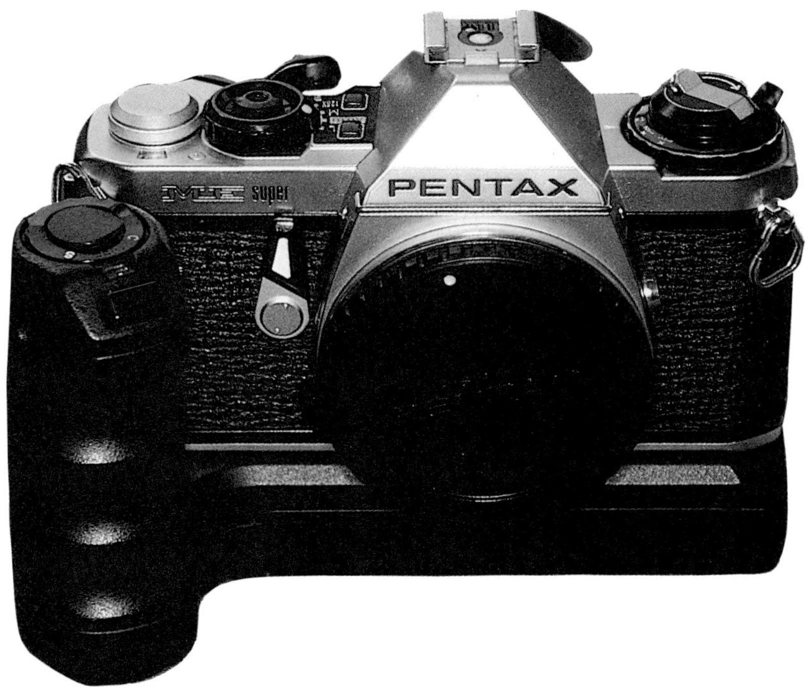

Pentax ME Super with Winder MEII.

enabled shutter speeds to be used up to $^1/2000$ sec. The function selector was located on the top of the hand-grip rather than on the back of the motor.

The success of the ME Super renewed and continued that of the ME and it remained in production longer than the ME, despite existing alongside the reflexes derived from third-generation electronics, equipped with programmed automatic working.

Pentax MV and MV1

The Pentax MV reflex was brought out simultaneously with the Pentax ME Super. The ME Super was the advanced version of the ME, whilst the MV was greatly simplified, for less demanding photographers who did not want to pay for facilities they did not require. It had the same body, the same light metering circuit and the same shutter as the ME. The function selector was decidedly simplified and the viewfinder practically devoid of information.

The selector offered AUTO, 100x and B. The viewfinder had a single signal which acted like traffic lights indicating the way to the best exposure. Green showed that the automatic exposure was correct, that the set aperture enabled the computer to choose a sufficiently high speed so as to avoid the risk of blurring.

Yellow advised the photographer to open up because the speed would be slower than $^1/30$ sec. If it stayed yellow even with the aperture fully open, this meant there was not enough light. In this case, the computer selected a slow speed and one had to take the shot with the camera on a tripod, or else be very careful about shake. Red meant that it was too bright for even the fastest shutter speed and in order to avoid overexposure it was necessary to close the aperture until the light turned green again.

A second light signal in the form of a cross indicated the state of the batteries on the dedicated Pentax AF 200S flash. The flash had to be mounted on the hot shoe bracket. When this was done, the light came on to signal that the flash was available for use.

With these kind of indications, the Pentax MV came within anyone's range, without being unnecessarily complicated or showing superfluous information. The information given by the camera was the barest essential and did not allow the photographer to know about the exposure.

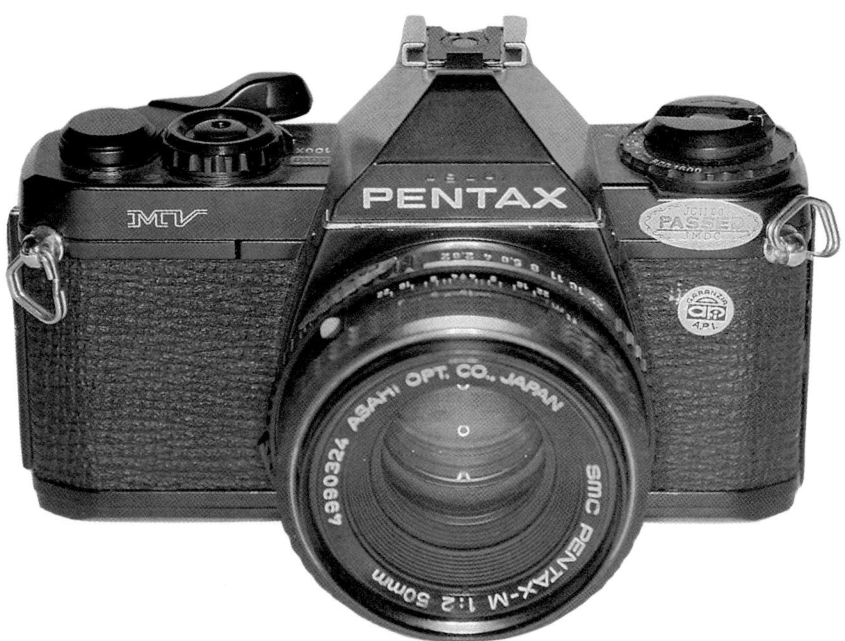

The Pentax MV was the simplified version of the ME, without speed scale in the finder and without winder arrangement. Here with SMC Pentax-M 50mm, f/2.

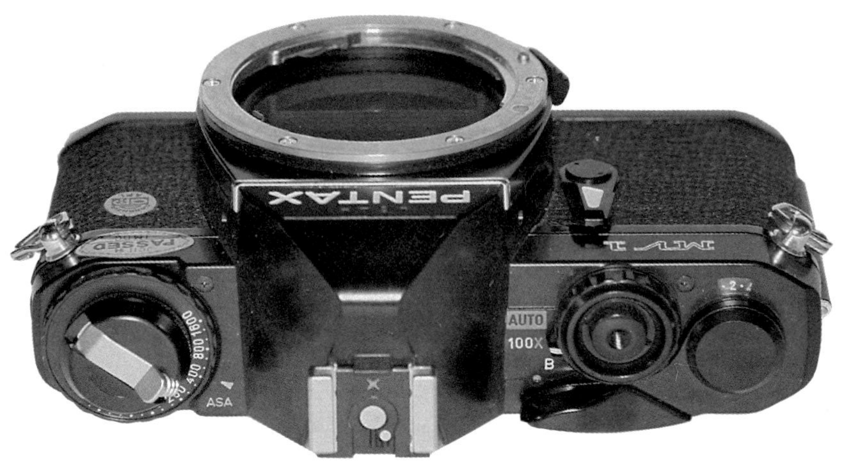

The Pentax MV-1 was the modified version of the MV, with winder arrangement.

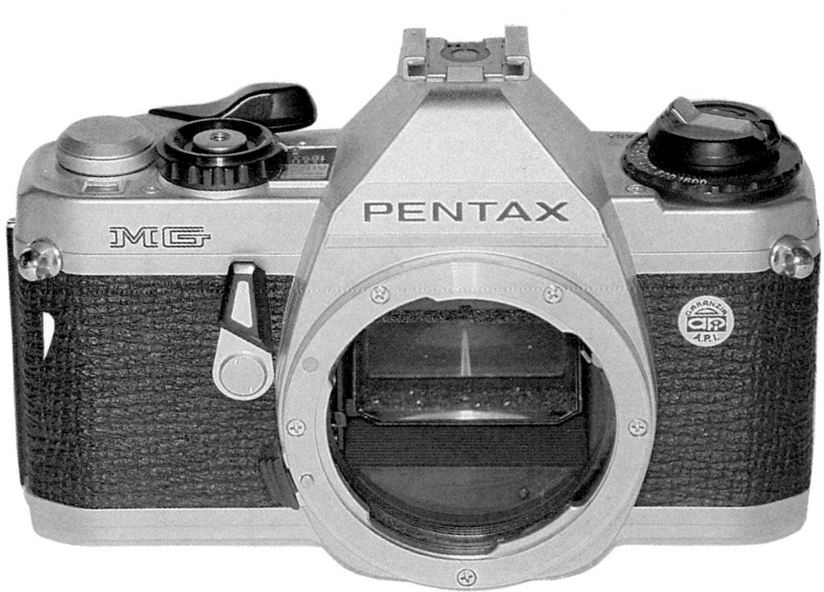

The Asahi Pentax MG was a simplified automatic camera, the last of ME-family.

It was possible with the MV to adjust automatic exposure to within plus or minus two stops. To do this, one had to raise the rewind lever and alter the film speed. There was no signal in the viewfinder to warn that adjustment had been made and it was easy to expose an entire roll at a sensitivity other than the nominal one.

Simplified in the extreme, it was not possible to fit the winder onto the Pentax MV. This limitation impaired the camera's success. In the era of computerized photography, one could forego anything but the wind-on motor for the film. To rectify this, the Pentax MV was suddenly replaced by the MV1 model, identical to the MV but fitted with a modified base for coupling with the ME winder.

The Pentax MV and MV1 were marketed at an extremely modest price. Despite their features, they did not remain in the catalogue very long and were replaced by a compact electronic camera originating from the ME. This last of the ME's daughters had features similar to its mother and bore the abbreviation MG.

Pentax MG

The Pentax MG was a compact electronic reflex which compensated for the over-simplicity of the MV and returned to the technical features introduced on the ME. The MG's most interesting features concerned the viewfinder. Contrary to the MV, the MG enabled visible checking of the shutter speed. The MG's viewfinder once more had the full range of speeds.

The body and controls of the MG corresponded exactly to those of the MV and ME. The function selector indicated the three positions AUTO, 100x, and B. The film speed selector did not allow for spontaneous adjustments without altering

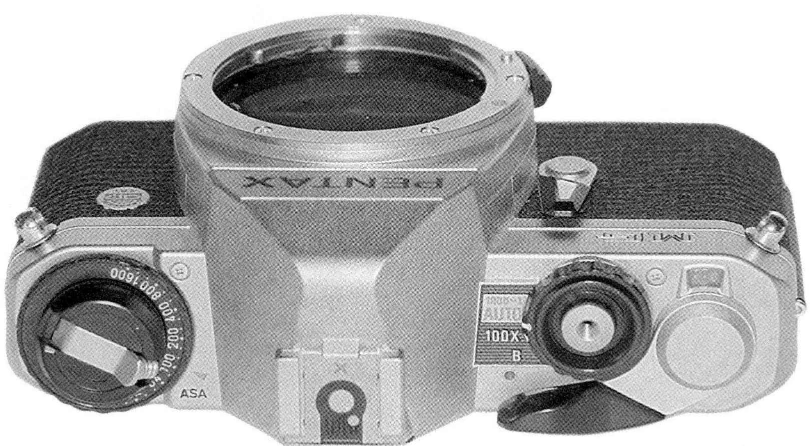

Top-plate of the MG.

the set value. The signal showing that the film was winding on correctly was taken off the back of the camera.

The viewfinder data were similar to those on the ME. The shutter speed range was from $^1/1000$ to 1 sec., plus OVER and UNDER and the symbol showing that the flash was available for use. By activating the exposure meter, a green diode indicated the release speed selected by the computer between $^1/1000$ and $^1/60$ sec. If the speed selected was slower than 30, the diode turned yellow to warn of the risk of blurring. If the speed selected was outside the range, a red LED showed either OVER or UNDER.

In designing the MG, the errors of the past were borne in mind. The MG offered motorization with the ME and ME II winders. Compared with the ME, the MG appeared simplified, but not rendered commonplace. The MG was a simple reflex to use and understand, but it was not stupid. It afforded more limited possibilities in comparison with the ME Super and the other electronic reflexes. The expert photographer using the Pentax MG could choose the aperture/shutter speed and personalize his own photographs. It afforded access to the full

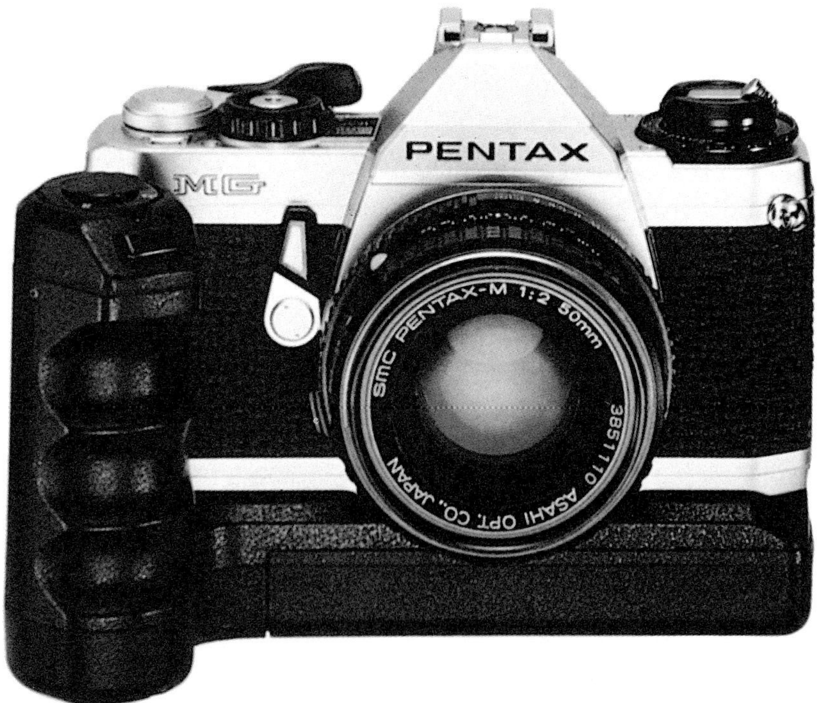

MG with winder.

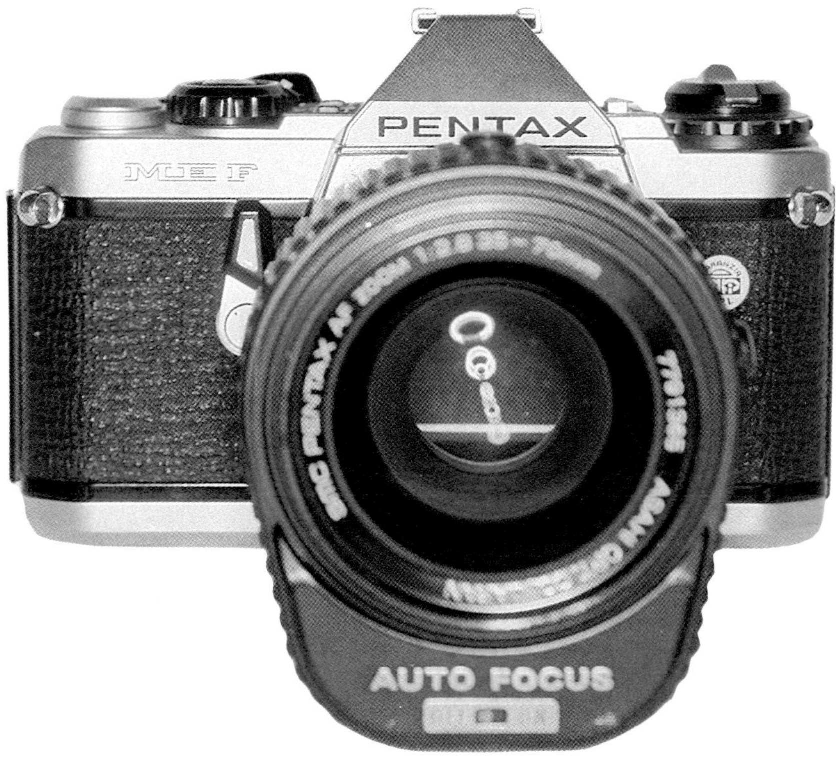

The Pentax MEF provided on auto focus facility with the special AF-SMC Pentax 35-70mm, f/2.8 lens.

range of Pentax equipment, lenses, motors, flashes and even the data backs. In the hands of less demanding photographers, the MG was perfectly capable of doing a decent job without any problems.

Pentax MEF

The last member of the Pentax ME family was the MEF, brought out in April 1982. Its introduction preceded that of the Canon AL1 by a few days. It was only by a fortunate coincidence that the Pentax MEF could glory in the title of the first autofocus reflex. History would reappraise that record. The growth in electronics was to give rise to a generation of SLR's for which the term autofocus was more appropriate. The automatic focusing control mechanism used on the Pentax MEF was quite primitive and not followed up. In spite of the MEF being destined for obsolescence, its feat assured its historic value.

The Pentax MEF derived from the ME Super. A number of supplementary controls were added in order to adapt it to the required functions. The viewfinder was adorned with data and the lens mounting embellished with a series of electrical contacts. The body was identical to that of the ME Super. From the light metering point of view, the MEF preserved unchanged the ME Super's possibilities of working fully automatically or in manual. It used the same accessories as the ME Super - the winders, data backs and dedicated flashes.

The right-hand part of the top plate accommodated the same function selector as on the ME Super. A new control was added on the left-hand side - an unusual

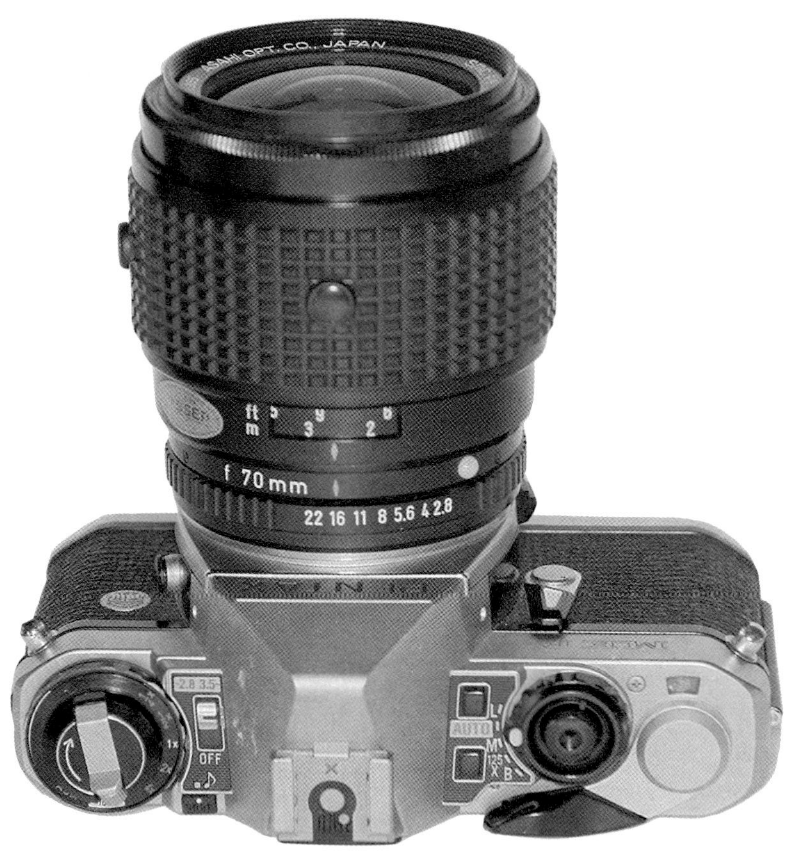

The three-position switch on the top-plate of the MEF governed the auto focus function.

switch with three positions: OFF, green and red. The green and red positions indicated the highest speed of the lens being used. The green had to be set with lenses faster than f/2.8. The red was used for lenses slower than f/3.5. The OFF position was for turning off the electronic focusing control.

Once the camera knew the maximum speed of the lens being used, it proceeded to frame and focus. Besides the light metering information, the MEF's viewfinder afforded additional data. In the lower part, three diodes gave focusing information. Two red arrows on the sides indicated incorrect focusing and the rotation direction of the focusing ring for adjustment.

It was not a very fast method and one needed to proceed by trial and error. It was really an assisted focusing system which was improperly described as auto-focus. An audible warning, which could be switched off, also signalled perfect focusing.

The focusing screen on the Pentax MEF was the same as on the ME Super and had a circle of microprisms and a split-image rangefinder at its centre. In order to use the assisted focusing facility, one had to centre the subject in the area taken up by the circle. The autofocus sensor was housed in the lower part of the camera, under the mirror. The mirror had a translucent middle area which allowed through a proportion of the light. The sensor on the MEF was of the MOS type and measured image contrast. When greatest contrast was achieved it signified correct focus. The autofocus mechanism was not efficient with subjects with low contrast in the central area.

Adequate power was required to supply the numerous electronic circuits and LEDs in the viewfinder. It needed four 1.5 volt batteries, double those needed for the ME Super. A larger compartment was made in the bottom to accommodate them.

The Pentax MEF was accompanied by a 35-70mm,f/2.8 zoom lens with a built-in motor for automatic focusing. A system of five electrical contacts on the ring of the bayonet mount enabled the camera body and lens to exchange information so that with this lens one had automatic focusing. By using the MEF with the Pentax K lenses, one had assisted focusing.

The introduction of the MEF gave rise to much debate. The electronic focusing system was compared with the visual systems. The speed and reliability of electronic focusing were criticised.

History has shown that the solution proposed by Asahi Optical was ahead of its time - it signalled an important stage in reflex development without gaining great commercial success. The competition imitated the assisted focusing system on some of their reflexes, but it did not become popular. It took three long years before autofocus was triumphant. Deprived of an autofocus lens system, the MEF was set aside, without marring the success of the ME Super. At the end of its brief and unsuccessful career the Pentax MEF was sold off at a lower price than the ME Super.

C H A P T E R   13

Pentax LX, The Big Professional

In the mid-1980s, Asahi Optical brought out their first modular reflex. It was only produced in black and was given the abbreviation "LX", ie: "60" in Roman numerals. The reason for such a designation was that the introduction of the camera coincided with Asahi Optical's sixtieth anniversary. The pentaprism bore the single word "Pentax" engraved in white on a black background. "LX" was engraved on the top plate next to the rewind lever. The name Asahi had finally disappeared from the photographic world.

The Pentax LX bore no ressemblance to the reflexes which preceded it nor to those which have followed. Like the MX, the LX was part of a special generation. It was launched fully-fledged and was not subjected to any revision, reworking or modification, except for a special edition with gold finish. The accessories for the LX were also fully developed at launch and afforded a multiplicity of possible uses.

The Pentax LX had an automatic, electronically-controlled shutter. The automatic working could be turned off and the camera used in manual mode. Accessories included motors, backs and interchangeable viewfinders. It was the only Pentax allowing the viewfinders to be interchanged. This feature had always signified reflexes intended for professionals and demonstrated the ambitions of the Pentax LX.

The professional aspirations of the Pentax LX showed in the construction of the camera's sturdy body. It had special trim on the parts subject to wear, and internally had a considerable number of sophisticated and reliable electronic circuits. With the Pentax LX, electronic reflexes broke out from the amateur market and achieved respectability. Its arrival coincided with the introduction of electronic professional models by Nikon, Canon and Leitz. The Nikon F3 was a masterpiece of mechanical and electronic engineering and was produced in several forms, with a titanium body, with a special HP viewfinder and in an autofocus version. Canon's model had the unwarranted designation "F1new", but it had nothing in common with the Canon F1, which went out of production. It was a highly specialized reflex which by using special viewfinders and motors, could be changed from a manual reflex to a reflex with automatic shutter or

148

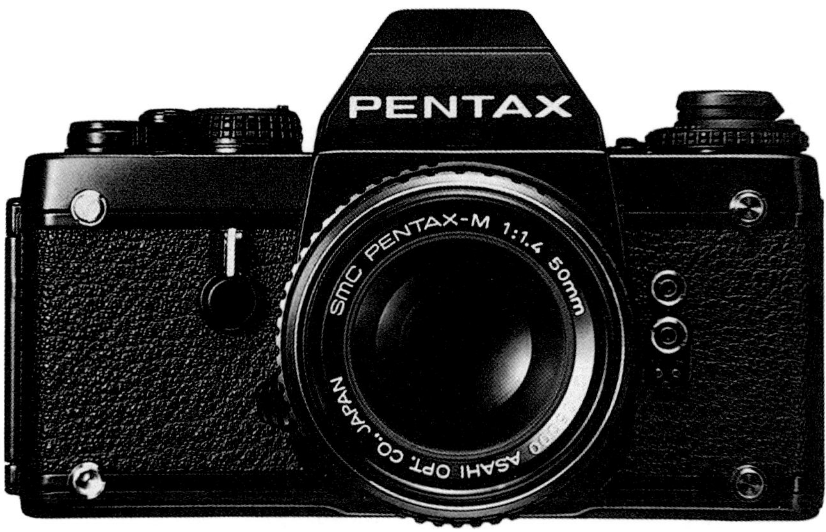

The Pentax LX was the top camera made by Asahi Optical for professionals. Interchangeable finders, waterproof shell and arrangement for high speed motors are points in favour of this reliable camera.

aperture priority, as the user chose. Electronics as applied to photography had reached a level of reliability such as to be offered to the most demanding of professionals without any worry.

The Pentax LX had quite a strong impact on the market. Its price was more than double that of the MX, justified on grounds of prestige and the high cost of components. Before the Pentax LX, Asahi Optical had aimed almost exclusively at the mass market. The company had gained some degree of success in its attempt to reach professionals and a more demanding public. The LX kept its promise and was sturdy, reliable, almost infallible. Its qualities were appreciated by some of the most demanding photographers and it was successful in its limited market.

The LX became Asahi Optical's crowning achievement and typified Japanese camera production. It symbolized a method of building cameras which made concessions neither on the production nor the conceptual levels.

Intended to stay on the market for a long time, the LX was created with a comprehensive and rational range of accessories and was designed with a wide variety of professional applications in mind.

The LX body was all black, reasonably compact and particularly sturdy. It was a pressure casting of a special aluminium alloy but was not too heavy. The body was 145mm long and, with the standard viewfinder, weighed 565g. The rival

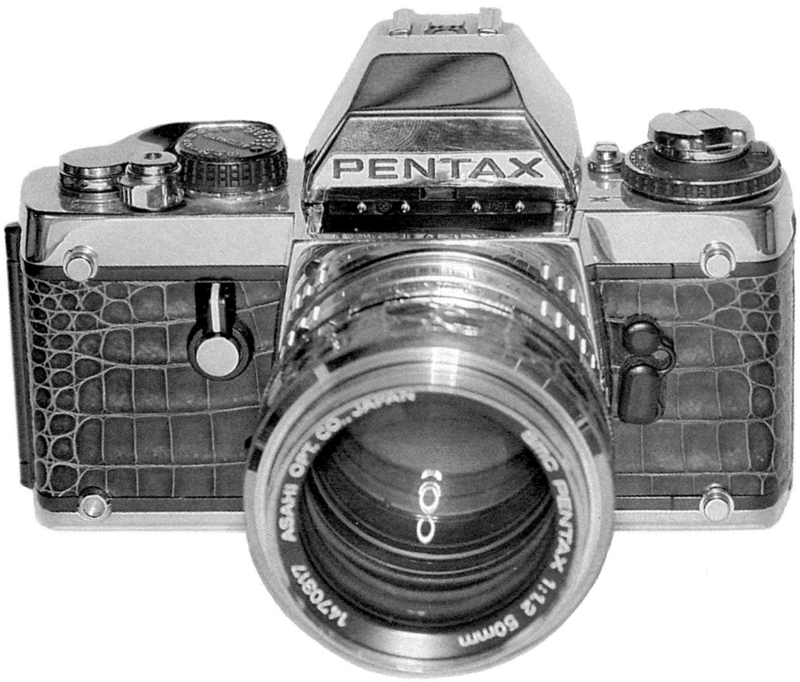

A special edition of the Pentax LX in gold finish was made for the 60th birthday of Asahi Optical Company

Nikon F3 measured 149mm in length and weighed 700g. The Spotmatic had measured 143mm and weighed 665g. Despite all its facilities, the LX was as compact as a Spotmatic.

The camera body was an unusual shape and departed from Asahi Optical's style. The corners were not sharp like the traditional Pentaxes, but were rounded and inclined slightly towards the front panel of the camera. The camera was easy to handle and comfortable to hold. Seen from the front, it appeared smaller than it actually was.

The heart of the camera consisted of an electro-mechanical shutter with titanium, horizontally running blinds. Shutter speeds from $^1/2000$ to 4 sec. could be set manually. When used automatically, the range of shutter speeds covered $^1/2000$ to $^1/125$ sec. The shutter's exceptional facilities were completed by a silicon light metering system. The photo-sensitive element was housed in the base of the camera and oriented so as to meter the light reflected from the blinds and film during exposure. When metering with the mirror down, a little auxiliary mirror directed part of the light towards the photocell located below the main mirror. Direct measurement of the light during exposure, called direct metering, was already used on a number of prestigious reflexes and was first introduced by Olympus on their first electronic reflex, the OM2, in 1975.

The exposure meter, shutter and all the electrical functions on the LX were powered by two 1.5 volt batteries accommodated in the base of the camera. Without batteries the camera could be operated manually, but without metering of course.

The LX shutter was electronically controlled for speeds slower than $^1/60$ sec. and mechanically controlled for faster speeds. Flash synchronization took place at $^1/75$ sec. Without batteries, the shutter functioned mechanically at the faster speeds, $^1/75$ to $^1/2000$ sec.

Controls on the LX were traditional and rational. The front panel had a few essential controls and three strap fastening points. The brightness of three chrome fastening points and the lug for the auxiliary hand-grip reduced the severity of the front panel. The self-timer lever incorporated several different functions. As on the MX, it served for closing the aperture manually and for direct viewing of the depth of field. It also served to fasten the mirror in the raised position. No other Pentax apart from the K2 had this professional feature.

The FP and X contacts were situated on the left-hand side of the front panel. Besides the traditional contacts, the LX used a bipolar socket for connection with the dedicated flashes.

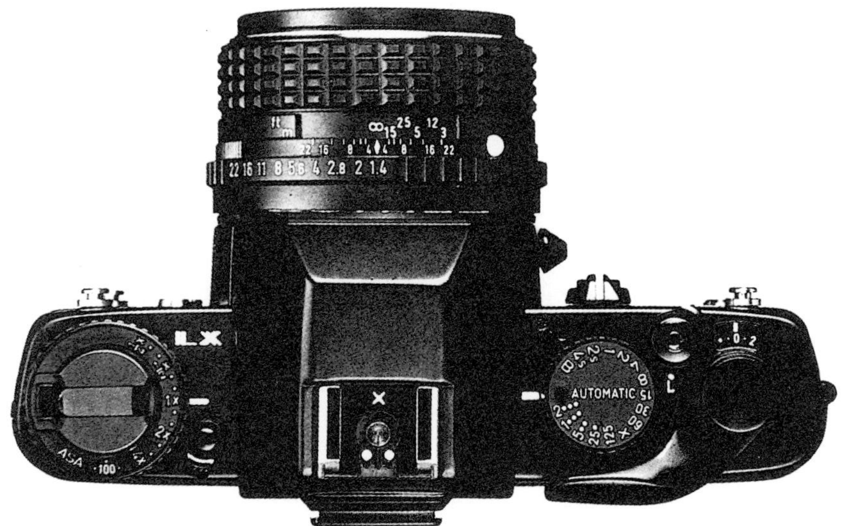

Controls on the LX were traditional and rational.

The top plate housed the traditional controls in their standard layout. The wind lever was large and accessible, the frame counter sunk into the camera body and shutter release was provided with a ring which acted as a safety lock.

The shutter speed dial was over-sized and had a ribbed rubber rim for better grip. It set manual speeds from $^1/2000$ to 4 sec. and X, B and AUTOMATIC.

The traditional rewind lever was located to the left of the top plate. The dial for setting film speed, from ASA 6 to 3200, and the dial for exposure compensation, from $^1/4x$ to 4x, were located around the axis of this lever. Exposure compensation could be set in $^1/3$ stops for really precise adjustment of the exposure. The adjustment dial had a ribbed rubber rim and could not be activated by mistake. Before rotating it, one had to unlock it with a button located on the top plate.

A button inside the camera body made it possible to open the focal plane shutter manually. To gain access to its internal components.

An unusual feature of the LX was the many seals on those parts of the camera which could be opened or moved. The back, viewfinder coupling, speed selector and rewind lever were all sealed against dust and damp. The LX was thus impermeable to dust and sand and adequately protected against rain and humidity. A number of minor construction details showed that nothing was left to chance. Two special mouldings on the base allowed the camera to sit firmly on a flat surface for shots at slow speeds.

The Pentax LX viewfinder offered a great deal of information about the exposure and the camera's functions. The shutter speed scale was situated to the right of the screen, as on the K2 and in contrast to the ME. It showed the values $^1/2000$ to 4 sec. The scale of values was preceded by "A" in Automatic and followed by the abbreviation "LT.B", which indicated an exceptionally long exposure. In manual, a blue mark indicated the speed selected by the operator. A green diode for values above 30 and a yellow one for those below 15 indicated the value advised by the exposure meter. The photographer could make his own judgement according to the indications given by the exposure meter. In automatic, the blue mark indicated position A and an LED showed the shutter speed chosen by the computer. By adjusting the exposure at will, a bright red mark reminded the photographer that a voluntary variation was being made. When working with the dedicated flashes, a red diode lit up at position X, between 125 and 60, advising that the flash was ready to be released.

The standard viewfinder for the Pentax LX was the FA1 pentaprism. It had a little window for viewing the set aperture and a hot shoe on the top. By pressing a button situated on the top plate, the pentaprism was unfastened and could be removed from its seating and replaced. The other viewfinders were:-

FA1W: Identical to the standard viewfinder except that the eyepiece could be adjusted from -3 to +1 dioptres to correct for eyesight.

FF1: The waist-level viewfinders of the Eighties were an inheritance from the past, but some manufacturers continued to provide them for professional modular reflexes. Regardless of the fact that virtually no one used a waist-level viewfinder any more, Asahi Optical put the FF1 viewfinder with folding hood and reverse image into its catalogue.

FE1: Offered a direct and magnified view of the LX screen. The fixed eyepiece gave a substantial magnification of the image and dioptric adjustment could be set between -5 and +4.

FB1: The most versatile of the Pentax LX viewfinders was a pentaprism with magnified vision and a 45^0 angle of view. The only similar one was in the Canon catalogue for the F1new modular reflex. This viewfinder made it possible to observe the aperture value and it could be supplemented by three different interchangeable bayonet mount eyepieces. The standard FD2 eyepiece permitted clear, sharp vision. The high magnification FD1 eyepiece had dioptric adjustment from -5 to +3. The FC1 eyepiece was extremely versatile. It could rotate fully around its own axis and afforded full, clear vision from any viewpoint, front, side or at an angle.

The coupling between the FB1 viewfinder and the FC1 eyepiece was one of the most interesting sight systems ever devised. It involved a sort of very high technology waist-level finder, reversible at any moment and at any position. The screen could be viewed from a distance and the image was always direct and not laterally reversed. Large, bulky and heavy, the FB1 viewfinder with the FC1 eyepiece was an ideal solution for telephotography, photo safari, micro- and macro-photography and photography of models. The LX system viewfinder was devised for those kinds of photography where the eye could not easily be brought up to the standard viewfinder and where additional right-angle finders would otherwise be needed.

FA2: This simple, linear viewfinder formed part of the LX equipment. The FA2 viewfinder comprised a very simple pentaprism without the little aperture window or hot shoe. Its clean pyramidal shape closely ressembled the Spotmatic pentaprism. The FA2 viewfinder emphasized the LX's sense of compactness and recalled the origins of the Asahi Pentax system.

The LX equipment afforded a wide choice of focusing screens to go with the viewfinder system. There were twelve focusing screens for the LX, as against eight for the MX. The analogy with the MX screens was not merely fortuitous. The interchange system was identical to that of the MX and screens were changed through the lens mounting. In spite of its viewfinders being fully interchangeable, the LX used the same system as used on the MX. The LX screens offered were the same as for the MX, with additional ones in standard and special versions for long telephoto lenses. The identification codes for the LX matched those for the MX screens. The SC screen was the standard one with microprisms and a split image rangefinder. The MX's SC screen was named SC1 and the LX had two SC screens called SC21 and SC26. The SA screen only had microprisms. It was available in a fine-grain SA1 version and a coarse-grain SA3 version for the MX. The LX had three similar screens named SA21, SA23 and SA26. The SB screen had only the split image device and was called SB1 for the MX and SB21 for the LX. The SD screen had central cross-hairs and was called SD1 for the MX. It was available in two versions, SD21 and SD11 for the LX. The MX had a plain ground-glass SE screen. On the LX, the same screen became SE20 and SE25. The SG grid screen and SI graduated scale screen became SG20 and SI20 on the LX.

Motorization of the Pentax LX followed the same criteria as motorization of the MX. It was possible to wind on the film in two ways, with a compact winder and with a fast motor.

The LX winder lacked a hand-grip and was powered by four AA-size batteries. The film wound on at a speed of two frames a second. The LX winder made possible a single release and rewinding of the exposed film. The function selector was on the back, as on the ME Winder. A lever similar to that of the mechanical self-timer controlled the motorized rewinding.

The Motor Drive LX could be programmed for speeds from 5 frames a second to one frame every 2 seconds. The LX's professional motor enabled fast shots and rewinding of the film. Aristocratic and exclusive, the LX motor could not be coupled to any other Pentax. It did not have an upper hand-grip and had to be powered by an outside source. The standard power pack was the vertical hand-grip containing twelve AA batteries and an independent shutter release. The most compact pack was the rechargeable Nickel Cadmium storage battery. When working in a studio, the Motor Drive could be powered by mains current. The function selector and speed selector were coaxial and located on the back of the motor unit, as on the Winder.

A motor appearing at the beginning of the Eighties could not offer less than remote control and programmable working, and the Motor Drive LX was no exception. The versatility of the Motor Drive LX was increased by the usual arsenal of cables, huge 250-frame backs, hand-grips and accessories.

Like all sophisticated reflexes, the LX had a number of special backs for replacing the standard one. The LX backs were similar to those available for the MX. The Dial Data LX back could be programmed with the day, month and year of the shot or with alphanumeric information. The Watch Data LX back had more sophisticated facilities. It was not confined to printing numbers and letters, but the face of a watch which gave the exact time at which the photo was taken. The central area could be used for personal data.

The Eighties technology had accustomed photographers to using dedicated flashes. The Pentax LX system afforded very high-level facilities. Thanks to the light metering system which metered the light simultaneously with the expo-sure, the Pentax LX allowed TTL automatic control of the flash.

By using the direct metering system and the exchange of information between the dedicated flash and central computer, the LX made it possible to integrate the light metered out by the flash with the ambient light. The LX had four dedicated flashes. The most versatile was the AF 280T, with a guide number of 28 with ASA 100 film and a directable flash head. The professional flash for the LX was the AF

400T. The abbreviation indicated the guide number 40 and TTL automatic working. Power could be by means of AA or NiCad batteries. There was also a little amateur AF 200T with guide number 20, and the AF 080C ring-flash for macro- and close-up photography.

The Pentax LX enjoyed the full range of lenses already available for the MX and the ME. The K-bayonet mount enabled the LX to use SMC Pentax K and SMC Pentax M lenses. Throughout its long life, the LX witnessed the continuous growth of the SMC Pentax lens system. The SMC Pentax A lenses, made for the programmed reflexes, functioned equally well with the LX. The SMC Pentax F autofocus lenses could also be fitted to the Pentax LX without any difficulty.

CHAPTER 14

The A-Family - The Programmed Pentaxes

Ten years on from the introduction of the first electronic reflex shutter and aperture priority automatic electronic reflexes had reached high levels of professionalism and robustness. Electronics applied to photography had won over amateurs and professionals. Nikon, Canon, Pentax, Contax and even Leitz had produced wholly reliable professional automatic reflexes. Alongside the professional reflexes, the popular automatic reflexes had conquered the mass market. But still more ambitious targets were set. Manufacturers' offerings for the second half of the Eighties were encapsulated in the word "Program". Reflexes with automatic shutter and aperture working were safe and reliable, but needed care and experience. Working with the aperture too small, the exposure was perfect but the photo could turn out blurred as a result of too slow a shutter speed. Working with the aperture too large, the photo could be burned out due to lack of speeds faster than $^1/1000$ sec. The automatic aperture reflexes could be deceived by manual setting of a shutter speed incompatible with the possible range of apertures.

The solution to the problem required the further application of electronics. A few reflexes used double automatic working which could be set as the photographer pleased. Some reflexes had the facility of cross automatic working which did not allow any margin of error. The concept of programmed automatic working came about.

Compact cameras with programmed automatic working had been on the market for some time. They had a non-interchangeable lens and central blade shutter. The combination of the aperture with the shutter simplified the adoption of electronically-controlled cross automatic working. On SLR's, focal plane shutters and interchangeable lenses necessitated sophisticated and accurate control mechanisms. In order to facilitate the exchange of information and controls between camera and lens, contact panels were needed on the lens mount and the outer ring of the camera bayonet.

Asahi Optical devised a programmed reflex based on the layout of the Pentax ME Super. It was named Super A and brought out at the 1983 Milan Sicof. The camera was awarded the title of "European Camera of the Year 1984". In the United States, it was called the Pentax Super Program. The Pentax Super A was the first Pentax reflex to have different nomenclature for the European and American markets.

Mainly available finished in black, the Super A vaguely ressembled the LX. The layout of the controls, compatability of the motors and electronic components betrayed its origins in the ME Super.

A second Pentax programmed reflex came out in the wake of the success of the Super A. The Pentax Program A was a year younger and renamed the Pentax Program Plus in the USA. It signified a return to the marketing policy of a cheaper version of a model riding on the success of its more expensive partner.

The Pentax Program A very closely ressembled the Super A but proved an ephemeral creature. It aspired to mass circulation, but failed to achieve its expected success. Whereas the Super A remained in the catalogue for a long time, the Program A was quickly replaced by a generation of compact reflexes.

The third programmed reflex was unimaginatively named A3 and offered interesting but limited facilities. In North America, it was called the A3000. The Pentax A3 offered extreme simplicity of operation. It only operated in the automatic mode. It had a built-in micro-motor for automatically winding on the film and DX-coding for automatic reading in of film speed. It sought the same success as the Pentax ME, but was not to find it. The A3 ingloriously concluded the short history of the A-family, which began most auspiciously with the Super A. For the A-family reflexes, Asahi Optical produced a series of K-mount lenses with automatic diaphragms. The lenses for the programmed Pentaxes were called SMC Pentax A and replaced the traditional lenses in a few short years. Some were of the old optical design, whilst others had original and interesting optical configurations.

Pentax Super A

The Pentax Super A was one of the most interesting items at the 1983 Sicof. It was Asahi Optical's first programmed reflex and, in contrast with many reflexes belonging to the same generation, offered many more possible applications.

The structure of the camera derived from that of the ME Super, to which it brought a number of modifications. It was nearly the same size as the ME Super, accepted its motors and weighed 490g. The Super A was finished in black to accentuate its compactness and professional outlook. The pentaprism was wider, with a hot shoe, and a white window. Shutter speeds were set by two small buttons, as on the ME Super.

In planning the camera, the basic requirements of photographers were considered. Its strong point was the program function, but it was also easy to use

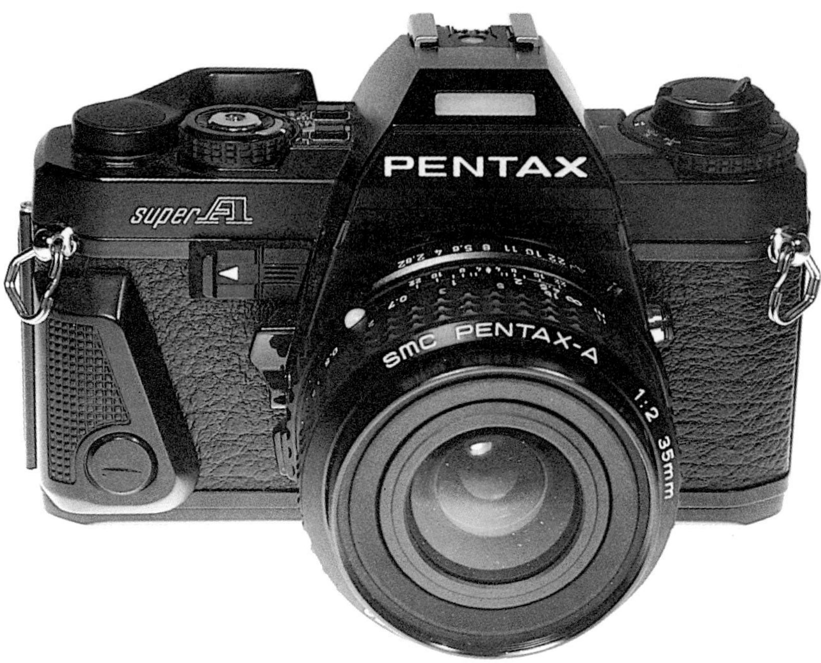

The Pentax Super A was an electronic automatic and programmed camera. The K-bayonet mount was modified with electrical contacts to communicate with SMC Pentax A lenses, here a 35mm,f/2.

in automatic with shutter and aperture priority and in manual mode. It offered a full range of facilities and was priced between the ME Super and the LX. In order to take full advantage of its facilities, the Super A had to be used with the SMC Pentax A lenses.

Aesthetically, the Super A was the result of sophisticated research into detail and by an excess of ornamentation. A plastic moulding screwed onto the right-hand side of the front panel to act as a hand-grip to make the camera easier to hold. There was a similar prominent feature fixed to the back incorporating the label-holder. The front hand-grip had to be removed to enable the winder to be used.

The arrival of the Super A signalled the end of production of the Pentax MEF autofocus reflex. The Super A did not break with tradition and fitted perfectly into the existing system of accessories, but obliged owners to buy the SMC Pentax A lenses for the program mode. With other lenses the Super A worked in manual and aperture priority, but not in program or shutter priority modes. The SMC Pentax A lenses could be used on all earlier bayonet models without restriction.

Controls on the Super A were slightly more complicated than on the ME Super, but conformed to the basic layout. Light metering data was displayed in the viewfinder. On the outside of the camera, a small-scale display showed the selected shutter speed and the program function. The viewfinder was clear; the display was located below the focusing screen and did not interfere with the image. It had two panels, one for apertures and one for shutter speeds. Aperture value was indicated by means of digital data and not direct viewing. The focusing screen was like the one on the ME Super and could not be removed.

The right-hand side of the top plate accommodated the wind lever, the frame counter sunk into the body, the display, shutter release and function selector. The selector allowed for five positions: L (off), AUTO, M (manual), 125x (flash synchro) and B. By selecting AUTO, the camera operated in automatic, but only when fitted with a SMC Pentax A lens with the aperture set at A. The external display showed the letter P and selected shutter speed. The internal display showed, in the left window, the speed, and in the right window, the value of the aperture selected in automatic working and preceded by the letter F. The information was clear and unambiguous.

By selecting AUTO with independant lenses or manually adjusted SMC Pentax A lenses, the Super A behaved exactly like an ME Super. It chose the shutter speed and transmitted it on the display without adding any other information. Aperture was not shown because it was selected manually.

By setting value "A" on the barrel of the lens for automatic selection of the ap-

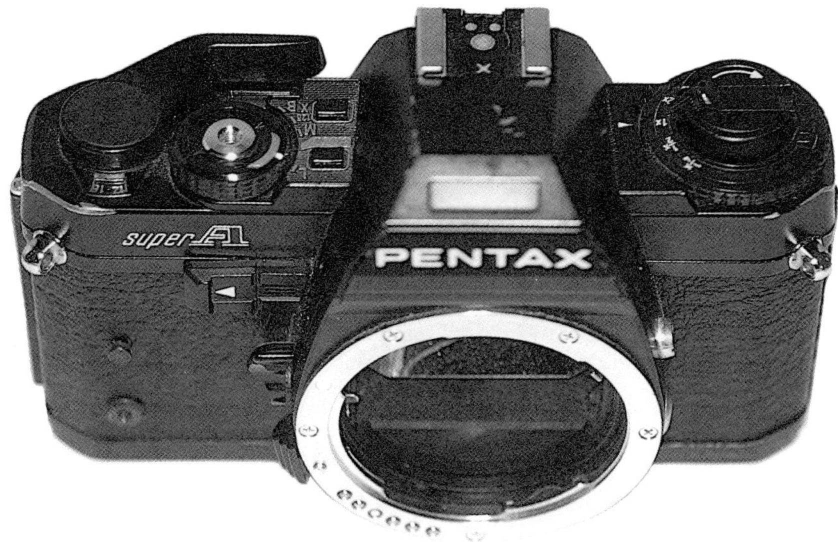

Controls of the Pentax Super A.

erture and setting the camera on M, one had the possibility of working with shutter speed priority. The display showed the automatically selected aperture and the manually selected shutter speed. The speed could be changed at will by means of the buttons and the aperture adapted.

By using the manual aperture and selecting function M on the camera body, a preferred aperture/shutter speed could be chose. Possible over- or underexposure was signalled in quite an original way. The value of the selected speed appeared on the first display, and a number, from one to three, appeared on the right-hand one, preceded by the plus or minus sign. When the exposure corresponded to the one selected by the computer, the figure 0 appeared. If the exposure difference exceeded three stops, the figure 3 began to flash. This practice made it possible to decipher the information fully and in an instant.

When working with the Super A, the fully manual function was rarely selected. For snapshots and working with telephoto lenses, the program function was preferable, thus ensuring sufficiently high shutter speeds. When working with wide-angle lenses, it was better to set aperture priority in order to avoid over large apertures that might have been selected by the program mode. It only made sense to work in manual when metering the light on a detail, or if the same exposure was wanted over the whole scene. As the Super A did not have a memory lock, it was necessary to use the manual exposure mode.

It was frequently necessary to compensate the automatically selected exposure, in order to saturate the colours better or give more prominence to light or shade. In these cases, it was better to make use of the appropriate dial for adjustment between +2 and -2. The helpful display warning the user about not being within the program, caused the letters EF to flash. The dial for adjusting the exposure corresponded to that on the ME Super and the other electronic Pentaxes and was coaxial to the rewind lever and film sensitivity disc.

The other controls for the Super A were located on the front panel. The self-timer was electronic. A sliding black switch showed a red warning light. By operating the shutter release, the light flashed at increasingly frequent intervals until the release took place. It was possible to turn the switch off again and block the self-timer while the flashing was going on without endangering the picture.

The depth of field preview lever was below the self-timer switch. Moving the lever with the light metering circuit open, the display would go wild, giving totally crazy data. The return of a depth of field preview facility on an electronic reflex was a sign of the professional aspirations of the Pentax Super A.

On the left-hand side of the lens mounting was a standard flash socket. Below, an unusual red and white button served to illuminate the display in the viewfinder. The method was similar to that used on digital watches. This night-time illuminator however absorbed more energy from the batteries than was needed to expose ten rolls of film.

The Super A was equipped with a number of energy-saving devices. The light metering circuit automatically switched off after thirty seconds. The first three blank releases occurred at a speed of $^1/1000$ sec., to avoid unnecessarily long exposures. By flashing a row of zeros, the display warned that the batteries were nearly exhausted.

The electronic shutter was a Seiko MFC E3, similar to the one on the Pentax ME Super. Its highest speed was $^1/2000$ sec. and it could be controlled in manual for exposures up to 15 sec. Without batteries, the shutter locked.

Two 1.5 volt silver oxide or alkaline batteries were needed to power the camera. The ME Super, MX and LX took the same batteries.

The Pentax Super A used all the accessories devised for the ME Super. When it was brought out, the Super A had a powerful winder, called Motor Drive A. This Motor Drive was compact and powered by eight AA batteries. An accessible hand-grip took in the shutter release, C/S function selector and H/L speed selector, from 3.5 to 2 frames a second. A power take-off made it possible to operate the motor by remote control up to a distance of sixty metres.

The system of flashguns compatible with the Super A corresponded to those for the Pentax LX and used the TTL flash system. For this, the main light metering

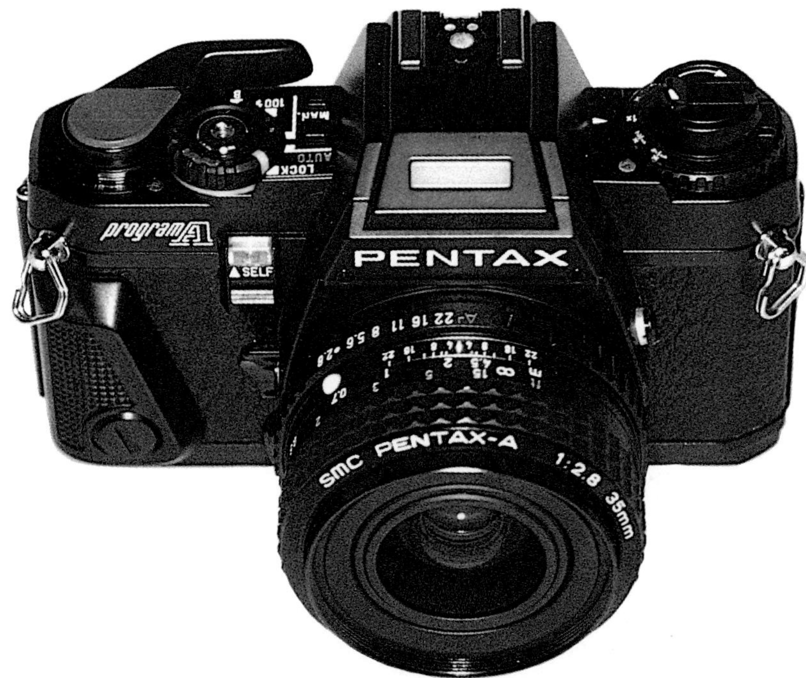

The Pentax Program A was the simplified version of the Super A. This example is fitted with a SMC Pentax-A 35mm,f/2.8 lens.

circuit, based on gallium phospho arsenide cells, was integrated with a secondary circuit which had a silicon cell directed at the focal plane shutter.

The Super A offered an original data-back called Digital Data M which included a calendar which could be programmed up to the year 2019. It could be adjusted to record the date or time.

Pentax Program A

Exactly one year after the introduction of the Super A, Asahi Optical doubled up by bringing out the Pentax Program A. For marketing reasons, the cameras intended for the North American market were given a different designation. Since the Super A had been called Super Program, the Program A was called Program Plus, making it difficult to distinguish between the two reflexes.

A little confusion also arose outside the USA, given the similarity between the two cameras, which barely differed in their front panels and had a lot of common features on the top plate.

The main aesthetic difference lay in the design of the pentaprism, which comprised a broad central moulding. The pentaprism of the Program A was fastened at the base by two visible screws. The self-timer switch moved vertically and the red warning light was continually in view. In order to distinguish between the two cameras better, the bottom of the shutter release was emphasized by a fine red line. The function selector had a black plastic covering and was not surrounded by a rubberized rim as on the Super A.

If the aesthetic differences between the two reflexes were minimal, those relating to the controls were even more imperceptible. The wind lever only changed the shape of its plastic covering which became indented rather than roundish. The external display disappeared from the top plate, leaving more room for the layout of the main controls. The function selector provided for five functions: L, AUTO, MAN, 100x, and B, like the Super A. The fact that flash synchronization was at $^1/100$ sec. rather than $^1/125$ sec. meant that a slower travelling shutter had been chosen than on the Super A. The vertical metallic-

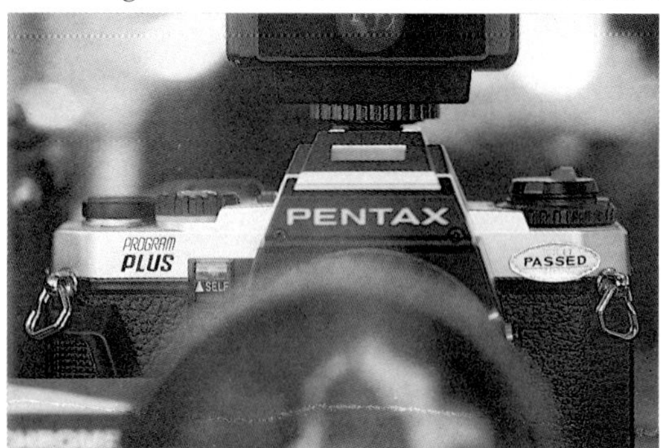

The Program A was called the Program Plus in North America. This example was photographed through a shop window.

blind shutter was a Seiko MCF, with the abbreviation E5, and allowed a maximum speed of $^1/1000$ sec.

The Program A and Super A offered almost identical facilities. The manual control was the same and both cameras had the same lever for closing the aperture manually. Both had the same removable hand-grip.

The exposure program on the Program A was the same as that of the Super A. Aperture priority and manual modes were also the same, as was the information given in the viewfinder. The same accessories, the same motors and the same Digital Data M back also applied.

But the Program A had fewer facilities, which justified its lower price. It did not have shutter priority mode or TTL flash control. It also lacked the display illuminator, the usefulness of which was very debatable. The limitations of the Program A were not drastic but in comparison with its bigger sister, Super A, the Program A exhibited less attention to design, owing to the way it was rushed onto the market, and it did not succeed in asserting itself as determinedly. It was in production less than three years, whereas the Super A easily kept going for six years.

Times had changed and cheap copies of successful reflexes could not find room in a demanding and overcrowded market. Asahi Optical's strategists did not learn anything from the partial failure of the Program A, and continued to offer cheap and poorly qualified reflexes.

Pentax A3

The third of the A-family's reflexes was simply called A3. This abbreviation was used in Europe and Japan, whilst in the USA it was called A 3000.

The Pentax A3 was marketed in the summer of 1985. It had a built-in motor, a large protruberance on the side that acted as a hand-grip and only one program exposure mode. It was a not very elegant square shape. It followed in the wake of motorized automatic reflexes like the Canon T50 and followed a logic which claimed to simplify photographic operations. An automatic which could not be turned off, like the 1976 ME, 1980 MV and 1982 MG, the Pentax A3 gave the photographer no opportunity of being creative.

Distinguished by the battery-carrying hand-grip, the Pentax A3 had a pentaprism similar to that of the Program A, without the upper window. The lens mounting was fitted onto a square plate. The top was flat and consisted of three levels with the minimum of controls. The shutter release was of the electromagnetic type. Large and round and edged in red it stood out on the end of the battery-carrying hand-grip. The cable release socket was situated at the base of the hand-grip. The name A3 was engraved behind the shutter release with the frame counter window behind it. The controls comprised a large selector with the PROGRAM function in the centre. The service functions indicated by the selector were LOCK and BATT.C (battery check). The alternative functions to PRO-

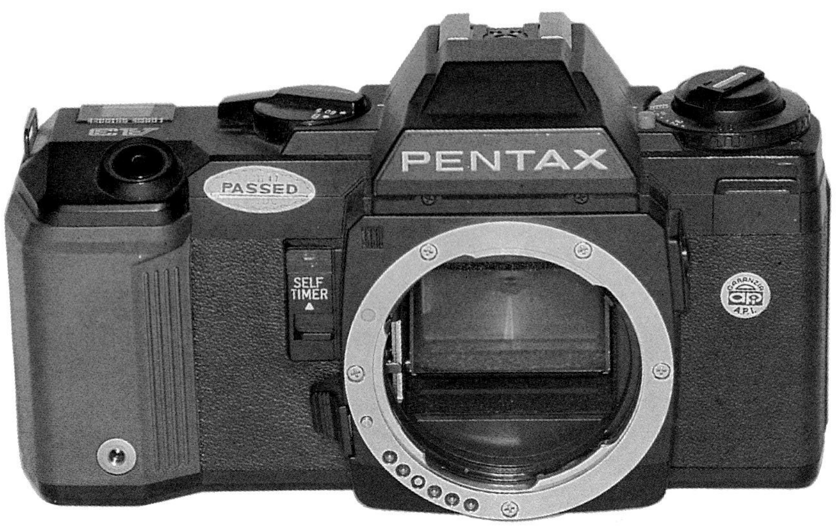

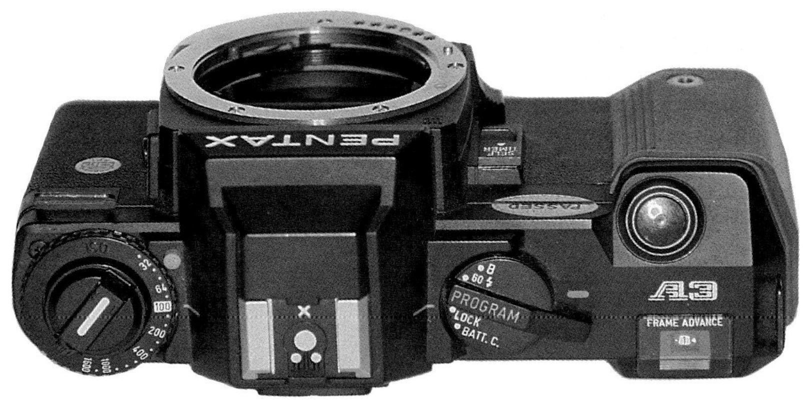

The Pentax A3 was a simple, programmed and manual camera, without provision for a winder.

GRAM were synchronization with the 60x flash and B setting. The vertical focal plane shutter was an electronic Seiko MFC E6 with $^1/60$ sec. synchronized mechanical speed.

The pentaprism had the inevitable hot-shoe. On its left, the rewind lever was surrounded by a ring for setting the film speed, calibrated in ASA/ISO. There was no provision for manual exposure, but on the side of the mounting there was a push-button for compensating for extreme back lighting, as on compact cameras. The electronic self-timer switch was like that on the Program A. Unbalanced by the motor, the A3 had two strong asymmetrical fastenings for the strap. The one on the left was on the front panel and the one on the right was on the side of the camera.

There was a simplified viewfinder which gave shutter speed indications between 1000 and 30. The slowest speeds were not shown, but the figure 30 flashed, indicating the risk of blurring. In the event of overexposure, the figure 1000 flashed and a buzzer warned of this risk. The signal P lit up whilst working in program and the signal that the flash was ready lit up to indicate correct exposure with the electronic flashgun.

Although fully benefitting from the excellent range of SMC Pentax A lenses, flashes and accessories designed for cameras with high-quality facilities, the A3 came over as an extremely limited reflex. It was 153mm long and weighted 530g without the batteries.

It came in at the bottom end of the market with other reflexes offering programmed integral automatic working and a built-in motor. The technology for the A3 derived from that used on compact cameras, at a much higher price than a compact and with considerably greater weight and clutter.

The great restriction of the A3 was the fact that the programmed automatic working could not be adjusted, except in the case of back lighting. With lenses not designed for it or by manually setting the aperture, the Pentax A3 behaved like an automatic reflex as far as shutter speeds were concerned. When using DX-coded film it automatically read-in the code. There was no possibility on the A3 of deceiving the exposure meter by setting a film speed other than nominal, nor of using a film beyond the stated sensitivity.

The A3 suffered from serious limitations for a reflex at the centre of one of the most advanced photographic systems of the time. It sought potential users from amongst less demanding photographers, but the experiment was not entirely convincing. To offer poorly qualified products was not the best way to go about winning over the market.

Shortly after bringing out the A3, Asahi Optical introduced a cheap reflex with completely different features. The Pentax P30 programmed reflex did not take a motor and could be turned off. With it was born a family of cameras which opened a significant chapter in the history of the company and closed the era of the A-family reflexes.

CHAPTER 15

The P-Family, Program and Multiprogram

Continuing its marketing policy aimed at satisfying the mass demands of less sophisticated photographers, Asahi Optical neglected the quality reflex sector for some years. Towards the mid-Eighties, it offered a number of cheap cameras accessible to the general public.

After the motorized and programmed automatic A3 reflex, a reflex of plain and simple appearance was produced. It was called P30 and ushered in a period of expectation. The P30 stressed economy and simplicity of use. It could not be motorized and did not have automatic exposure with TTL flash like the last generation. On looking at it, it was obvious that it had been constructed with maximum overall economy. In contrast with the Pentax A3, the P30 was not fully automatic and was wisely designed for manual use.

It was not a camera with great pretensions. It came about as an alternative to the cheap automatic reflexes which were invading the market and could compete with the most sophisticated compact cameras. With its automatic working which could be turned off, the Pentax P30 aimed to satisfy those photographers who did not just want to frame and release, but sought to learn to master the situation.

With the manufacture of the Pentax P30, the marketing policy which had characterized the previous years was overturned. The simplified reflexes like the Program A and A3 were derived from the success of sophisticated reflexes like the Super A. The cheap and simple Pentax P30, on the other hand, opened the way for a younger sister, the P50, offering more facilities and the choice of two different exposure programs.

In contrast with the P30, the P50 offered the possibility of motorization with the existing winders from the ME Super and Super A equipment. Like the P30, it offered the facility of manual control but not of deceiving the exposure meter. The DX-code set the film speed.

In the United States, the P30 was called the P3 and the P50 was called P5.

The market turmoil caused by the first successful autofocus reflexes led to a revision of plans for traditional reflexes and the Pentax P50 was eliminated from

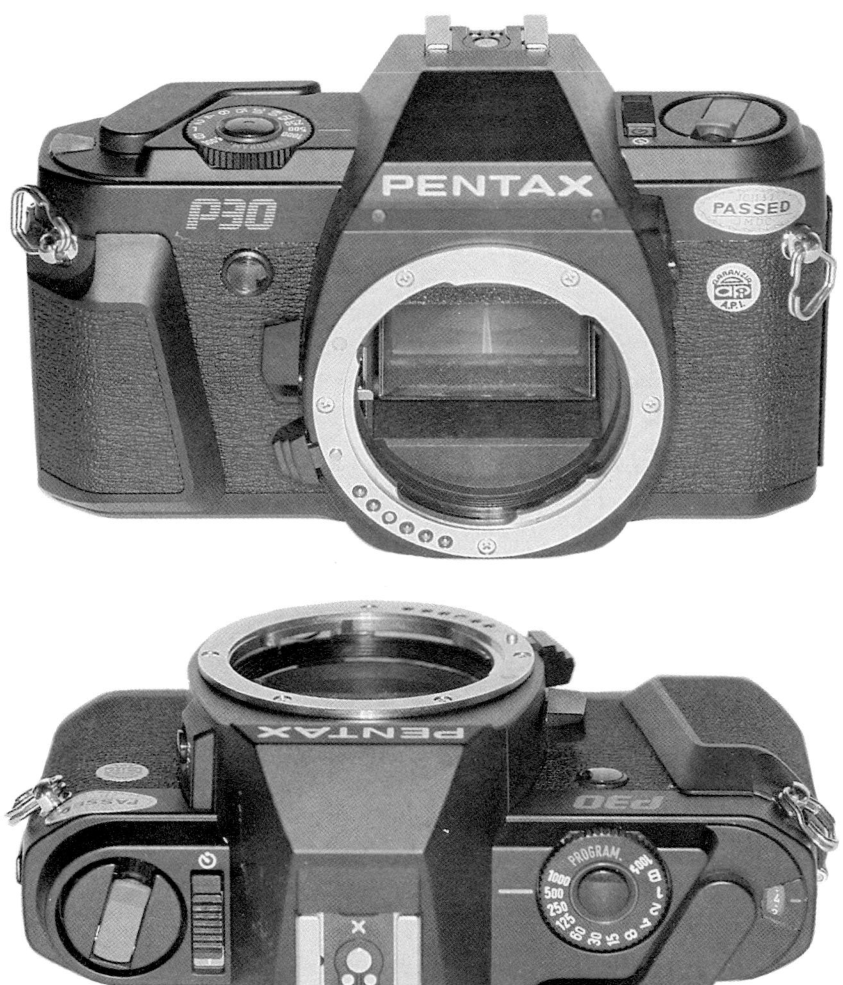

The Pentax P30 was a simple, programmed and manual camera, without arrangement for winder.

the game. The Pentax P30 survived by its body being adapted to that used on the autofocus cameras in the Pentax SF family and by changing the name to P30n, P3n in North America. The Pentax P30n was equipped with SMC Pentax F autofocus lenses and was the cheap alternative to the spearhead autofocus reflexes, SFX and SF7.

Pentax P30

The Pentax P30 was very compact in shape, the front panel being completely smooth and the corners rounded and it was only available in black. The body was designed to disguise the actual dimensions of the camera which, with its 137mm length and 87.5mm height, exceeded the standards of compactness introduced by the Asahi Pentax ME ten years earlier. The weight also, at 510g without the batteries, slightly exceeded that of the preceding generation reflexes.

The metal vertical focal plane shutter was a Seiko MCF E7 with a maximum speed of $^1/1000$ sec. and synchronization at $^1/100$ sec. The GPD photocell and electronic shutter were powered by two 1.5 volt silver oxide or alkaline batteries.

The front panel of the P30 was smooth and plain. The lens plate was lengthened and followed the curve of the lens. A fixed side projection acted as a hand-grip and was discreetly emphasized by a broad smoothed part. On the front panel, a round ostentatious red eye winked during the self-timer delay. The control activating the self-timer was located on the top plate next to the camera's general switch.

The top plate was arranged on a raised plate which accommodated a few essential controls and made the body of the camera seem higher than normal. The wind lever had a similar shape to the one on a compact camera, and in rest position it fitted tightly to the top plate to form a single unit with it. The frame counter was sunk into the camera body and the little window was situated on the right-hand side of the top plate.

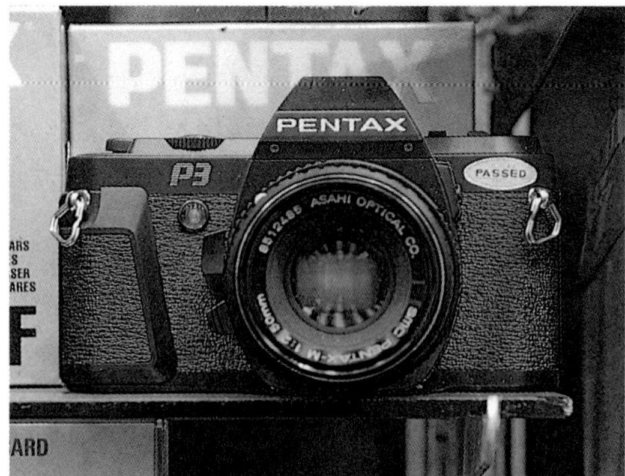

The P30 was the P3 in North America. This example photographed through a shop window.

The shutter speed dial was of traditional form, making an unexpected return on a mid-Eighties reflex. It projected slightly over the front panel. To select the program function or manual speeds it was only necessary to bring pressure to bear on the projecting rim. The dial enabled selection of manual speeds from 1 sec. to $^1/1000$ sec. in addition to B, 100x and PROGRAM. In the centre of the disc was the electromagnetic shutter release.

The rewind lever was at the opposite end of the top plate and sunk into the raised control plate. Alongside the lever, an elongated double switch served to activate the camera's circuits and the electronic self-timer mechanism.

The depth of field preview button, similar to that on the Super A, was located at the side of the lens mount. This was a happy exception on a simple reflex. On the opposite side of the lens mount was the cable release socket, surmounted by a little button labelled "ML" which acted as a memory lock for the automatic exposure.

Such a device had never before been installed on the electronic Pentaxes, nor on the very advanced ME Super and Super A. Its appearance represented an intelligent choice and welcome surprise. For the first time, a popular automatic reflex included a number of facilities which went some way towards catering for the photographers creative urges. The Pentax P30 did not have an exposure compensation control nor a manual film speed setting, being DX-coded.

On the back of the camera there was no film flap slot. A little window, becoming common on many SLR's, made it possible to read directly from the cassette the kind of film in the camera.

The P30's viewfinder was a mine of information, and it did not skimp on the most important details. Shutter speeds were shown on the left of the screen, as on the ME, and an LED indicated the selected value. The other information provided in the viewfinder were the set functions, manual or program, and the signal that the flash was ready. By using dedicated flashguns, it was possible to use flash in programmed automatic working. When working in manual mode, the slow shutter speeds were indicated by a yellow diode to warn of the risk of blurring.

By setting the P30 to program mode and the lens aperture to A, it was possible to obtain programmed automatic exposure as on the A-family reflexes. The P30's program differed slightly from that of the Super A, it was faster and favoured wide apertures and high shutter speeds, favouring fast actions to the detriment of the depth of field. Under identical light conditions and with the same film, the Super A exposed with the combination $^1/60$ sec. at f/4 whilst the P30 used the combination of $^1/125$ sec. at f/2.8. It was not a question of hues, but of accurate design and marketing choices. The Pentax P30 was a reflex for snapshots and aimed at photographers in a hurry with unsteady wrists. Alongside the programmed facilities, it offered interesting possibilities for manual manipulation unusual on such a reflex.

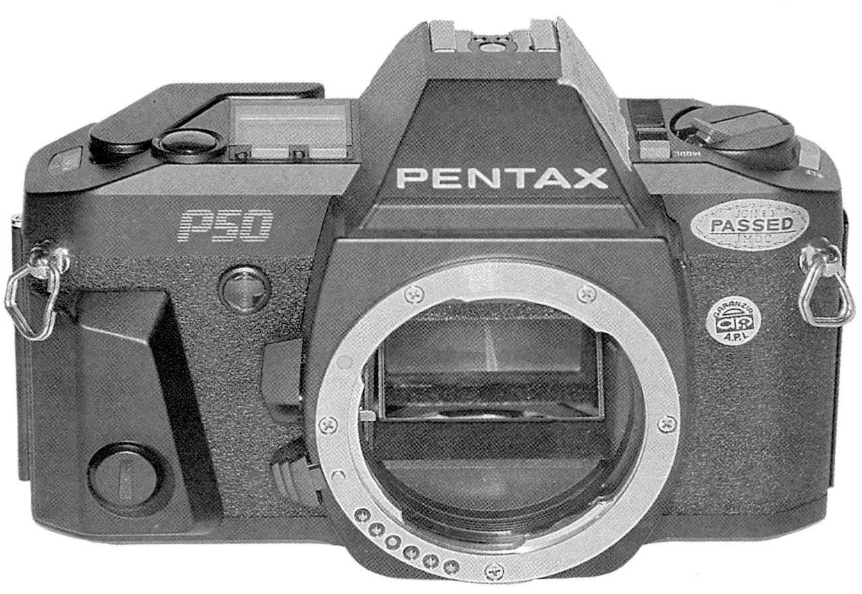

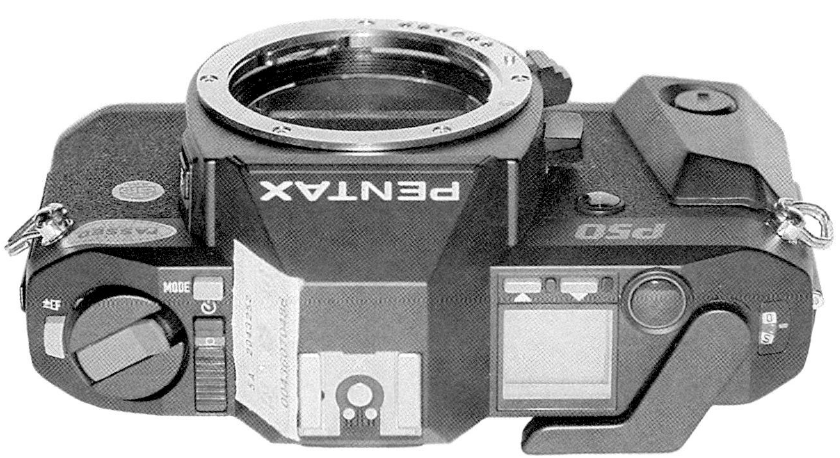

The Pentax P50 was the first multiprogram SLR camera made by Asahi Optical.

Pentax P50

The Pentax P50 was the younger but more advanced sister of the P30. It was exhibited at the 1986 Photokina exhibition, exactly one year after the P30.

The two cameras shared the same shutter and focusing screen, offering the same information in the viewfinder, being powered by the same batteries and having the same measurements and size. The P50 weighed 15g more.

The front panels of the cameras were almost identical, on the P50 the hand-grip could be removed, being fastened by a large screw as on the Super A. Wide smoothed parts on the sides of the top plate made the Pentax P50 appear lower than the P30. The lens plate of the P50 was square-shaped on the upper part. On the right was the depth of field preview button and on the left the lens release button, the memory lock and the cable release socket.

The top of the P50 housed numerous controls, which were different from those on the P30, being more complex and enigmatic. The shutter speed dial was replaced by an anonymous pair of press-buttons and the space filled by a wide digital display. The electromagnetic shutter release was emphasized by a fine red line and moved to the front panel. On the left-hand side, the general switch was supplemented by the MODE button and the rewind lever by the EF button for manual adjustment of the automatic exposure.

The back of the camera had a fixed protuberance as a hand-grip and the window for reading the film cassette information. The base of the P50 was designed for coupling with the motors of the ME Super and Super A. Mounting of the Winder ME II and Motor Drive A motors was only possible by removing the front hand-grip. A rubber eyepiece shield completed the accessories for the P50.

There were four functions that could be set on the Pentax P50 by means of the MODE button and they appeared on the external display. There were two program modes, plus an automatic and manual mode. In PROGRAM mode, the P50 had the benefit of two different programs, a fast one identical to that of the P30, and a slow one which favoured small apertures.

When in programmed automatic working, the prominent word PROGRAM occupied the upper part of the screen. The type of program selected was indicated by a symbol showing a little man running or a little man against a mountain background. In the lower part of the screen, a figure indicated the selected shutter speed.

The wording AUTO indicated aperture priority automatic working and MAN indicated that the camera was being used manually. In both cases, the screen showed the selected shutter speed. To go from one operation mode to the other, one simply had to press the MODE button and look at the four programs, selecting the one required.

Film speed was entered by DX-coding. Exposure compensation allowed manual adjustment of the automatic working up to plus or minus two stops in half-stop intervals.

When working in manual, the Pentax P50 advised a shutter speed in the viewfinder, leaving the photographer free to select the speed he preferred by means of two buttons similar to those on the ME Super and Super A. When working with SMC Pentax lenses not designed for the program or when manually setting the aperture, the P50 functioned like an automatic reflex as regards shutter speeds. When using dedicated flashguns, the P50 shutter self-adjusted to the synchronized speed of $^1/100$ sec. and programmed automatic flash could be used.

The Pentax P50 was extremely adaptable in the hands of the demanding photographer. The memory lock made it possible to use it intelligently. Once activated, about thirty seconds elapsed to vary the shutter or aperture values, automatically obtaining an equivalent pair. The exposure value was fixed and remained the same even if one half of the aperture/shutter speed parameters was changed.

Most of the multiprogram reflexes on the market offered three exposure programs identified as NORMAL, WIDE ANGLE and TELE. The Pentax P50 only catered for the extreme programs, leaving out the so-called normal one. There were considerable differences between the two programs. The TELE program or action program was identical to that used on the Pentax P30. The slow or depth program selected a shutter speed of between $^1/30$ and $^1/60$ sec., gradually closing the aperture with increasing brightness. Only in very bright light and with the aperture closed to minimum value did the slow program begin to set the faster speed of $^1/60$ sec.

The choice of program led to very different pictures and would be governed by the photographer's conceptual approach to the subject. To hold the action at the moment of climax, for pictures being taken in a hurry or for capturing the split second, the best program was the TELE program, regardless of the lens focal length. To photograph a still subject or one offering its cooperation, and to relate it to a particular background and to obtain maximum sharpness, the slow program was indicated, in line with the focal length employed.

The program most often used on a reflex like the P50 was the fast program. With static subjects, it never mattered losing a few seconds in exchanging the fast program for the slow one. With unpredictable moving subjects there was often no chance to go from the slow program to the fast one. The action could be over while the photographer was busy selecting the right program.

The slow program was not always suitable for still subjects. Sometimes it was better to use aperture priority and select a sufficiently small aperture. The digital display did not tell the photographer about the aperture selected by the computer, so when depth of field was a determining factor in the composition, it was better to choose the best aperture manually.

Like all of the last generation reflexes, the Pentax P50 hid its numerous qualities under a standardized and not very individual body. Black and anonymous, it did not exhibit a sharp style like the earlier Pentaxes. Technological and cultural uniformity had subjected the SLR to the exposure program, the black cloak, the clumsy pentaprism and the almost obligatory hand-grip.

The Pentax P50 proved to be an extremely manageable and adaptable camera. It did not have the facilities of the Super A, but appealed to a completely different public. It cost a third less than the Super A, which remained in production, and had the benefit of the motors and accessories, with the sole exception of the flashguns in TTL automatic working. This was not significant and did not harm the image of the Pentax P50, which for some years was the most advanced programmed reflex in the Pentax family. The introduction of the Pentax SFX autofocus multiprogram dislodged the Pentax P50, which was prematurely sacrificed on the altar of progress and market demands.

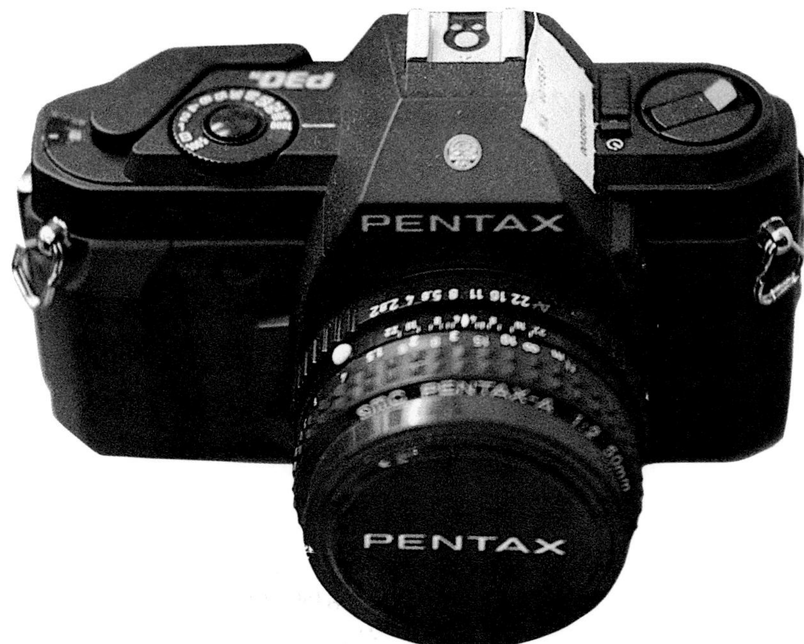

The Pentax P30n is the redesigned version of the Pentax P30 and offers the same performance.

Pentax P30n

When the SFX and SF7 autofocus cameras came out, the P30 survived as a simple programmed, non-autofocus SLR, but was redesigned and named P30n. It was introduced at the same time as the SFXn which replaced the SFX. It was the first Asahi Optical SLR ever to be given a face-lift.

The controls and facilities of the P30n exactly matched those of the P30. The shutter was the same Seiko MCF E7 and the operating modes were manual, aperture priority, and programmed. The general switch and shutter speed selector were practically unchanged. The program function was indicated simply by the letter A and the exposure program remained fundamentally unchanged.

The differences between the Pentax P30 and P30n were limited to the front panel design. As on the SF autofocus reflexes, the front panel was smooth and soft. The name P30 was printed on the hand-grip at the side and was not emphasized in colour. "P30n", on the other hand, was stamped in white on the top plate, behind the speed selector. The screw-cover of the battery compartment was replaced by a hinged cover.

Equipped with the SMC Pentax F lenses which matched the design of the front panel, the Pentax P30n found itself assigned the role of reserve camera, to be paired off with the nobler and more sophisticated autofocus Pentaxes in the SF family.

CHAPTER 16

Pentax Today - The Pentax Autofocus Reflex Cameras

The Pentax autofocus SLR cameras are too new to be placed in their historical context, and they have not yet become collectors'items. However, they will be briefly mentioned here to complete the story.

Minolta took the photographic world by storm in 1985 when they launched the world's first successful autofocus SLR - the 7000. Previous attempts by other makers at an autofocus SLR had been either clumsy or restricted to one or two

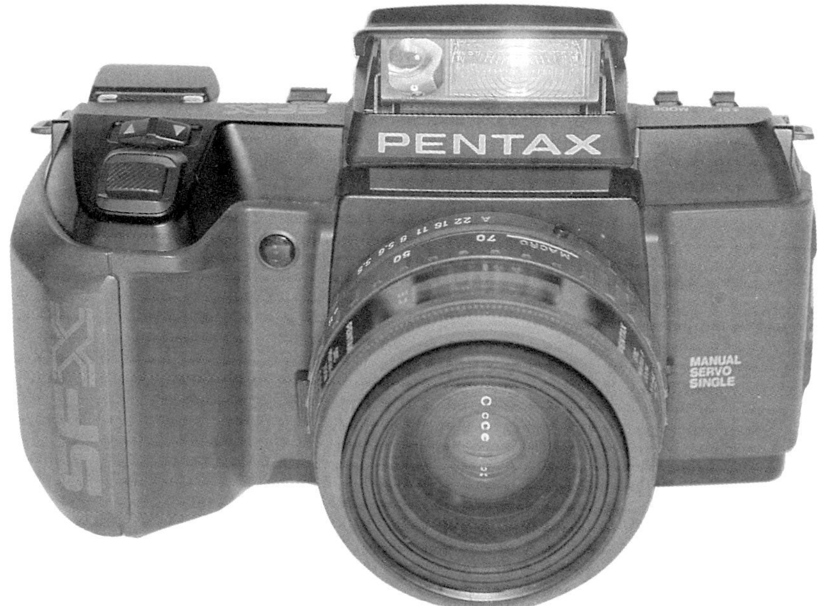

Above and overleaf: The Pentax SFX is a multiprogrammed, autofocus camera with built-in motor drive and electronic flash.

175

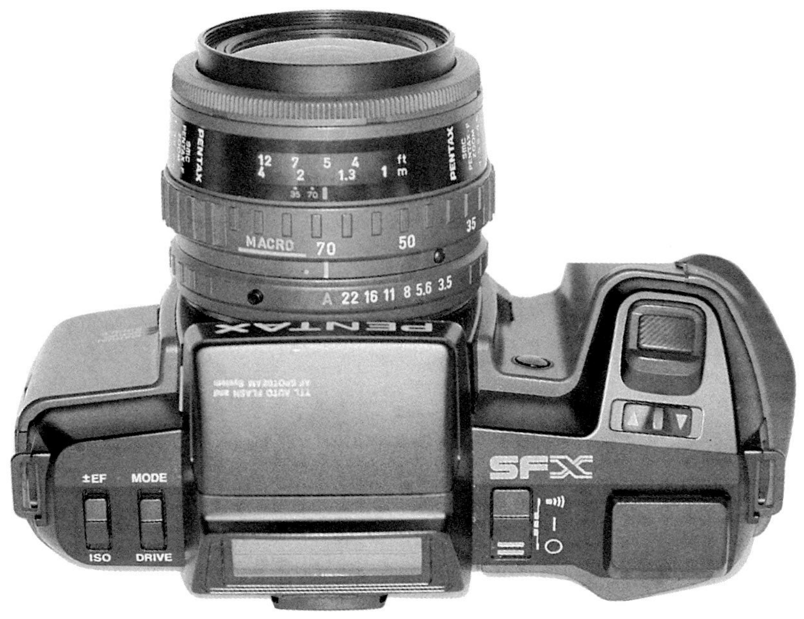

special lenses. Autofocus had been well established on compact cameras for a decade or so, but the problems of coupling interchangeable lenses to a distance measuring and focus control system in an SLR body had proved very difficult to overcome. Minolta's 7000 was a total, highly practical system. But it required a wholly-new lens bayonet, which meant that no previous Minolta lenses could be used on the new autofocus camera. Canon later took a similar route with their EOS range.

Nikon followed with their first autofocus SLR, the F-501, (N 2020 in North America) and a different strategy, no doubt conscious of the huge investment many Nikon uses had in Nikkor lenses. Nikon retained their traditional bayonet, making it possible for photographers to continue to use their old lenses on the autofocus body. Although the autofocus facility was not directly available to the old Nikkor lenses, the system could be used to check when a manually focused lens was in focus. Nikon also brought out an adapter which made autofocus available to older lenses at the cost of an extension in focal length and reduction in lens speed.

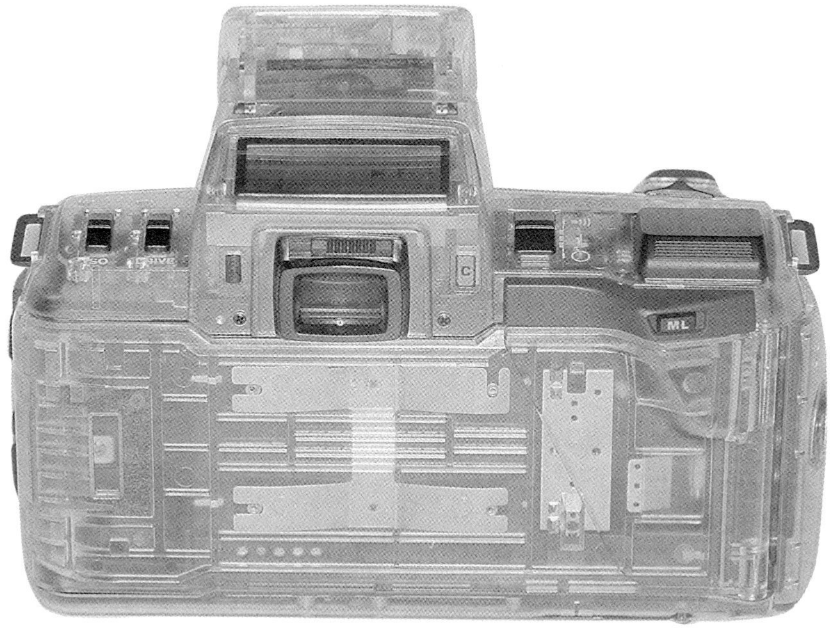

The Pentax SFX in a transparent shell showing the electronic and mechanical components.

Pentax agreed with the Nikon philosophy and entered the autofocus SLR market with the SFX, called SF1 in North America, in 1987. The K-bayonet proved to have been a wise choice all those years ago in that it was still suitable in the autofocus era. Consequently, all K and KA bayonet lenses can be used directly on the Pentax SF cameras, but without the autofocus facility, or by means of the SMC Pentax-F AF Adapter 1.7x they can be coupled to the autofocus system, extending the focal length 1.7-times in the process.

A new range of autofocus lenses, the SMC Pentax-F series, have also been introduced. Some of these have the same optical design as the equivalent SMC lenses, others have completely new optical systems.

The Pentax SFX has the two automatic focusing modes now customary with autofocus SLR cameras. These are AF single and AF Servo (for following a moving subject) as well as manual, for which the auto system can still be used to indicate when the image is in focus. In dim light, or darkness, an infra red beam is available to assist focusing. The SFX offers three normal AE programs: for wide, standard and tele lenses, as well as an action program and depth of field program. In addition to these, aperture priority AE and shutter priority AE are also available, as well as metered manual control of exposure. A novel feature for an SLR is the built-in, pop-up flash.

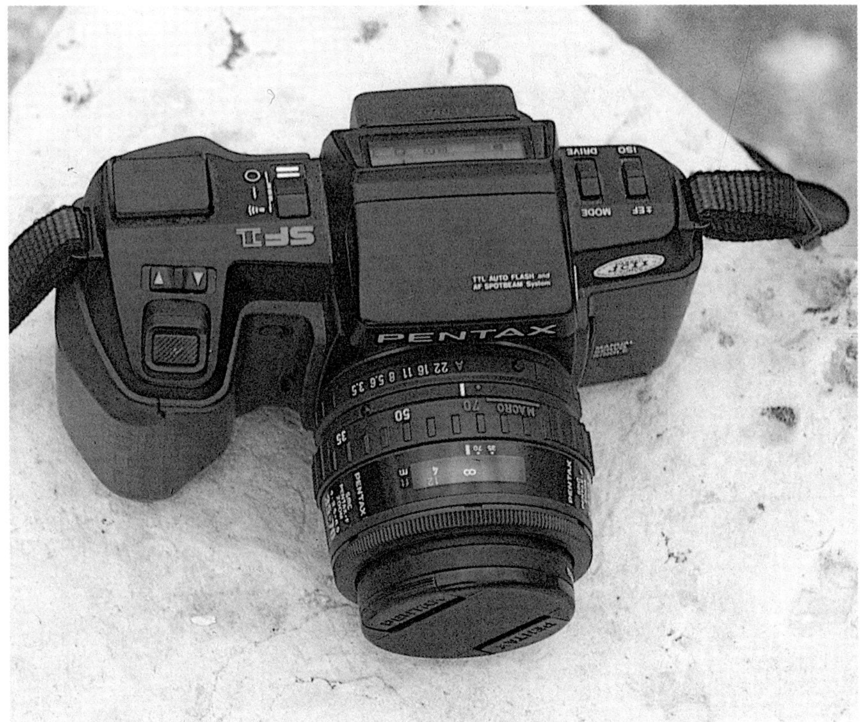

The Pentax SF1 is the American version of the SFX.

The SFX was succeeded by the SFXN in 1989, adding automatic exposure bracketing to the facilities, as well as a few other improvements such as $^1/4000$ sec. maximum shutter speed. The camera is called SF1N in North America.

A simpler camera, the Pentax SF7 (SF10 in North America) supplements the Pentax AF range. This omits Servo AF mode and has only a single programmed exposure mode.

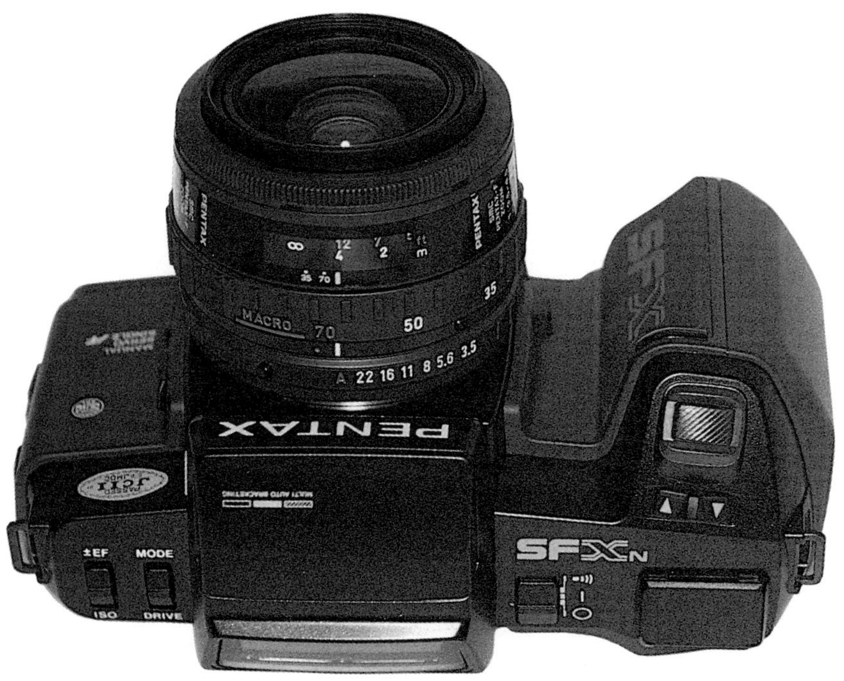

The SFXn is the current and improved version of the SFX.

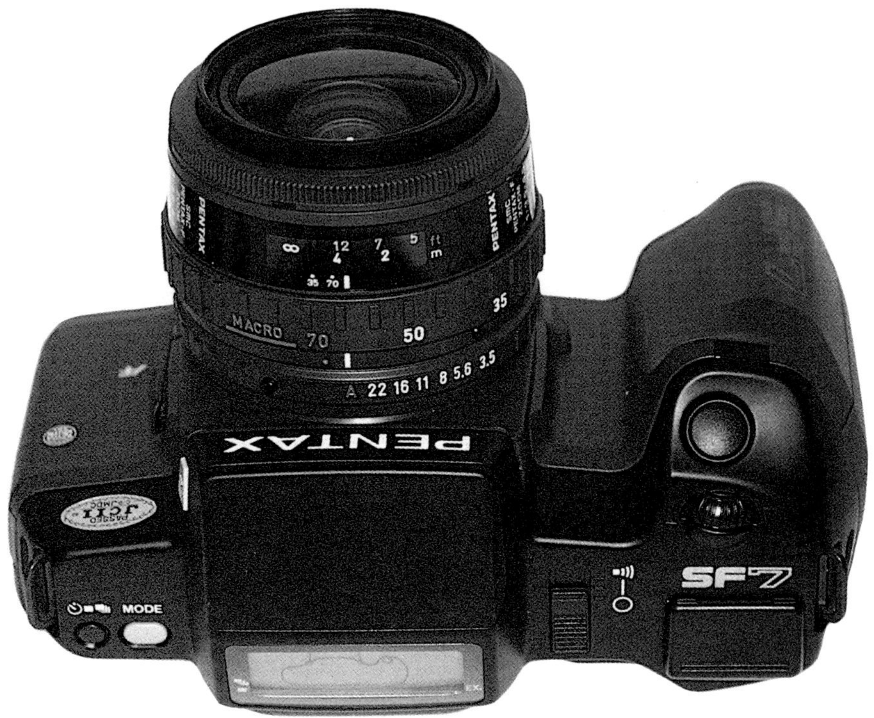

The Pentax SF7 is the simplified version of the SFX.

CHAPTER 17

The Pentax Bayonet Mount Lenses

In 1975 the screw-mount SMC Takumar lenses were taken out of production together with the screw mount Asahi Pentax cameras and were replaced by K-bayonet mount lenses.

The optical quality of the SMC Takumar lenses was renowned throughout the world and they ranked among the best of Japanese lenses. The bayonet mount Asahi Pentax cameras had been hastily introduced onto the market and it had not been possible to equip them with a series of fully redesigned bayonet mount lenses. The optical units of the SMC Takumar lenses were assembled on bayonet mounts and reintroduced onto the market under a different name.

Asahi Optical's new marketing policy provided for the use of the name "Pentax" as a single trade mark intended to identify the company's entire range of production. So the SMC Takumar lenses were renamed SMC Pentax. The Takumar trade mark continued to survive in a number of special markets and was limited to the most widespread focal lengths.

SMC Pentax Lenses

The SMC Pentax lenses, with their K-bayonet mounts, were decked out in square black rubber covered barrels, with a wealth of engraved data, highlighted in colour. The aperture was closed by rotating the ring to the right, as on the SMC Takumars. A white pip on the mount made it possible to fit lenses even in the dark. The name, focal length, maximum aperture and serial number were engraved on the ring surrounding the front element.

The following SMC Pentax lenses derived directly from the equivalent Super Takumar lenses, with identical optical constructions, but in some cases with a smaller minimum aperture and standard filter diameter as noted below:

181

17mm,f/4   SMC Pentax Fish-Eye
24mm,f/3.5 SMC Pentax - minimum aperture f/22
35mm,f/2 SMC Pentax - minimum aperture f/22
35mm,f/3.5 SMC Pentax - filter diameter 52mm
50mm,f/1.4 SMC Pentax - minimum aperture f/22
50mm,f/1.8 SMC Pentax - filter diameter 52mm
50mm,f/2 SMC Pentax (This was the standard lens for the Asahi Pentax K1000)
105mm,f/2.8 SMC Pentax - minimum aperture f/32, filter diameter 52mm
120mm,f/2.8 SMC Pentax - minimum aperture f/32, filter diameter 52mm
135mm,f/2.5 SMC Pentax - minimum aperture f/32,
135mm,f/3.5 SMC Pentax - minimum aperture f/32, filter diameter 52mm
150mm,f/4 SMC Pentax - minimum aperture f/32 filter diameter 52mm
200mm,f/4 SMC Pentax - minimum aperture f/32
400mm,f/5.6 SMC Pentax
500mm,f/4.5 SMC Pentax - 52mm filter on rear element
1000mm,f/8 SMC Pentax
50mm,f/4 SMC Pentax macro - minimum aperture f/32, filter diameter 52mm
85-210mm,f/4.5 SMC Pentax Zoom - minimum aperture f/32

15mm,f/3.5 SMC Pentax This super-wide-angle lens was introduced in a screw mount version at the 1972 Photokina exhibition but was relatively unknown. It was offered in a bayonet mount version without modifications. Minimum aperture was f/22 and comprised thirteen elements in eleven groups. It included four filters, UV, Skylight, Y2 and O2.

20mm,f/4.0 SMC Pentax This lens had a 12-element optical construction, in 10 groups compared with the 11-element layout of the 20mm,f/4.5 SMC Takumar. Minimum aperture was f/22 and filter diameter 58mm, in line with that of the other wide-angle lenses in the family.

24mm,f/3.5 SMC Pentax; 28mm,f/3.5 SMC Pentax This lens had the same focal length and speed as the 28mm SMC Takumar lens, but its optical layout gained an additional, becoming eight instead of seven elements. The minimum aperture was f/22, filter diameter 52mm. Minimum focusing distance became 30cm.

50mm,f/1.2 SMC Pentax The normal 50mm,f/1.2 lens was a new optical design introduced as the standard lens for the Asahi Pentax K2. It comprised a seven-element, six-group layout, with minimum aperture f/22 and taking standard 52mm filters.

85mm,f/1.8 SMC Pentax The odyssey of Asahi Optical's 85mm lens gained a new chapter which did not conclude its story. After being redesigned and going from the 85mm,f/1.9 Super Takumar to the 85mm,f/1.8 SMC Takumar without modification to its five-element optical layout, it reappeared as the 85mm,f/1.8 SMC Pentax, with an optical layout of six elements in six groups. The minimum aperture went from f/16 to f/22 and the filters size, from 58mm to 52mm. Minimum focusing distance remained 85cm.

300mm,f/4.0 SMC Pentax A new seven-element, seven-group layout was adopted for the 300mm telephoto. The minimum aperture was f/32 and the filters diameter 77mm. The minimum focusing distances was 550cm.

100mm,f/4.0 SMC Pentax Macro The 100mm,f/4.0 SMC Bellows Takumar without the automatic aperture and designed for use on the extension bellows was replaced by a 100mm,f/4.0 SMC Pentax Macro lens. This had the same five-element, three-group optical layout and its own focusing mount. Minimum aperture was f/32 and the minimum focusing distance without accessories was 45cm. The filters were the standard 52mm.

45-125mm,f/4.0 SMC Pentax Zoom The optical construction comprised fourteen elements in eleven groups. Minimum focusing distance was 150cm and minimum aperture f/22. Filter diameter was 67mm. The aperture closed automatically.

135-600mm,f/6.7 SMC Pentax Zoom This massive cannon weighed four kilos and offered a focal range of over four times the basic focal length. It did not have an automatic aperture. Minimum aperture was f/45 and the standard 52mm filters were mounted at the back. The optical layout comprised fifteen elements in twelve groups.

The sophisticated and costly 85mm,f/4.5 and 300mm,f/5.6 Ultra Achromatic UA Takumar lenses, unsuited to general photography, were taken out of production owing to their high cost and meagre public demand.

The initial equipment of twenty-six bayonet mount SMC Pentax lenses grew in the period immediately after 1975. When the MX and ME compact reflexes were brought out in 1976 they were accompanied by compact lenses called SMC Pentax M and characterized by redesigned optical layouts. The SMC Pentax M lenses replaced many of the focal lengths in the initial equipment, whilst a number of non-compact SMC Pentax lenses were also introduced which supplemented the existing focal lengths.

18mm,f/3.5 SMC Pentax This lens covered 100^0 on the diagonal. Its optical layout comprised twelve elements in eleven groups and the minimum aperture was f/22. The lens weighed 328g and had four standard built-in filters. Minimum focusing distance was 25cm.

24mm,f/2.8 SMC Pentax After little more than a year, the 24mm,f/3.5 SMC Pentax super-wide-angle lens was replaced by the 24mm,f/2.8 SMC Pentax lens, with a nine-element, eight-group optical layout. The minimum aperture was f/22 and it accepted standard 52mm filters.

28mm,f/2.0 SMC Pentax At the same time, the 28mm, f/3.5 wide-angle lens was replaced by the fast 28mm,f/2.0 SMC Pentax lens, comprising nine elements in eight groups. It weighed 423g, minimum aperture was f/22 and filter diameter 52mm.

30mm,f/2.8 SMC Pentax Asahi Optical introduced a lens with the unusual focal length of 30mm. It weighed 215g, consisted of seven elements and took 52mm filters. The minimum aperture was f/22.

200mm,f/2.5 SMC Pentax This faster 200mm lens, consisted of six elements in six groups and weighed almost a kilo. The minimum focusing distance was 200cm and the minimum aperture f/32. Filter diameter was 77mm.

100mm,f/4.0 SMC Pentax Bellows The 100mm,f/4.0 Bellows lens reappeared in the catalogues one year after the introduction of the bayonet mount Asahi Pentaxes. It preserved its five-element, three-group optical layout unchanged. The manual aperture closed down to f/32. It could only be used on the Pentax Bellows.

28mm,f/3.5 SMC Pentax Shift This first Pentax shift lens deserves particular mention. With a manual aperture closing to f/22 and the shift facility, the lens consisted of twelve elements in eleven groups, weighed 611g and focused down to 30cm.

1000mm,f/11 SMC Pentax Reflex Alongside the 1000mm conventional tele-photo lens, Asahi Optical also introduced a mirror telephoto lens with the same focal length. It weighed 2300g, less than half the weight of the equivalent refracting telephoto, and of course had no diaphragm. Its minimum focusing distance was 8m.

SMC Pentax M Lenses

Designed for the MX and ME compact reflexes, the SMC Pentax M lenses were particularly light and compact. Their optical layouts were the result of careful study and sophisticated computer calculations. The SMC Pentax M lenses replaced many of the existing focal lengths in the basic bayonet mount Asahi Pentax equipment and could be used freely on all Pentax SLR's. Their introduc-tion meant the disappearance from the catalogues of almost all the non-compact SMC Pentax lenses, with the exception of the most recent and unusual optical constructions.

20mm,f/4.0 SMC Pentax M The 20mm,f/4.0 SMC Pentax wide-angle lens was replaced after little more than a year by an SMC Pentax M wide-angle lens of equal speed and focal length. With an eight-element optical layout, the 20mm,f/ 4.0 SMC Pentax M weighed 150g, exactly half the weight of its predecessor, while projecting half as much at 29mm from the camera. The minimum aperture was f/22 and the filter diameter 49mm, characteristic of the SMC Takumars and almost all SMC Pentax M lenses.

28mm,f/2.8 SMC Pentax M; 28mm,f/3.5 SMC Pentax M The replacement of the 28mm,f/3.5 lens with the fast 28mm,f/2.0 made room for the 28mm,f/2.8 and f/3.5 SMC Pentax M compact wide-angle lenses. The slower and less successful lens consisted of six elements and weighed 180g. The faster lens consisted of seven elements and weighed barely 156g. Both lenses closed to f/22 and took 49mm filters.

28mm,f/2.0 SMC Pentax M In 1983, the 28mm,f/2.0 SMC Pentax wide-angle lens was replaced by the compact version, with a simplified optical layout of eight elements in seven groups and weighing 215g as against the 423g of its predecessor. The filters were standardized at 49mm.

35mm,f/2.0 SMC Pentax M; 35mm,f/2.8 SMC Pentax M   The 35mm SMC Pentaxes were replaced by the seven-element 35mm,f/2.0 SMC Pentax M, which was 80g lighter than its predecessor of the same speed, and by a six-element 35mm,f/2.8 SMC Pentax M wide-angle lens weighing 174g.

40mm,f/2.8 SMC Pentax M   The most compact of the SMC Pentax M lenses had a hybrid focal length of 40mm and was introduced as the standard lens for the MX and ME compact reflexes. The lens projected barely 18mm from the camera, weighed 110g and comprised five elements in four groups. The minimum aperture was f/22, standard 49mm filter and minimum focusing distance, 60cm.

50mm,f/1.4 SMC Pentax M; 50mm,f/1.7 SMC Pentax M   The 50mm,f/1.4 and 55mm,f/1.8 SMC Pentax standard focal length lenses were replaced by the compact 50mm,f/1.4 and f/1.7. The 50mm,f/1.4 comprised seven elements in six groups and weighed 238g. The 50mm,f/1.7 had one element less and weighed 185g. The minimum aperture was f/22 and filter diameter 49mm.

75-150mm,f/4.0 SMC Pentax M Zoom   This lens consisted of twelve elements in nine groups, weighed 465g and used the standard 49mm filters.

80-200mm,f/4.5 SMC Pentax M Zoom   This lens replaced the 85-210mm Zoom. The lens consisted of fifteen elements in twelve groups and weighed only 555g.

35mm,f/1.4 SMC Pentax M   At the beginning of the Eighties, Asahi Optical brought out their fastest 35mm lens. This consisted of ten elements in eight groups and weighed 420g. It appeared only very briefly in the catalogues.

2000mm,f/13.5 SMC Pentax Reflex   Two years after the introduction of the 1000mm catadioptric lens, Asahi Optical introduced a 2000mm mirror-lens weighing 8kg and with an external diameter of 18cm. There were four built-in filters and minimum focusing distance was 20m.

24-50mm,f/4.0 SMC Pentax M Zoom   A twelve-element, ten-group optical design weighing 380g.

35-70mm,f/2.8 SMC Pentax AF Zoom   With the arrival of the MEF autofocus reflex, Asahi Optical introduced a zoom lens fitted with an internal focusing motor. This had a special mount, weighed 580g and comprised seven elements.

400-600mm,f/8-12 SMC Pentax Reflex Zoom   Defying convention, Asahi Optical constructed an unusual and huge mirror zoom lens with a focal length range from 400 to 600mm and a speed of f/8 to f/12. This catadioptric zoom weighed 730g and was barely 108mm in length.

200mm,f/4.0 SMC Pentax M   The 200mm,f/4.0 SMC Pentax telephoto lens was replaced by this compact version, which had an optical layout of six elements in five groups and weighed 405g as against the 516g of its predecessor. The filters became 52mm rather than 58mm.

50mm,f/4.0 SMC Pentax M Macro; 100mm,f/4.0 SMC Pentax M Macro

Asahi Optical's macro lenses were redesigned using the same number of elements and became lighter and more compact. The 50mm,f/4.0 SMC Pentax M

Macro came down in weight by almost 80g, whilst the latest 100mm optical construction gained only 15g.

The process of restructuring the set of lenses continued during the second half of the Seventies.

300mm,f/4.0 SMC Pentax M; 400mm,f/5.6 SMC Pentax M Asahi Optical's long distance telephoto lenses were brought out at the beginning of the Eighties in a lighter version. The 300mm,f/4.0 SMC Pentax M telephoto used an eight-element optical layout and weighed 815g, as against the 924g of its bulkier predecessor. A gain in weight for the 400mm focal length lens was unavoidable but it was barely 20g in 1240g.

24-35mm,f/3.5 SMC Pentax M Zoom With a nine-element optical layout and weight of barely 290g, this lens was the lightest and most compact zoom in the family. The filter size was 58mm.

28-50mm,f/3.5-f/4.5 SMC Pentax M Zoom Consisting of ten elements in ten groups, this Zoom weighed 315g and only projected 52mm from the camera.

35-70mm,f/2.8-f/3.5 SMC Pentax M Zoom Relatively fast for a zoom spanning the standard focal length, this zoom had seven elements and weighed 470g.

40-80mm,f/2.8-f/4.0 SMC Pentax M Zoom Made up of seven elements, this zoom weighed 395g, took standard 49mm filters and enabled close-up shots in Macro position.

50mm,f/2.0 SMC Pentax M The cheap Asahi Pentax K1000 reflex was equipped with a standard 55mm,f/2.0 SMC Pentax lens which was replaced by the lighter and cheaper 50mm,f/2.0 SMC Pentax. Weighing only 137g, it consisted of five elements in five groups, and like the other standard lenses, it closed up to f/22, focused down to 45cm and took 49mm filters.

85mm,f/2.0 SMC Pentax M The 85mm,f/2.0 SMC Pentax M compact lens supplemented and replaced the old 85mm,f/1.8 SMC Pentax lens. Consisting of six elements in six groups, the medium telephoto lens weighed 250g and took the standard 49mm filters.

100mm,f/2.8 SMC Pentax M The 105mm telephoto lens was replaced by a compact five-element 100mm. This telephoto lens weighed 225g, used standard filters and closed up to f/22.

120mm,f/2.8 SMC Pentax M The 120mm,f/2.8 SMC Pentax lens was replaced by a compact lens with the same speed and focal length and redesigned optical layout. It was reduced in weight to 270g.

135mm,f/3.5 SMC Pentax M The most typical of Asahi Optical's short telephoto lenses was replaced by this M compact telephoto. Although using a layout with one additional element, the compact telephoto lens weighed 50g less than its predecessor.

150mm,f/3.5 SMC Pentax M Asahi Optical's original 150mm telephoto lens was redesigned and made faster. There was no change in the number of elements and the weight was reduced from 340 to 290g. The smallest aperture was f/32 and filter size 49mm.

SMC Pentax A Lenses

In Spring 1983, Asahi Optical brought out the Pentax Super A reflex, with programmed automatic exposure and aperture working. In order to function it required special lenses, equipped with electrical contacts matching those on the camera body. The camera was followed one year later by the sister Program A.

Lenses named SMC Pentax A were put into production for the programmed reflexes, and designed to operate in programmed automatic working. They were perfectly compatible with the earlier reflexes. Asahi Optical's engineers seized the opportunity to create a completely new design of lens, which supplemented and eventually replaced the SMC Pentax and SMC Pentax M lenses.

Fourteen lenses were introduced in 1983 for the Super A. Their optical layouts largely originated from earlier series.

In the following list, where the lens is identical with an equivalent from a previous series, the name of which is simply noted in brackets.

24mm,f/2.8 SMC Pentax A (SMC Pentax)

28mm,f/2.8 SMC Pentax A (SMC Pentax M)

35mm,f/2.8 SMC Pentax A (SMC Pentax M)

50mm,f/1.4 SMC Pentax A; 50mm,f/1.7 SMC Pentax A (SMC Pentax M)

135mm,f/2.8 SMC Pentax A The optical construction of this lens was original and consisted of four elements in four groups. The lens weighed 340g and it took 52mm filters.

200mm,f/4.0 SMC Pentax A (SMC Pentax)

300mm,f/4.0 SMC Pentax A* This lens was an original optical construction comprising eight elements in seven groups. The asterisk following the A indicated a particular design in the elements making up the lens. It weighed 850g.

ED IF 600mm,f/5.6 SMC Pentax A* An original optical construction consisting of eight elements in six groups. The abbreviations ED and IF indicated respectively the use of low-dispersion glasses and a focusing system operating by means of an internal shift in the lens groups. This 600mm canon weighed 3280g and was 386mm long. It was in a white casing, in common with the trend in long focal length lenses, to reduce heat absorption from the sun.

50mm,f/2.8 SMC Pentax A Macro The 50mm,f/4.0 SMC Pentax A Macro was redesigned with a six-element, four-group layout and became the 50mm,f/2.8 SMC Pentax A Macro, faster by one stop and heavier by 50g.

24-50mm,f/4.0 SMC Pentax A Zoom (SMC Pentax M)

35-105mm,f/4.0 SMC Pentax A Zoom With a focal range of more than three times the basic focal length and a fifteen-element, thirteen-group layout, this lens weighed 615g.

28-135mm,f/4.0 SMC Pentax A Zoom A seventeen-element, fifteen-group construction, weighing 820g.

70-210mm,f/4.0 SMC Pentax A Zoom Thirteen elements in ten groups made up this lens, which weighed 680g and projected 149mm from the camera.

The SMC Pentax A lenses became very closely integrated with the SMC Pentax and SMC Pentax M lenses. Together they comprised the equipment for the bayonet mount Pentaxes in the years between 1983 and 1987. The arrival of a lens designed for the automatic exposure program did not always push the older-generation lens out of the catalogue, but at the end of the Eighties, replacement was almost complete.

In 1984, eleven SMC Pentax A lenses and four focal length extenders were brought out. In 1985, the family grew by a further twelve lenses. They mostly involved new and interesting optical constructions, characterized by special glasses, high speed and better facilities, but some were identical with lenses from previous series as noted in brackets.

15mm,f/3.5 SMC Pentax A (SMC Pentax)

28mm,f/2.0 SMC Pentax A The 28mm,f/2.0 SMC Pentax fast wide-angle lens was completely redesigned, brought up to eight elements in seven groups and reduced to 215g in weight.

35mm,f/2.0 SMC Pentax A (SMC Pentax M)

50mm,f/1.2 SMC Pentax A (SMC Pentax M)

85mm,f/1.4 SMC Pentax A* This medium telephoto lens replaced the M-series lens of the same focal length. With a new seven-element, six-group optical layout, it used aspherical elements and weighed 555g. Filter diameter was 67mm.

100mm,f/2.8 SMC Pentax A (SMC Pentax M)

135mm,f/1.8 SMC Pentax A* This lens afforded great speed for its focal length, used special glasses and was an original seven-element, six-group optical construction. It weighted 865g and the filters were 77mm.

ED 200mm,f/2.8 SMC Pentax A* The use of low dispersion elements facilitated the construction of this telephoto lens. Its optical layout consisted of six elements in six groups. It weighted 850g and took 77mm filters.

ED IF 300mm,f/2.8 SMC Pentax A* This telephoto lens was distinguished by a white casing, low-dispersion glasses, internal focusing and high relative speed. The optical layout consisted of eight elements in eight groups. It weighed nearly 3kg and the standard 49mm filters had to be rear-mounted.

400mm,f/5.6 SMC Pentax A The 400mm,f/5.6 SMC Pentax M lens was redesigned with the addition of two elements. The minimum focusing distance was reduced from 500cm to 280cm but the weight was almost unchanged.

35-70mm,f/4.0 SMC Pentax A Zoom This compact zoom lens consisted of seven elements in seven groups, weighed 330g and facilitated close-up focusing at 25cm in the macro position on the maximum focal length. However, it only stayed in the catalogue for little more than a year and was replaced by more complex optical constructions.

Rear Converter A 1.4XS Rear Converter A 2XS Rear Converter A 1.4XL Rear Converter A 2XL

In order to widen the use of its telephoto lenses, Asahi Optical introduced four focal length extenders. The extenders with the letter "S" could be coupled with the majority of existing lenses and with the zooms. Those with the letter "L" were designed to work with the longest and fastest focal lengths.

16mm,f/2.8 SMC Pentax A Fish-Eye This replaced the 17mm,f/4.0 SMC Pentax Fish-eye. Consisting of nine elements in seven groups, it weighed 320g and included four filters.

20mm,f/2.8 SMC Pentax A The new optical construction of this super-wide-angle lens consisted of ten elements in nine groups and replaced the M-series lens of the same focal length. In comparison with the earlier lens, it was almost 100g heavier and the filters were 67mm.

50mm,f/2.0 SMC Pentax A (SMC Pentax M)

ED IF 400mm,f/2.8 SMC Pentax A* The 400mm focal length was supplemented by the superb 400mm,f/2.8 SMC Pentax A*, with exceptional speed, an elegant white casing and a new optical layout consisting of eight elements. It weighed 6kg. The 49mm filters were applied to the rear element.

ED IF 1200mm,f/8 SMC Pentax A* A nine-element, eight-group layout 8.5kg in weight, minimum focusing distance of eight metres and an automatic aperture were the features distinguishing this super-telephoto lens. The abbreviations indicated the use of low-dispersion lenses and internal focusing.

100mm,f/2.8 SMC Pentax A Macro This Macro was distinguished by its original seven-element optical construction. Minimum focusing was 31cm., weight 470g, filter diameter 58mm.

100mm,f/4.0 SMC Pentax A Macro (SMC Pentax M)

ED 200mm,f/4.0 SMC Pentax A* Macro The optical layout of this lens consisted of ten elements in nine groups, and included low-dispersion glasses. The lens weighed 880g, and took 58mm filters. At the minimum focusing distance of 55cm, reproduction scale was 1:1 without accessories.

28-80mm,f/3.5-f/4.5 SMC Pentax A Zoom Twelve elements in nine groups, a moderate weight of 335g and 80cm. minimum focusing distance made this an extremely interesting lens.

35-70mm,f/3.5-f/4.5 SMC Pentax A Zoom Consisting of eight elements and weighing 265g, this lens was suitable for replacing the standard lens in many photographic outfits.

35-210mm,f/3.5-f/4.5 SMC Pentax A Zoom Consisting of seventeen elements in fourteen groups, this fabulous zoom lens covered a focal range equal to six times the basic focal length. The lens weighed 775g and with a 67mm filter size. Minimum focusing distance was 160cm. However, it was in the catalogue for less than a year.

85mm,f/2.2 SMC Pentax Soft This soft-focus lens did not have electrical contacts for the programmed reflexes nor an automatic diaphragm aperture. It consisted of only two elements in a single group. An adjustable soft filter facilitated the shooting of portraits and scenes softened as if by a luminescent mist. Only suitable for use in special shots, the Soft lens took standard 49mm filters and weighed 235g.

SMC Pentax F Lenses

The introduction of the Pentax SFX autofocus reflex required new lenses as well. A 1.7x focal length extender made it possible to use the earlier series, bayonet mount SMC Pentax lenses in autofocus. The lenses designed for autofocus working with the Pentax SFX were called SMC Pentax F. The SMC Pentax F lenses preserved the original K-bayonet, had a smooth barrel with the focal length stamped in red and belonged to a special generation.

In the following list of lenses, when the optical construction is the same as the equivalent SMC Pentax A lens this is noted in brackets.

50mm,f/1.4 SMC Pentax F; 50mm,f/1.7 SMC Pentax F

ED IF 300mm,f/4.5 SMC Pentax F* This telephoto lens used a new optical layout of nine elements in seven groups, weighed 880g and automatically focused from 200cm. The filters were 67mm. Internal focusing made it possible to restrict the overall length of the lens to 160mm. The external casing was white.

100mm,f/2.8 SMC Pentax F Macro Nine elements in eight groups, focusing down to 31cm. It was 590g in weight and took 58mm filters.

24-50mm,f/4.0 SMC Pentax F Zoom (SMC Pentax A)

28-80mm,f/3.4-f/4.5 SMC Pentax F Zoom (SMC Pentax A)

35-70mm,f/3.4-f/4.5 SMC Pentax F Zoom (SMC Pentax A)

35-135mm,f/3.4-f/4.5 SMC Pentax F Zoom

70-210mm,f/4.0-f/5.6 SMC Pentax F Zoom The layout of the SMC Pentax A Zoom with the same focal range was modified to thirteen elements in nine groups to produce the 70-210mm,f/4.0-f/5.6 SMC Pentax F Zoom lens. The overall weight came down from 680 to 555g.

1.7X SMC Pentax F AF Adapter If it is true that every revolution demands its victims, Asahi Optical, unlike Canon and Minolta, sought to limit damage to the minimum. The SMC Pentax F lenses which came with the Pentax SFX could be used on earlier Pentax reflexes with a bayonet mount, by selecting manual focus. Vice versa, it was possible to mount the SMC Pentax, SMC Pentax M and SMC Pentax A lenses on the autofocus reflexes by turning off the autofocus mode. These SMC Pentax lenses could be used on the SFX, preserving the automatic exposure workings unchanged and losing only the integral autofocus function. It was possible to use these SMC Pentax lenses with the autofocus function by means of a 1.7x focal length duplicator which changed SMC Pentax A lenses greater than f/2.8 into autofocus lenses, at a cost of one stop.

The list of SMC Pentax lenses compatible with the Pentax SF reflex autofocus system came to nineteen, from the 16mm Fish-eye to the 400mm,f/2.8 lens. All the SMC Pentax A lenses with a length of 20mm, 24mm, 28mm, 35mm, 50mm, 85mm, 100mm, and 135mm could be turned into autofocus lenses, in addition to the 200mm, 300mm, and 400mm,f/2.8 telephoto lenses. Even the 35-105mm,f/3.5 SMC Pentax A Zoom could be used in autofocus, except in macro position. Obviously, the special Shift, Soft and Macro and Bellows lenses could not work in autofocus.

The introduction onto the market of the Pentax SF7 autofocus reflex was accompanied by a number of lenses with an autofocus mounting which supplemented the SMC Pentax F-family.

28mm,f/2.8 SMC Pentax F (SMC Pentax A)

IF 135mm,f/2.8 SMC Pentax F This was an original optical construction consisting of eight elements in seven groups with internal focusing. The lens weighed 400g and the filters were 52mm.

ED IF 600mm,f/4.0 SMC Pentax F* Distinguished by its white casing and considerable speed, this lens had an original optical layout of nine elements in seven groups. The weight was 6830g. The 43mm filters were applied to the rear element.

50mm,f/2.8 SMC Pentax F Macro The 50mm Macro lens was completely revised in its optical layout, which consisted of eight elements in seven groups. Minimum focusing distance was 20cm. Filters 52mm.

35-105mm,f/4.0-f/5.6 SMC Pentax F Zoom This zoom consisted of fourteen elements in twelve groups. Minimum focusing distance was 140cm in normal position and 42cm in macro position. The weight was 345g and the filters were 58mm.

ED 250-600mm,f/5.6 SMC Pentax F* Zoom With a layout consisting of seventeen elements in fifteen groups, its white casing and a weight of 5400g, this lens was the most powerful and heaviest of the zooms built by Asahi Optical. Its extreme focal lengths and relatively high speed made it an exclusively professional instrument.

The optical equipment of the bayonet mount Pentax cameras was modified often during the period 1975-1989. Each development was the fruit of long research. Each improvement was paid for by the disappearance from production of a good lens. The transition from the SMC Pentax to the SMC Pentax M signified a revision in optical design in favour of compactness. The transition from the SMC Pentax M to the SMC Pentax A signified the introduction of low-dispersion glasses and internal focusing. The transition to the SMC Pentax F lenses signified the abandonment of fixed-focus in favour of zoom lenses. Each advance had seen the end of production of very good lenses in favour of more prestigious optical designs.

The introduction onto the market of the individual lenses had never been accompanied by a great advertising rumpus. With the exception of optical monsters with sensational features, the lenses arrived almost unnoticed to enrich photographic equipment. Many lenses had disappeared from the catalogues just as silently. Some had only made quick forays and never reached the market.

Despite the restraint with which new designs often sprung up and died, there was a story behind each one, often stirring and inseparable from the history of the cameras on which they were mounted.